To Mom from Aunt Christmas

W9-CRH-720

To Mom from Aunt Christmas

The Heart of a Priest

FATHER FRED'S LIFE AND MINISTRY

The Heart of a Priest

FATHER FRED'S LIFE AND MINISTRY

By Paul LaPorte

Foreword by Fr. Edwin Thome

MISSION COMMUNICATIONS

Traverse City, Michigan

Mission Communications will donate the profits from the sale of this book to enhance the work and preserve the legacy of Father Fred.

Published by Mission Communications, 2011

664 Hidden Ridge Drive,
Traverse City, MI 49686

ISBN 978-0-615-50842-9

Published September 2011

Printed in the United States of America

Fr. Edwin Frederick
1925 - 2000

This book is dedicated to the thousands of people whose lives have been touched by Father Fred: family, friends, parishioners, patients, foundation clients, donors, and volunteers. Without you, this beautiful and inspirational story would not have been possible.

Contents

FOREWORD

The true value of a person is measured by what happens after he dies.
Benjamin Franklin

Often, I wondered what it took to be asked to write a foreword to a book—a recognized scholar? A famous personality? Someone well-known by the author with more than a usual knowledge of the subject matter of the book? I am neither famous nor a recognized scholar, but I have known our author for several years as pastor and friend. We share a lot in common, especially when we meet at the gym with the same quizzical look, as if to ask: *Is this doing either of us any good at all?*

As far as the subject matter of this book, the life of Father Edwin Frederick, I am among the very few alive who knew him from his first year in college, at the seminary in Grand Rapids, Michigan—our common birthplace. "Ed-Fred," as we all called him in the seminary, was four years my senior. There are thousands of Father Fred stories, and our author has done a good job of telling some of them in this book. However, I want to tell you about the three times my friend Ed-Fred asked me a particular question. The situation and consequence of each of the times he asked this same question tell volumes about his character, his compassion, and his love for everyone he met. He was a wonderful friend and a guide in my life, as I watched him bring people closer to God in his unique and special (often unconventional) way.

I was only thirteen when we first met, the homesick seminarian fresh from the farm, when one day he approached me and asked: *"What's the matter, Eddie?* You had better pick up your face before it scrapes the ground." He sensed my need and disorientation over being away from home. I knew immediately, then and there, I was with someone who cared. It was the beginning of a long and valued friendship. I thought of this scene often during the eight years I sat behind his desk at The Father Fred Foundation. He listened. He cared. He shared.

Father Ed-Fred was assigned as chaplain at the State Hospital in Traverse City, Michigan, during the short time I was the pastor at Immaculate Conception Parish in the same city. Once more, he found me in a perplexed mood, as we happened to meet in front of a store. *"What's the matter, Eddie?"* came the familiar question in that unmistakable, confident voice. Once more, he was able to read my concern. I told him about a runaway lad who came to me asking for shelter. This was in a day before such problems were not suspect of anything but goodness and generosity. I explained that I had called an attorney and even talked to the lad's parents, who were happy their boy had a safe place to stay. "So what's the problem?" my understanding priest-friend asked. I explained that I didn't have the bishop's permission. His retort was swift and disarming: "Since when do you need the bishop's permission to be a Christian?" The young man stayed until he married. In the meanwhile, I sent him to the neighboring parish for instructions in the Catholic Faith.

Father Fred died in January 2000—eight months before my retirement as pastor at a different Traverse City area parish. I was well aware of the desperate search for his successor at The Father Fred Foundation. I remained very quiet as I heard that people had backed down on their donations to The Foundation. Like Saint Peter did to Jesus, after Jesus died, I wanted to leave town to avoid being asked. But the Lord had His ways and asked me: *"Quo Vadis?"* Where are you going? A mutual priest-friend who knew both Father Fred and me well told me that I was the next "anointed one," stating that Father Ed-Fred would be pleased to know that I would give it a try.

When I finally accepted the appointment at The Father Fred Foundation, I must have repeated a thousand times: "Fools rush in where even angels dare to tread." For sure, I did not "rush in." Out of reverence and respect, I did not move anything on Father's desk for a good long period of time. The only thing I took with me was my statue of Saint John Vianney who, at the time, was the only diocesan priest to be declared a saint. I had little illusions about becoming number two. A martyr, maybe, but certainly not a saint! It was a difficult time for me and for The Father Fred Foundation.

I am grateful to our author for adequately describing the various problems that emerged during the transition period from an iconic leader to his unfortunate successor. The rejoicing over someone new stepping in doesn't last long. First comes the comparisons, then the complaints. One day, after a rather strenuous conflict at work, I almost decided to make that my last day. I drove up the Old Mission Peninsula, to the cemetery where Father Fred was buried. I found his grave and I could all but hear him ask a third time, *"Hey, Eddie, what's the matter?"* He seemed to say to me: "Don't let them get you down. The Lord and I will help you." I went back to work the next day and stayed for eight more years. During those years, I had the backing of the Traverse City community, most of The Foundation's board of directors, as well as the ever-faithful volunteers. The miracles continued.

Each of us would like to be associated with success or even better, with a successful person. During the eight years that I was "on the job" at The Foundation, I was delighted to be in the presence of the successful initiative started by Father Fred. We worked as a team, trying to preserve his legacy while we built a more sustainable, on-going source of goodness in our community. During that time, I heard many persons speaking for Father Fred, telling me and others what he would want and what he would do. Maybe he was speaking through them, maybe he wasn't. In any event, we kept his vision alive and helped its growth and success.

I was happy to read that Paul referred to Father Fred as a man of *Faith*. I wonder how many people who read this book really understand what that means. Father was so convinced that God was on his side that he was willing to give a client in need the last dollar in the till, the last food on the shelf, the last item of clothing on the rack, knowing that God would provide more dollars, food, and clothing for others. Some would call such extremism poor business. They forget what Jesus told His followers: "I have chosen you out of this world. You are to live *in* this world but not *of* this world" (John 17:14).

Some wonder about how long The Father Fred Foundation will last. As this book is being written, it is in good (and Godly) hands. People of faith will keep donating. How long it will be known as "The Father Fred Foundation" depends upon the faith expressed by the Board and Administration. Otherwise, it will become just another social services organization doing good work according to philanthropic convictions. I hope this never happens!

May this biography help all of us to better understand why Father Fred was held in such high esteem and adulation by those he served and those who served side by side with him. It is now eleven years since he has passed on to meet the Lord, with whom he shared a common priesthood for fifty years.

Those of us who knew him do not need a book to remind us of this gentle yet strong personality. May others who never knew him in a personal way come to know and appreciate the priest who did extraordinary and ever-miraculous things in an ordinary way by listening, caring, and sharing. I hope this book helps us remember that the "heart of the priest" is still beating in The Father Fred Foundation.

I know that I made it to the top, one day, when a client who never knew the real Father Fred came to me for help. On her way out my office door, she hesitated, and turning said, "Thank you, Father Fred!" Nothing could have pleased me more. If, at that moment, I'd heard him ask, *"What's the matter, Eddie?"* I would have had to say: "Nothing, Ed-Fred, nothing at all."

Sincerely in Christ Jesus,

Father Edwin A. Thome

Father Edwin A. Thome, Former Spiritual Director
The Father Fred Foundation

INTRODUCTION

The best time to plant a tree was twenty years ago.
The second best time is today.

Chinese Proverb

Father Fred was an extraordinary man yet, in many ways, he was quite ordinary.

He was the Yin and also the Yan. He dealt with the oppressive complexities, distresses, and hardships of peoples' lives, yet he could be amazed with a childlike wonder and the simplicity of a sunshine day. He was strong, and he was gentle. He held strict disciplines, yet he was peacefully flexible. He was equally at ease with mental patients, the poor, and millionaires. He had an unerring instinct for the Gospel message of Jesus and an insatiable appetite for helping people. He was authentic.

So begins the dichotomy that is Father Fred. In his time, he touched the lives of thousands of people and now, after he's been gone for eleven years, his work lives on in the ever-expanding Father Fred Foundation. Many people know about the foundation he started, yet fewer people are around who knew him. His story is a wonderful inspiration that must not be lost.

I knew Father Fred and considered him a friend. That doesn't really make me unique, however, since everyone who knew Father Fred felt like he was a friend. He was a genuinely humble and gracious man who made everyone feel as though they were the only person who mattered to him. Even if you disagreed with him, he was still your friend.

In a work like this, it is easy to sanctify someone like Father Fred. It is effortless to carry on in generalities about what a great guy he was, or how compassionate, devout, or generous he was. It is my desire to have this book accomplish all of that and more. Even though he was an unbelievably devoted and pious person, I made it a goal to also portray him as an astonishingly ordinary man. He was not pretentious or especially worldly. It's not that he didn't enjoy the good things that came his way. He did. That simply wasn't his focus. He lived rather modestly and nothing was more joyful for him than helping someone. It was his sustaining source of energy and direction.

Young Edwin Frederick distinguished himself within his own family, with friends, in sports, and in school. His friends in the seminary and in his priesthood knew him as "Ed-Fred." His service in parish work was outstanding, and he made history at the Traverse City State Hospital. When the hospital closed and his ministry there ended, any single aspect of his life to that point would have been noteworthy. Yet, he moved forward, bringing all his experience and expertise together, to meet the challenges facing "his people." He started the eponymous Father Fred Foundation. It is as though he had lived his entire life for that culmination moment: to do what lay ahead.

His capacity and energy for giving were unrelenting, and he demonstrated that in his work at The Foundation. Then, when he was sixty-five years old, in 1990, he became pastor of a parish for the first time in his vocation. This is a time when many men consider retirement.

When he died, his parish endured within the structure of the Diocese of Gaylord and the Catholic Church. The foundation he started, however, nearly succumbed to the vacuum he left behind, as the leadership scrambled to find a new direction. Under some skillful guidance and inspired leadership, The Father Fred Foundation survived and is now helping nearly 7,000 families annually.

Researching and writing this story was like making and assembling a jigsaw puzzle of a watercolor image that was being painted at the same time. I'd find a story or an impression, or a date or photo or genealogical fact, and have to see how it fit into the final image that was also coming together on the paper in front of me. The research process was met almost universally with smiles and genuine enthusiasm. People who shared their stories with me were delighted to do so. Some people laughed out loud in their recollections of him. Others wept in their reminiscence. Everyone who knew him and talked about him misses him.

I met several people whose grief over losing this wonderful friend is still so great they could not share with me. I heard refusals from some of the people who were closest to him. As puzzling and frustrating as this is, I respect it. It seems that everyone had a unique and special relationship with him. His personality and demeanor were so unusually charismatic that, for many people, sharing it would somehow devalue their individual relationship with him. Several people told me: "I don't want to tell you about my memories of Father Fred. I just want to keep them as they are." Others shared openly and heartily and then, in an interview, abruptly stopped. They might tell me something like, "Oh, I've got a few more stories for you, but they aren't going to make it into your book." I respect these decisions.

I was humbled by the people I met and the stories I heard as I worked to preserve this beautiful story. When we started, we made the decision to specifically not identify, by name, any client of The Foundation, nor any patient at the State Hospital. Names that appear in the story are either with permission or have previously been made public. In cases where we want to protect the anonymity of the person in the story, that name is fictitious and is shown in italics the first time it is used.

After interviewing nearly two hundred people and digging through countless boxes of newspaper clippings, writings, letters, and artifacts, certain themes emerged and certain stories were told from different angles. Consequently, I have taken the liberty to combine some of these multiples into one, in an effort to tell a better story. However, even in the attempt to tell a good story, I have tried to portray the events, people, and concepts as accurately as I am able. I have focused on responsible research and have generally taken as truth, the things people have told me. There have been a few instances when memories have drifted a bit with time. Some conflicting stories have come to me. In those cases, I considered them and presented the version I believe to be most accurate. I take full responsibility for any errors or inaccuracies and beg the forgiveness of the reader.

I also take full responsibility for the content: what was included, what was excluded. The primary reason for any exclusion is simply the volume of material we sifted through in our research. There will likely be readers dissatisfied with the product. "Not enough about the State Hospital," they may claim. The same might be said for family history, sacramental experiences, The Foundation, or his parish work.

In researching this book, I uncovered hundreds of stories by and about Father Fred. There were so many we could not jam them all between the covers of this book. My intent, in presenting a volume that can still be lifted off the table, is to provide an overall narrative of this wonderful, sweet, compassionate, ordinary man and preserve a few of the stories of how he touched the lives of so many. Only a fraction of them could be included.

Of course, everyone has advice for the writer. "Don't make it too 'priest-y'," said one man. "Make him look like an ordinary guy who helped people." Another told me, "Don't make him look too worldly. The readers might get the wrong impression, that maybe he wasn't a good priest." Well, he was a priest, and yet he was also a regular man of the world.

For me, there has been the pleasure of seeing him through the eyes of many people. It is as though I can look at him through one of those optical toys that presents a hundred points of view. A nephew may see him through one perspective, a patient through another. A fellow priest may see him from his own perspective, while a volunteer at The Foundation will see him through hers. In that regard, I am fortunate to have looked at him from all these angles—through their eyes.

Because of the nature of his work, he touched the lives of people in special and intimate ways. As with any priest, minister, or religious, he dealt with issues that were profoundly personal and meaningful for the people he came in contact with. Consequently, I heard stories that are deeply personal. I have permission to share some of these stories with you. Many others involve information that I, alone, have decided not to present. I ask the reader to believe that it is in the best interest of Father Fred and those he cared for so deeply that these stories live only in the hearts of those whose lives they involve.

My friend, Doug Stanton, says, "We are a race of storytellers." In that context, I have attempted to tell a good story. It is also important to know I want it to be truthful. Most important, to me, however, is that I not embarrass or hurt anyone in the telling.

At the end of some chapters, I have included a section with the subtitle "Here's One For You." This is in the classic Father Fred tradition. So many people have told me about his wonderful and meaningful sermons. "Every one had a beginning, a middle, and an end," they'd tell me. "There was always a punch line and Father Fred would announce, 'Now here's a little something to take home with you.'" These tidbits made the sermon more memorable and brought the Gospel message to life for many parishioners. In that fashion, the stories at the end of some of the chapters are "a little something to take home with you."

To paraphrase the Chinese proverb in the chapter heading, there were many days I wished I'd started this project twenty years ago. It would have been so easy to be able to ask a few questions and have Father Fred sort out the important events and parts of his life. Oh, to be able to pick up the phone and have him clarify something or verify a date for me. Certainly, that would have made my research a lot easier. That fantasy, however, would have diminished the project. I would not have had the wonderful and inspirational experience of discovery over the past two years. I would not have met the hundreds of people who generously shared their Father Fred stories with me. It has been my honor and my pleasure to synthesize them into this book.

What did I learn in writing this book? Many have asked me if there were any surprises in the research and presentation of this story. There is one aspect that stands out. Like the rest of us, in his lifetime, Father Fred encountered several periods of extreme disappointment. While these episodes of loss affected him quite deeply, he overcame them and they were invisible to most of the people who knew him. One such disappointment was his assignment to the state psychiatric hospital in Traverse City. At thirty-four, he was excelling in his vocation, and was destined for a leadership position in the Church. He was surprised as he accepted this unusual change in pastoral direction. Thirty years later, when the hospital closed he was puzzled by the decision and was deeply concerned about what would happen to "his people." Shortly after that, he and the community were sadly unsuccessful in the attempt to preserve All Faiths Chapel, the popular inter-faith facility from which he met the spiritual needs of the faithful for so many years. In each of these unexpected instances and others, he continued to serve as an obedient priest, helping people find their way to God. He not only survived, but in each case, he thrived. Thus, we have the title of this work: *The Heart of a Priest.*

The biggest benefit from writing the book at this time is seeing the effects his life and work have had on the people whose lives he touched, after he has been gone for eleven years. His vision and work have extrapolated themselves through The Father Fred Foundation. That spark he ignited in Traverse City, in 1989, has grown into a phenomenal community asset, fueled by the spirit he left behind. He put a face on the vulnerable and challenged members of the community for us. The lasting effects of his goodness would not be as evident had this book been written twenty years ago.

I truly believe Father Fred guided me through this process by what he left behind. It seems as though he was beside me the entire time and I find myself thinking, If I'd known I was going to be writing his biography, I'd have gotten to know him better. I hope you enjoy reading the story as much as I did writing it.

Paul LaPorte
June 2011

Father Fred Chronology

c1882	Maternal grandfather Joseph Szczepanski arrives in Grand Rapids, from Poland
1891	Paul and Myrtle Frydryszek leave Poland to come to Saginaw Valley, in Michigan
October 9, 1897	Fr. Fred's dad, Joseph Frydryszek, is born in Saginaw, Michigan
January 16, 1899	Fr. Fred's mother, Antoinette Szczepanski, is born in Grand Rapids, Michigan
June 27, 1922	Parents are married at Sacred Heart Church in Grand Rapids
September 19, 1923	His sister, Dorothy, born in Saginaw
April 17, 1925	Edwin born in Grand Rapids
February 4, 1927	His sister, Theresa, born in Grand Rapids
April 20, 1928	His brother, Joseph, born in Grand Rapids
September 11, 1939	Edwin enters St. Joseph Seminary in Grand Rapids
August 15, 1940	Dorothy enters the Carmelite Monastery in Grand Rapids
December 30, 1945	Theresa enters Carmelite Monastery in Santa Fe, New Mexico
July 2, 1948	Dorothy takes her final vows in Traverse City, Michigan
June 3, 1950	Fr. Fred is ordained in Grand Rapids
June 1950	Fr. Fred is assigned to Sacred Heart Parish in Mount Pleasant, Michigan
June 1951	Fr. Fred is assigned to St. Joseph Parish, Manistee, Michigan
April 1953	Fr. Fred is assigned to St. Michael Parish, Muskegon, Michigan
June 16, 1959	Fr. Fred is assigned to the Traverse City State Hospital as Chaplain
May 18, 1965	All Faiths Chapel dedicated at the State Hospital
May 28, 1968	Fr. Fred is certified as Mental Health Chaplain Supervisor
1974	Michigan institutes new Mental Health Code, establishing Community Mental Health

August 20, 1989	Fr. Fred celebrates the last Mass at All Faiths Chapel
September 29, 1989	State Hospital is officially closed
December 6, 1989	Father Fred Foundation is incorporated and registered with the State of Michigan
January 1990	First Foundation facility opens on Fourteenth Street in Traverse City
March 24, 1990	Fr. Fred becomes Pastor at St. Joseph Parish, Mapleton
January 25, 1991	Fr. Fred recognized with Distinguished Citizen Award by the Chamber of Commerce
July 14, 1991	Fr. Fred named as one of President George H. W. Bush's "Thousand Points of Light"
August 8, 1991	Foundation moves to Griffin Street location
1993	Fr. Fred recognized as "Friend of AMI" by Alliance for the Mentally Ill of Michigan
November 1994	Foundation moves to Hastings Street location
December 9, 1994	Sara Hardy Memorial Award, Traverse City Human Rights Commission for Fr. Fred
December 26, 1995	Foundation building donated to the Foundation by anonymous donor
August 1, 1996	Fr. Fred retires from St. Joseph Parish
March 7, 1999	Fr. Fred's sister, Dorothy dies in St. Agatha, Ontario, Canada
January 4, 2000	Fr. Fred dies in Traverse City
January 7, 2000	Over 1,000 attend Fr. Fred's funeral at St. Francis Church in Traverse City
May 2000	Fr. Edwin Thome joins Father Fred Foundation as Spiritual Director
June 2000	Mike Shockley joins Father Fred Foundation as Administrator
June 2006	Martie Manty becomes Executive Director of Father Fred Foundation
July 2008	Fr. Iakovos Olechnowicz joins The Father Fred Foundation
January 2009	Fr. Thome retires from The Father Fred Foundation
April 10, 2009	Fr. Fred's sister Theresa dies in Jefferson City, Missouri
December 29, 2009	Fr. Fred's brother Joe dies in Eaton Rapids, Michigan

Frederick Family Tree

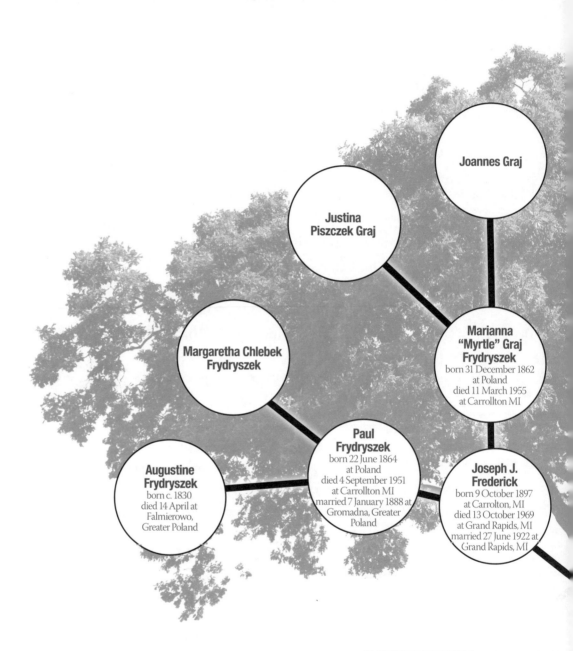

Joannes Graj

Justina Piszczek Graj

Margaretha Chlebek Frydryszek

Marianna "Myrtle" Graj Frydryszek
born 31 December 1862
at Poland
died 11 March 1955
at Carrollton MI

Paul Frydryszek
born 22 June 1864
at Poland
died 4 September 1951
at Carrollton MI
married 7 January 1888 at
Gromadna, Greater
Poland

Augustine Frydryszek
born c. 1830
died 14 April at
Falmierowo,
Greater Poland

Joseph J. Frederick
born 9 October 1897
at Carrolton, MI
died 13 October 1969
at Grand Rapids, MI
married 27 June 1922 at
Grand Rapids, MI

Fr. Fred's siblings
Dorothy 1923 - 1999
Theresa 1927 - 2009
Josaeph 1928 - 2009

Joseph Szczepanski
born 19 March, 1840
at Poland
died 13 March, 1911
at Grand Rapids, MI,
Married 16 November,
1868 at Potulice,
Greater Poland

Francisca Radlicki Szczepanski
born 12 December,
1849 at Zelice,
Greater Poland, Poland
died 28 September, 1932
at Grand Rapids, MI

Joseph Szczepanski
born 30 January 1872
at Zelice Greater Poland
died 31 August 1953
Grand Rapis, MI
married 8 Nov. 1897
Grand Rapids, MI

John Nowakowski
born November 1850
at Poland (Germany)
died 6 November, 1925
at Grand Rapids, MI
married Circa 1872

Antionette C. Stepanski Fredrick
born 16 January 1899
Grand Rapids, MI
died 28 February 1983
Grand Rapids, MI

Ursula Nowakowski Szczepanski
born 1877
at Poland
died 5 March 1932
Grand Rapids, MI

Pietronella Zielinski Nowakowski
born 17 February, 1856
at Poland (Germany)
died 17 June, 1907 at
Grand Rapids, MI

Edwin J. Frederick
born 17 April 1925
at Grand Rapids, MI
died 4 January 2000
Traverse City, MI

Prepared by
Tom McCarthy

BUDDY

Honor your father and your mother, that you may have a long life in the land which the Lord, your God, is giving you.

(Exodus 20:12)

When Father Fred died, the headline on the *Traverse City Record-Eagle* was, "The Faithful Father Fred: TC's 'Mother Teresa' leaves lasting legacy." Over a thousand people packed St. Francis Church in Traverse City, Michigan, as Bishop Patrick Cooney led the celebration of his funeral Mass. After seventy-four years of unrelenting service, this friendly, inspirational man, with twinkling blue eyes and a quick smile, was laid to rest. Those big, strong hands of his were no longer reaching out to comfort, to build, and to help.

The entire community mourned: not just Catholics, not just parishioners, or Foundation volunteers and clients; not just former patients and hospital staff. Everybody mourned. Who was this man? How did he capture and guide the heart of everyone he met? How did he earn the comparison to Mother Teresa?

The answer to these questions is very simple: he loved people and people loved him. In the pages of this book, we will get a glimpse at a few of the stories of his life and see, in a small way, how this love directed and defined his life. As a priest, he preached the Gospel message of Christ. As a man, his life *was* the Gospel message of Christ.

Fr. Fred's dad, Joe, was a stonemason and called him "Buddy." It is a nickname, with its variation "Bud," that persists within the family and close friends—even now, eighty-five years later. From all indications, he and his dad were pretty good friends. Joe died when Bud was forty-four, and when he celebrated his dad's Funeral Mass and laid him to rest, Fr. Fred must have been flooded with great memories of his dad.

As a young man, Bud worked side by side with his dad learning the skills of a builder and stonemason. When Bud bought a little cottage on the Boardman River, near Traverse City, Michigan, his dad joined him in remodeling it to be his home, a private sanctuary, away from town. Bud's huge, strong hands were like his dad's. For both of these men, their hands were instrumental in their professions. Just as his dad's hands lifted thousands of pounds of brick and rocks, Bud's hands lifted and comforted thousands of heavy souls.

As much as Buddy learned from his dad, he also learned from his mother. Anna was devoutly Catholic and ran a loving household that nurtured the family and was devoted to the Blessed Virgin Mary. From her, he derived different strengths: piety and tenderness. From both his parents came his lifelong pattern of compassion and dedication—to help and to give.

The disciplines of work and faith that came together in Bud were evident in at least three generations. All eight of his great-grandparents were born in Poland and represented an ethic of hard work and strong faith. Through the years, Bud never lost sight of either one of those two elements of his heritage. They shaped his life.

Bud's Grandparents: Paul and Myrtle Frydryszek

Paul and Myrtle Frydryszek were Father Fred's paternal grandparents, who came to America from the west-central region of Poland, in the County of Pila, and Provence of Greater Poland (Wielkopolska), a flat region interspersed with forests and lakes in the Warta River basin. Throughout history, this region has been part of Poland, Germany, and Prussia.

Paul was the oldest of three boys, born in 1864. His brother Joseph was born in 1870 and his brother Michael in 1875. At age twenty-four, Paul was living in the farming village of Falmierowo, when he met the widow Marianna Schultz. Although christened as Marianna Grei (also "Graj"), in the village of Gromadno, only a few short miles from Falmierowo, she went by the name of Myrtle. She was the twenty-six-year-old single mother of Martha and

Paul and Myrtle Frydryszek at home in Carrollton, Michigan.

Thomas. There is no record of her changing her name to Myrtle, although it was the name she lived by throughout her life and is on their tombstone in Mount Olivet Cemetery, in Saginaw, Michigan. They were married January 7, 1888, in her village of Gromodno and went to live in Paul's village. At the time of their wedding, Paul was identified, in local records, as a laborer.

They emigrated from Poland to the Saginaw Valley in 1891. With them were three children: Martha, Thomas, and Marie. Another child, John, born in 1888, died either prior to immigration or in transit. The young couple built a home and lived on Elm Street in Carrollton, in Saginaw Township. At the time they built that home, the location was quite rural. After settling in, they had and raised seven more children. A daughter, Delegree, was born in 1894 and died prior to the 1900 census. Fr. Fred's dad, Joseph, was born on October 9, 1897, in Carrollton. Neither Paul nor Myrtle spoke much English beyond a simple "ya" and "no" in the early days.

On March 24, 1892, Paul filed a Declaration of Intention to become a citizen of the United States in the circuit court in Saginaw, Michigan. On October 30, 1896, in that same court, he was granted U.S. citizenship:

> *... having solemnly declared, on his oath, in open Court, that he would support the Constitution of the United States, and that he did absolutely and entirely renounce and abjure all allegiance and fidelity to any foreign Prince, Potentate, State or Sovereignty, and particularly the Emperor of Germany, of whom he was then a subject.*

An itinerant photographer posed the Frederick kids behind their home in Grand Rapids. L. to R.: Edwin, Dorothy, Theresa, Joe.

Paul was known to his grandchildren as *Dziadzia*, Polish for "Grandpa." He was a hardworking bricklayer and builder. Paul (and later, with his son, Joe) built homes for at least three of his children—Joe, Frank, and Virginia—in Carrollton. They also did commercial work, including the masonry on Arthur Hill High School in Saginaw, whose tall chimney is a lasting testimony to their craftsmanship. Along with his reputation for hard work, he enjoyed cooking and making his own wine for the family and their guests. He lived in the shadow of the St. Josephat Rectory, so there were constant reminders for his kids and grandkids to behave. None of this, however, stopped him and his son-in-law, "Huntz," from slipping into Heck's Bar in the morning for a beer "to get things started." Sunday dinners were magnificent, delicious affairs.

Myrtle was affectionately known to her grandchildren as *Busia*. She was a very small woman with lots of energy, an avid gardener, and a wonderful cook. Her granddaughter, Joanne, has memories of watching *Busia* go into her backyard, capture a chicken, kill and dress it, and fix it for dinner—scary memories for a child.

We get a good picture of the family's Polish heritage through the eyes of granddaughter Margaret (Marge) Kaczmarek, the daughter of Fr. Fred's aunt, Marie, who was the last of Paul and Myrtle's children born in Poland. Marge remembers her mother as a "spitting image" of the tiny and highly energetic *Busia*—a woman who would do anything for anyone. Marie learned well from her mother. She cooked everything from scratch and had a cure for everything. She spoke both Polish and English. She was an excellent seamstress who made all her kids' clothes, and sang them to sleep every night.

As Margaret remembers *Busia's* cooking, a delightful smile lights her ninety-nine-year-old face. "Oh, I remember all the Polish cooking, especially the homemade bread, sauerkraut, and the mashed potatoes," she recalls.

Paul and Myrtle had eleven children:

Martha (Faltyn) 1	1885-1985
Thomas	1886-1935
John (died in infancy)	1888-?
Marie (Garsky)	1889-1959
Angeline "Nellie" (Szczesniak)	1892-1936
Delegree (died in infancy)	1894-?
Blanche (Sister Adamine)	1895-1982
Joseph (Fr. Fred's dad)	**1897-1969**
Frank	1901-1945
Virginia	1903-1990
Josephine "Josie"	1906-1996

Bud's Grandparents: Joe and Ursula Szczepanski

Bud's maternal grandparents also came from Poland. Joseph Szczepanski (1872-1953) immigrated *circa* 1882, when he was about ten years old. His wife, Ursula Nowakowski (1876-1932), came to America around 1888, when she was about twelve years old. In 1897, at the time of their marriage, both were living in Wyoming Township near Grand Rapids, Michigan. By 1900, they had moved to Walker, also near Grand Rapids; then by 1910, to a home on Watson Street, in Grand Rapids. Joe worked in a plaster mill as a miller, shipping clerk, and laborer.

---

1 Martha and Thomas were from her first marriage to Thomas Schultz. Records are unclear about her other child, John, born after the marriage to Paul, who died in transit to America.

Joe and Ursula had six children:

Antoinette (Fr. Fred's mother)	**1899-1983**
Stella	1900-1987
Frank	ca. 1903-1915
Frances (Przbysz)	1904-1954
Josie	1906-1991
Joseph	1911-1968

Maternal Great-Grandparents: the Szczepanskis and the Nowakowskis

Fr. Fred's maternal great-grandfather, Joseph Szczepanski (born *circa* 1845), married Francisca Radlicki (*ca.* 1855–1932). They immigrated in 1882 from Poland, with at least five children, from the village of Zelice (parish of Potulice), Wagrowiec County, Greater Poland, about thirty-three miles south of Falmierowo, where the Frydryszeks came from. He was a blacksmith in a Grand Rapids plaster mill, and by 1910, they had moved from Walker Township to a home on Park Avenue, in Grand Rapids. Joseph died between 1910 and 1920, and Francisca stayed in the home on Park Avenue. By 1930, she had moved into an old folks' home in Grand Rapids and was there until her death in 1932.

Bud's other maternal great-grandparents were John Nowakowski (b. *ca* 1850) and Pietronella Zielinski (b. *ca.* 1854). They also immigrated around 1888, from Ostrowite Parish, about seventy miles southeast of Potulice. In 1900, John was a laborer and owned his home on Third Street, in Walker Township. In 1910, he had a job as a laborer in a Grand Rapids furniture factory and was retired by 1920. Pietronella died between 1900 and 1910. John died between 1920 and 1930.

Father Fred's Parents: Joe and Anna Frydryszek (Frederick)

Joseph Frydryszek was born in Saginaw on October 9, 1897. He was the seventh child of Paul and Myrtle. In high school, during the summers and weekends, he began working with his father as a builder and a stonemason. Together, they built homes for family members in Carrollton, in addition to those they built for customers. After high school, he served in World War I as a cook in France.

Joe and Anna's wedding portrait in Grand Rapids.

When he returned from the war and work was slow in the Saginaw area, young Joe went to Grand Rapids and found work as a stonemason, bricklayer, and builder. It was during this time he changed his name from Frydryszek to Frederick. There is no record of any legal name change, but supposition is that it was for one of two reasons. One reason might have been that it was to make it easier for the people in the union office to spell the "Americanized" name and remember him for work assignments. The other theory is that during that time there were lots of inter-ethnic prejudices in Grand Rapids, especially with the Polish. He may have changed his name to avoid some of that brouhaha. He was simply interested in getting work, and changing his name was a way of streamlining that process. Grand Rapids was also where he met and fell in love with Antoinette Szczepanski.

Joe, home on leave. He served as a cook in France in WWI.

Joe was always known as a hardworking, strong, and capable man who taught his two sons the work ethics of his life that he learned at the knee of his father, Paul. He is remembered by his niece, Margaret, as having a fun-loving and devilishly spirited side. He died on October 13, 1969, and on Thursday, October 16, his son Edwin, Father Fred, celebrated his funeral Mass and laid him to rest in Holy Cross Cemetery in Grand Rapids.

Joe takes a break from bricking the house on Watson Street to hold his little "Buddy."

Fr. Fred's mother, Antoinette "Anna" Szczepanski, was born on January 16, 1899, in Grand Rapids, to Ursula and Joseph Sczcepanski (also Stepanski). She was quiet, ladylike, and devout in her religion.

When Joe met her, Anna worked as a "cigar girl" in a factory in Grand Rapids. This was not unusual, since thousands of young women were thus employed in the local cigar industry. On August 16, 1910, *The Grand Rapids Press* reported that the G.J. Johnson Cigar Company in Grand Rapids was the largest cigar-producing factory west of Detroit. They produced nineteen million cigars a year, down from nearly thirty million in 1899. The majority of workers at this factory were young girls who performed a variety of jobs, working constantly throughout the day in complete silence.

From *The Grand Rapids Press* article, we learn that "250 girls performed a variety of tasks but the constant hard work, and frequent departure of girls due to marriage, resulted in rapid worker turnover." The unskilled girls were responsible for stripping the stems from tobacco leaves, making just $4 a week. These working girls and women performed the filling and binding of the cigars or worked to place wrappers and labels on them. Workers were expected to meet a quota each day and were released from work if they could not consistently achieve what was expected of them.

Her niece, Marge, remembers Anna as a "sweet and quiet woman, who was a wonderful cook and baker, who, at home, always wore an apron." Others remember her cooking and baking late into her life, with hands knotted and curled with arthritis, and after tasting nearly anything, would declare, "Needs another salt."

In 1975, she was happy and proud to celebrate the twenty-fifth anniversary of Bud's ordination. "He's such a good boy," she told his cousin Marge.

Anna died on February 23, 1983, at her son Joe's home in Eaton Rapids, Michigan.

Joe and Anna Build Their Family

Fr. Fred's parents married on June 27, 1922, in Sacred Heart Church in Grand Rapids, where Anna's family had been founding members of the young Polish parish. They began their married life in Saginaw where Joe and his dad, Paul, had built a brick home for themselves, not far from his parents' home on Elm Street, in Carrollton.

As Joe continued to work with his father, their first child, Dorothy, was born. Not long after that, missing her family in Grand Rapids, Anna announced to her young and handsome husband that she was returning to Grand Rapids "with or without you." So, in 1924, they moved to Grand Rapids. Joe and Anna bought the lot next to her parents' home on Watson Street, and he and his dad built a second home for her. It was a replica of the one they had built in Saginaw. Joe and Anna lived at 1033 Watson Street, and her parents lived at 1031.

Their home was a sturdy and handsome brick structure with special attention given to the stonemason's detail. He even built a grotto for the Blessed Virgin Mary in the backyard, which is evident in vintage photos of young Bud playing with his sisters. This is just one of hundreds of references to the family's life long commitment to the Blessed Virgin.

Bud was born at home on Watson Street, at 4:10 a.m. on April 17, 1925, and the attending physician was Dr. Ballard. He was the second of Joe and Anna's four children. An older sister, Dorothy, was born in 1923, and two siblings, Theresa and Joseph, completed the family by 1928. Examination of the birth certificate shows Bud was originally named Joseph John Frederick, Jr. That name was crossed out and changed to Edwin Joseph Frederick, in the same spirit of his dad who simply changed the family name from Frydryszek without any legal action. On that same birth certificate, his mother's family name is shown as Stepanski. Later, on Bud's graduation diploma from St. Joseph Seminary, his name was entered as Edwin

L to R: Dorothy, Theresa, Joe, Bud, Anna, Joe, Jr. at their Watson Street home.

Michael Frydryszek. Where did that come from? It is little wonder that throughout his life, he had scant interest in details others thought were important. It started when he was born.

Marge Kaczmarek, Fr. Fred's first cousin, tells lots of stories from the 1930s when her parents would drive the family from Saginaw to Grand Rapids to visit her aunt, uncle, and cousins. She says whenever her folks would announce a family trip to Grand Rapids to visit with Uncle Joe and Aunt Anna, there was huge excitement. During the entire ride to Grand Rapids, the kids were warned to be on their very best behavior. They enjoyed visits with their cousins, playing ball and croquet in the yard, laughing so hard they would fall down on the ground.

The Frederick household was filled with holy reminders of their deep Catholic faith. Marge tells of a time when she and her father, on a visit to Grand Rapids, counted over a hundred religious statues, pictures, rosaries, and other religious artifacts in Uncle Joe and Aunt Anna's home. She says everyone felt blessed when she walked through their door. Her parents told her and her brother, Chet, that they had to watch what they said while they were there, since they were unaccustomed to such reverence in their own family. "Whenever a letter arrived from Aunt Anna," Marge remembers, "my mother would say, 'Don't squeeze that letter, or you'll squeeze Jesus' since there was always a holy card or picture of Jesus or Mary in every letter."

Even when he was a kid, Bud was prankish, witty, and fun. He was known to have an impish sense of humor. Those who knew Bud later in his life could see that this mischievous behavior stuck with him. He loved to have a good time. He was always fun-loving and playful, and being with him was the highlight of any trip to Grand Rapids for the family visitors. "His dad, Uncle Joe, was pretty devilish, too," Marge recalls. When they arrived in Grand Rapids, after the long ride from Saginaw, Uncle Joe would greet them with a warm and enthusiastic welcome. His first words to her father often were, "C'mon in, Hunz. Let's hoist one."

Sunday dinner after Mass was the highlight of every weekend trip. There was always plenty of good homemade wine and bowls and platters of Anna's aromatic Polish cooking. They were very gracious hosts. "You kids had better mind yourselves," Marge's mother kept drilling into them. "Aunt Anna and Uncle Joe's house isn't like ours. They behave themselves, there." The Kaczmarek kids really had to mind their manners. That reverence, however, wasn't wasted on Bud.

Often, at Sunday dinner, after a devout prayer, and knowing very well that his cousins had been warned to behave, Buddy would secretly fling a small piece of food into Marge's face. When she began to giggle, her mother gave her "the eye." The more she giggled, the more her parents scolded her, as the seemingly angelic Bud watched it all, cracking just a hint of a smile.

Looking back over the past eighty years, after telling that story, Marge fondly remembers her cousin:

> *You couldn't get mad at him. He was such a great guy and we loved him so much. There was no way we could get him in trouble. It was just great fun. Bud was such a devil, and he was a wonderful cousin. He was always a good student and he grew into a wonderful man and a good priest. Later in his life, we loved to go to his place on the river. Every time we knew we were going to go see them it was so exciting, from the time he was real small. We went there lots of times. Right at home is where he got his impish personality.*

Susan Bielecki is a second cousin of Bud. While Susan obviously didn't know Fr. Fred as a child, she remembers growing up in Grand Rapids. Often, when Fr.

Fred would come to town to visit his family, he'd bring food and things for her growing family. She is insightful about family dynamics and some family tension that developed because "Father didn't always come down from Traverse City to officiate or attend various events because he had to be with his people. He was so dedicated to the patients at the hospital and the people of Traverse City. He loved them."

Susan's mother, Geraldine, grew up in the house immediately across the street, at 1032 Watson, and often played with her cousins. "Bud was always so generous," she recalls, "even as a kid. When he was a priest, he'd come from Traverse City at Christmas with a pillowcase stuffed with candy, cookies, and gifts for our eight children. Times were so tough for us, and he was so good to our family."

Bud's Siblings

Bud had two sisters, Dorothy and Theresa, and one brother, Joe. Both girls became nuns in the Carmelite Order. Joe married and raised a family.

The two sisters were quite different in their personalities: Dorothy was outgoing, gregarious, and athletic. Theresa was quiet and contemplative and is often described as the "holiest" of the four kids. Mother Marie Therese, head of the Carmelite Monastery (the Carmel) in Jefferson City, Missouri, re-tells stories told to her by Theresa. This one captures the differences between the two girls:

The Frederick kids, l. to r.:Joe, Dorothy, Theresa, Bud

The Frederick kids with their dog Topsy.

All four little Fredericks played musical instruments: Ed the violin, Joe the trumpet, Dorothy the piano, and Theresa both piano and organ. It seems Mom had a problem with the girls. According to "Tessa," Dorothy was the tomboy and preferred going outside to play baseball, etc. with the boys. She hated practicing the piano. Theresa, on the other hand, loved it almost too much. When Dorothy would come inside, after playing, Mom would ask, "Did you practice?" "But, Mom, Tessa's on the piano all the time and I can't get to it" was the excuse provided. Then Mom had to get after Tessa: "Leave that piano and go outside! You need your exercise!"

It is interesting that both girls joined the Carmelite Order. We might expect that Theresa would opt to lead a quiet, contemplative, and prayerful life. On the other hand, those who knew Dorothy thought she would have entered an order where she could express her activism and personality in a more worldly setting, perhaps in a classroom.

In 1950, Fr. Fred's sisters collaborated in making the vestments for his ordination. They were entirely hand-sewn, and Dorothy did all the intricate embroidery. When Fr. Fred died, his family returned these beautiful sacramental garments, along with his chalice, which had been given to him by his parents, to the Carmelite Monastery in Jefferson City, Missouri, where they are still in use.

The Carmelite Order

The first Carmelite Order was founded on Mount Carmel, in Israel, in the twelfth century as an order of hermit men who chose to seek God in solitude and silence and to honor the Blessed Virgin Mary. Although historical records about its origin remain uncertain, Saint Bertold has traditionally been associated with its founding, but few clear records of early Carmelite history have survived. Women began joining the order as Sisters in 1452, where they initially lived under the direction of Carmelite friars until independent convents were formed.

The Order has gone through many changes and reformations, most notably the reformation of the convents in the sixteenth century by St. Theresa of Jesus, founder of the Discalced (shoeless) Carmelites, and the influence of St. Therese of Lisieux, a nineteenth century Carmelite nun, who wrote of the "little way," rather than great deeds, in which anyone could show their love for God.

In modern times, the Carmelite Order has consisted of cloistered nuns and friars who adhere to strict vows of poverty, dedication to continual prayer, penance, self-sacrifice, and a belief that the prayers of the Order will lead to an "outpouring of redemptive blessings from God on this world." Generally, the Carmelites spend their days in prayer, work, recreation, and reading within the walls of the monastery, having little contact with the outside world. Their days are closely ordered, beginning at 5:30 a.m. with the morning Angelus, and ending at 10:30 p.m. at the conclusion of *Matins* (reading from the Divine Office) and the final evening blessing. Today, there are nearly 13,000 Carmelite nuns in 895 communities around the world.

Dorothy Frederick, Sister Dorothy Marie of the Immaculate Conception, OCD

Bud's older sister, Dorothy was born in Saginaw, on September 19, 1923, just before her parents moved to Grand Rapids. She was only sixteen when she entered the Carmelite Monastery in Grand Rapids on August 15, 1940. Because of her youth, her time as a novice was prolonged. At first, she was an extern sister, but before long, she experienced the desire to dedicate her life entirely to God within the cloister. Her religious name was Sister Mary of the Immaculate Conception. Later, she returned to her baptismal name: Sister Dorothy Marie of the Immaculate Conception. She received the holy habit of Carmel on December 8, 1941, in the Carmelite Monastery in Grand Rapids. She made her profession of temporary vows there on June 3, 1943.

Dorothy on the day of her initial vows.

Dorothy and Bud in the backyard on Watson Street.

Shortly before she was to take her final vows, Sister Dorothy Marie generously volunteered to join some others in an effort to establish a new Carmelite community in Culiacan, Mexico. From May 1946 until September 1967, Sister Dorothy assisted in beginning, building, and growing that community. On July 2, 1948, in Culiacan, Sinaloa, Mexico, she made her final vows and received her black veil.

In 1967, Fr. Fred went to Mexico to bring Sister Dorothy Marie home to the United States to have knee surgery. It was then that she joined the Carmelite Monastery in Traverse City. There, on February 6, 1968, she pronounced her solemn vows, a total form of consecration reserved for cloistered nuns. This final commitment had been postponed because of the political and religious environment in Mexico during her twenty-one years there.

Cousin Marge remembers Dorothy as a spirited, outgoing, and humorous woman who was a lot like her brother. Many times, Marge recalls, she and her husband drove from Saginaw to visit Dorothy at the Carmelite Monastery in Traverse City. They had to converse with her "from the other side of the screen" since she was a member of the cloistered order. She remembers being surprised when, during their visits to the convent, Sister Dorothy would offer them some of the nuns' homemade wine. No doubt, the craft of making wine had travelled down through the Polish vine of ancestry.

Mother Mary of Jesus, current prioress in the Traverse City Carmel was a young nun when she knew Sister Dorothy. "When I knew her (she would have been at least sixty by then), she was a big, strong woman; an energetic worker; extremely talented at embroidery and needlework. She could also play the organ well," she recalls.

In April 1985, Sister Dorothy Marie transferred to the monastery in St. Agatha, Ontario, Canada. Her sisters, there, remember her:

> *Sister Dorothy Marie was an extremely talented person. She was fond of music and excelled at needlework of any type. She was also a marvelous cook and baker. In the St. Agatha community, she served as sacristan[2] from 1987 until November 1994, when she developed a severe heart condition. She continued to make beautiful altar linens and other handcrafted items as long as she was able.*

> *On June 3, 1993, Sister Dorothy Marie celebrated her Golden Jubilee of Religious Profession. The main celebrant was Father Peter Hundt, the Chancellor of the Diocese of Hamilton. Father Fred concelebrated. Sister's brother Joseph and his wife Colette attended, as well as other friends from Michigan.*

Sister Dorothy Marie died at the Carmel in St. Agatha, on March 7, 1999. She is buried in the cemetery, there.

Theresa Frederick, Sister Agnes of God, OCD

Bud's younger sister, Theresa, was born February 4, 1927, in Grand Rapids, the third of Joe and Anna's four children. She was baptized on February 20, 1927, at Sacred Heart Church. She celebrated her First Communion in May 1935, and Confirmation a few years later on May 6, 1941, at the same church. She attended elementary school at Sacred Heart School and graduated from Grand Rapids Catholic Central High School.

Late in life, Theresa would often tell her religious sisters how, as a high school girl, she missed her sister, Dorothy, who had entered the Carmel in Grand Rapids. Often, the family would go over to the Carmel and help the sisters. Her father was a wonderful handyman—a person much appreciated at the Carmelite Monastery. Theresa ("Tessa") and her mother would often help the Sisters in the chapel and around the monastery. Also, the whole family frequently attended Holy Mass at the monastery. We cannot help but believe these visits had an effect on her decision to join the Carmelites. Cousin Marge, when asked to describe

---

2 A person in charge of the sacristy and ceremonial equipment.

her cousin in three words, replied without hesitation, "Oh, that's an easy one. Holy, holy, and holy!"

Mother Marie Therese, in Jefferson City, recalls some stories told by Sister Agnes:

> *Sister Agnes told us how they would all go to visit their grandparents in Saginaw. There, they had a great time with their cousins. Grandpa Frydryszek had several cherry trees, and this was a good time to get all the kids to help pick the cherries. All the trees were sour cherries, except one, and that one had big, dark sweet cherries on it. No one was to touch the "Tree in the Middle of the Garden" until all the sour cherries had been picked. When all the other trees had been picked, the kids could finally have the sweet cherries... and oh, how good they were!*

Sister Agnes left home for the Carmelite community in Santa Fe, New Mexico, on December 28, 1945. Fr. Fred and his brother, Joe, were home for Christmas vacation. Fr. Fred was in the seminary at the time. He was to accompany his sister on part of her journey, ensuring that she safely boarded the train to Santa Fe. After boarding the first train, he refused to sit next to her. He was already wearing his clerical "blacks" and was afraid someone would see him sitting next to this girl. Instead, he occupied a seat two rows in front of her. Poor Sister Agnes would say: "I could not understand why he wouldn't. After all, I was his sister. I thought maybe it was because just before I left, a friend of the family had given me a beautiful corsage. Maybe that's what scared him." Her Carmelite sisters would tell Sister Agnes, the only mistake anyone might make would be to think the two of them were twins—they so closely resembled each other.

Theresa entered the Carmelite Order on December 30, 1945, in Santa Fe, New Mexico, and received the holy habit of Carmel on October 3, 1946, when she took the religious name of Sister Agnes of God. Her first profession of vows was on October 15, 1947. She made her solemn profession on January 9, 1954.

Sister Agnes's parents and brothers, visited her in Santa Fe in July of 1955. It was the first time Fr. Fred and Sister Agnes had seen each other since their journey in 1945. After that, Fr. Fred saw her only a few more times in their lives.

Sister Agnes was a council member, sub-prioress for many years, and served one term (three years) in the Office of Prioress. She served as sacristan, was an excellent seamstress, community organist, avid gardener, and devoted community member. Sister Agnes was one of the original founding sisters of the Jefferson City Carmelite community, coming from Santa Fe. She completed sixty-four years in the Carmelite Order, the last fifty in Jefferson City.

On October 15, 1997, Sister Agnes of Jesus celebrated the 50th anniversary of taking her final profession of vows. Fr. Fred was in Jefferson City and concelebrated Mass with retired Bishop Michael McAuliffe, and Bishop John Gaydos, who had been appointed a few months earlier. It was the last time Fr. Fred saw his sister.

Sister Agnes of God celebrates the 50th anniversary in the Order with her brothers, Fr. Fred and Joe, and Joe's wife, Colette.

Late in her life, Sister Agnes wrote to Marge about the family. She told her one of the things she often prayed for was a closer relationship between her brothers. She rationalized that it was probably natural since one was a family man and the other a priest, and that they had simply concentrated on different priorities.

Sister Agnes of God died in Jefferson City on April 10, 2009. She is buried in the cemetery, there.

Bud's Brother: Joe Frederick and His Family

Joseph "Joe" Paul Frederick was born three years and three days after Bud, on April 20, 1928. Like Bud, he attended grade school at Sacred Heart. Again, following his older brother, he entered St. Joseph Seminary in Grand Rapids. However, that turned out to be a short-lived interest for him, and he went on instead to earn a Master of Social Work from Michigan State University.

Joe met Colette Weber in the hospital in Chicago where Colette was working as a registered nurse. At the time, he was going to school at DePaul University during the day and working nights at the hospital. Fr. Fred presided at their wedding in

Joe and Buddy.

1955. Joe and Colette raised four children: Paul, John, Mary, and Jim. The family lived in Eaton Rapids, Michigan, where he worked with the emotionally impaired as a consultant for the Ingham County Schools for twenty years, until retirement. Colette recalls that he always had a tendency to favor the poor.

By the time Joe was fifteen, his siblings were all gone from home. Bud was in the seminary and both of his sisters had entered the Carmelite Order. Consequently, he had more of an extended time with his parents. As they aged, Joe looked after them with increasing responsibility. He was also very helpful to his two maiden aunts, Josie and Stella Szczepanski, who lived next door. Like his father and grandfather Frydryszek, Joe was handy at building and maintenance projects.

As an adult, Joe made weekly trips from Eaton Rapids to Grand Rapids to take his mother grocery shopping and care for the home on Watson Street. He made sure his parents got to church, to the doctor and other appointments, and ran weekly errands for them, through the end of their lives.

Joe's family describes him as a very private, bookish, and intellectual person. His hobbies included carpentry, reading, writing, gardening, and anything nature-related. They say he was patient, never used foul language, and was a great role model. He had a great, though dry, sense of humor. Joe liked watching and listening to sports, especially being an MSU fan. Like his brother, he was loyal to the Detroit Lions and Tigers.

Christmastime was always special. Joe would take his family to Grandma's house in Grand Rapids, where Bud and his dog, Brucie, would arrive with pheasants he had shot, and his favorite dessert of pumpkin pie. Each year, there were a couple Christmas trees atop Bud's car—one for Joe's family and one for his parents. It was always Bud's pleasure to arrive home after his Mass schedule in Traverse City was complete and help his mother decorate their tree. Joe's oldest son, Paul remembers: "After dinner, Santa would suddenly arrive with a bag full of toys. Santa had a very high-pitched voiced and some years later, I recognized that voice as that of our Aunt Josie from next door."

For years, it was a custom for Joe and Bud to talk on the phone at nine o'clock every Sunday night. Often, these conversations would last an hour. Topics would include family well-being, kids' activities, the Detroit Lions and Tigers, and The Father Fred Foundation. Joe was fiercely proud of his older brother, and loved hearing about Bud's work at the State Hospital and The Father Fred Foundation.

In a similar effort, Joe talked, when he could, with his two sisters. Calling to the monastery was sometimes difficult because of their strict hours and telephone rules. So, he mostly communicated through letters and cards. His son, Jim, relates this story:

> *Later on, he talked a lot with Theresa on the phone. We visited Missouri a few times to see her. I remember the last time he saw her before she passed away. She was in the hospital and was actually having a great day. She was wide-awake, alert, and very talkative. Usually, at the monastery, he had to visit and talk through a screened wall, but this time was different. She was out in the open. It was the first time in more than sixty years that my Dad was able to give her a hug and kiss.*

Overall, Joe is remembered as a private man of great faith, and a dedicated family man. He was proud of his children and grandchildren and supported them in all they did. His faith was his greatest treasure and he passed it on to his children. Like the rest of his family, he had a life-long devotion to the Blessed Virgin Mary and was faithful about praying the Rosary. His rosary was in his hand when he died at home, surrounded by his family, on December 29, 2009.

Joe Frederick and his family. L. to R.: John, Mary, Joe, Colette, Jim, Paul.

The Maiden Aunts: Stella and Josie Szczepanski

After Anna's (Bud's mother) parents died, her sisters, Josephine, "Josie," and Stella, continued living next door. Stella and Josie had also worked at the cigar factory, and neither ever married. After his time in the Army, their bachelor brother Joe (Szczepanski) moved in with them and worked as a maintenance man at St. Joseph Seminary, in Grand Rapids. They all lived in that house until they died.

Bob Kimball, married to Marianne, one of Anna's cousins, tells about a visit to Joe and Anna's home. During the course of the late autumn afternoon visit, Josie and Stella came over from next door. One was carrying a jug of their latest homemade wine. As they were pouring the suspicious looking fluid, someone asked, "What kind of wine is it?" "Tomato," was the reply.

"Hmm," was the reaction, as each of the people sitting around the circle tasted it. It was dreadful. Nobody wanted to say anything to hurt their feelings, but when they weren't looking, each one spit it out and poured the rest on the ground. "Oh yes, very good."

As these two aunts aged, they continued to rely on the visits and attention from their nephews, Joe Frederick and Fr. Fred. The 1980 census of Sacred Heart Parish shows that Stella (80) and Josephine (74) still lived in the house they grew up in—at 1031 Watson.

Here's One For You: Straight Talk

Here, as in some of the following chapters, is presented a story or two in the method of Fr. Fred. At the end of a homily, he would add a memorable little story and say something like, "Now, here's a little something to take home with you."

Quite naturally, Bud became the spiritual center of the family. He was their rock and provided guidance. His second cousin, Suzanne Rehmann, a daughter of Bud's cousin, Marge, remembers a time when she was the subject of Fr. Fred's guidance. Suzanne was about seventeen and had a boyfriend that her parents didn't approve of. The more they talked to her about it, like any teenager, the more she insisted on being with him. "Okay, as soon as school's out, we're going to send you up to stay with Bud for a week. He'll straighten you out." That made Suzanne even angrier—and embarrassed. "How could these parents of mine," she thought, "make me go be with a *priest* for a week? Do they think I'm a lost cause?"

So, Suzanne went to stay with her mom's cousin at his home – his sanctuary on the Boardman River. They had a great time all week, tubing down the river, roasting marshmallows, hiking, and of course, talking as their feet dangled in the fast-moving Boardman. She remembers,

> *I was treated like a queen. We would sit and listen to the river and talk for hours —just Bud and I and his beautiful German shepherd, Brucie. During that visit, I learned he was no ordinary cousin. He was such a humanitarian. I still think of him every day.*

He even took her to work with him and she saw, firsthand, what he was doing at All Faiths Chapel and the State Hospital. She remembers being frightened by the patients, at first. After she saw how they responded to Bud's compassion, his humor, and his calming hands, she felt protected when she was with him.

Bud and his bike, dressed up for the Decoration Day Parade.

When she tells the story now, she says that while she was with him in Traverse City, the topic of the boyfriend hardly ever came up, and he didn't beat anything into her by preaching about it. It was merely hours and hours of an easy, weeklong, real-world conversation. At one point, she thought maybe he didn't even know why she was there.

On the last night, before returning home, Bud asked Suzanne, "You know why you're here, don't you?"

"Yup," she responded.

"Then do the right thing."

A week later, the guy was history.

Here's Another One For You: Satellite Dish Installation

Bud gave his nephew, John, the nickname "Rebel." John tells of the time when he called his Uncle Bud, who was at his home on the Boardman River. "Hey, Uncle Bud, how are you doing?" It was a chatty and pleasant and ordinary conversation. Well, it was an ordinary conversation until John heard *BOOM!* — a tremendous blast rang through the earpiece.

"Uncle Bud, are you okay? What just happened? What's going on?"

"Oh, the guy was out today to install my new satellite dish..." *BOOM!*

"Bud... are you okay? What the hell was that?" asked a worried John.

"Yeah, I'm okay. The guy was out to install my new satellite dish today, and I can't get good reception. Hang on a minute. I gotta go inside. Nope, that didn't do it."

BOOM! A third explosion reported a few seconds later.

"Uncle Bud, what's going on?"

"Well, the guy said the trees are in the way of my getting good reception, so I'm shooting the tops off with my 12-gauge shotgun." *BOOM!* A fourth report was heard. "I'm walking inside to check the reception. Oh, that's a lot better. Now I can talk. How you doin', Rebel?" By this time, John was laughing so hard he had to tell him he'd call back. Next time he went up north to visit his Uncle Bud, John looked up and sure enough, the jagged line of treetops was open enough to let in a nice, clear satellite signal.

Here's Another One For You: Carmelite Rudeness

John also tells that he visited his Uncle Bud in Traverse City quite often. Occasionally, Bud would have him take something back to Grand Rapids to drop off at the Carmelite Monastery. He remembers telling his uncle after one such trip, "They were really rude, Uncle Bud. They wouldn't even talk to me."

Bud smiled, as he told John, "Well, they can't Rebel. They're cloistered nuns!"

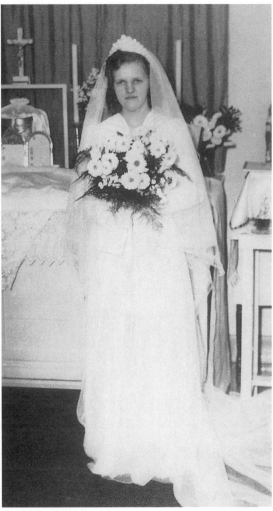

August 15, 1940, on the day Dorothy leaves home to enter the Carmelite Order.

Sister Agnes of God (Theresa) on the day of her initial vows in New Mexico.

Sister Dorothy celebrating her 50th anniversary in the Carmelite Order.

INTROIBO AD ALTÁRE DEI

Send your light and fidelity, that they may be my guide,
And bring me to your holy mountain, to the place of
your dwelling, That I may come to the altar of God,
to God, my joy, my delight.

(Psalm 43:3-4)

W e begin this chapter on Father Fred's faith formation and vocation as a priest with the opening words of the old Catholic Latin Mass: *Introibo ad Altáre Dei*—"I will go unto the altar of God." He entered his priesthood before the changes in the Catholic Church, brought about by Vatican II, so he opened Mass with these words for nearly twenty years. The liturgical changes, in the mid-1960s, must have suited him and his personality well. He would have felt more comfortable celebrating Mass in the vernacular English, facing the congregation. Even though he often appeared to operate outside some of the traditional Catholic norms, he was infused with a very traditional Catholic theology. To many, his popularity was based on his not being like other priests, yet he never strayed too far

Bud's baptism day with his parents.

Bud's First Communion, 1933.

from conservative Roman Catholic theology, a tradition that had been carried for generations in his family.

A strong Catholic upbringing and a pathway toward priesthood started early for young Edwin. Raised in a devout home and family, with roots that extended to the beginning of the local parish, he responded to the disciplines of religion from an early age. His first sacramental experience was at nine days old, his baptism, on April 26, 1925, at Sacred Heart Parish, in Grand Rapids. He was baptized Edwin Joseph Frydryszek by Fr. Sydlowski.

Sacred Heart Parish, Grand Rapids

In his book, *The Sacred Heart Story*, Eduard Skendzel does a masterful job of telling the history of Father Fred's family's parish in Grand Rapids, Michigan. Sacred Heart Parish was founded in 1904, by a small and growing group of Polish Catholics who wanted a new parish on the west side of Grand Rapids. The expanding Polish population wanted a parish in the highly ethnic Ninth Ward, where the walking distance to St. Adalbert's had become an inconvenience for many parishioners.

The early history of the parish, the eighth Catholic parish in Grand Rapids, is marked by difficulties, largely due to the diverse and mixing ethnicities of the area as well as some ethnic resistance from the ecclesiastical establishment. For more history of the parish, see Skendzel's book, from which much of this account is derived.

On September 11, 1903, Father Krakowski, the recently appointed pastor of the new congregation, received written permission from Bishop Richter to purchase five lots in the block bounded by Valley, Park, Dayton, and Garfield, on the eastern edge of the beautiful, new John Ball Park for $1,900. The first parish building was a combination church and school, dedicated on Thanksgiving Day in 1904. Twenty years later, there were 800 students in the new school, and in the parish census of 1925, the year Fr. Fred was born, 500 families are listed.

The new church, which still stands as a west side icon, was finished in time for Christmas Eve Mass, 1923. According to Skendzel:

> *This church has been built in the style of the Basilica of St. Paul Outside-the-Walls in Rome. The coffered ceiling is masterfully executed. The pillars have been placed on the sides so that they do not obscure the altars and the pulpit. Experts have affirmed that this church can be considered one of the most magnificent, not only in the diocese, but in the entire area. This church will forever remain a monument to the faith and love and generosity of the people of "Heart's."*

Among the group of contributors and founding parishioners thirty-year-old Joseph Szczepanski and his wife, Ursula, were busy raising their family just a few blocks away from the site of the new church, at 1031 Watson. Joseph was a member of the St. Ladislaus Society, a Catholic young men's society that was founded in September 1903 to support the new pastor and parish. In 1905, he is listed as a trustee, officer of that organization.

On Labor Day—September 3, 1923—the huge bells in the towers of the church were dedicated. Each of the four bells in the north tower has a name: St. Joseph, Sacred Heart, Guardian Angel, and St. Mary. Embossed on the side of each bell are the names of the contributors for that bell. Looking closely, on the side of St. Mary, one can find the name (in Polish) of Józef Szczepanski, Fr. Fred's grandfather.

Buddy's Time at Sacred Heart

Buddy attended Sacred Heart School, taught by the School Sisters of Notre Dame, the *"Notredamki."* He and his brother Joe were altar boys, serving Mass for the pastor, Fr. Joseph Karas; and associate pastors Fr. Francis Kupinski, Fr. John Bozek, and Fr. Bernard Sikorski. Edwin and Joe were among the altar boys who were strictly and lovingly directed and affected by Sister Mary Karola (Carola). This incredible woman took her first and only teaching assignment in 1918, and stayed at Sacred Heart fifty-four years, teaching grades second through eighth, until September 1972. She got to know all the students and their families as well as their children, grandchildren, and great-grandchildren. No other teacher in the history of Sacred Heart School had as much tenure or effect on the students as Sister Carola.

In 1933, Edwin, along with ninety-four other boys and girls, made his First Communion at neighboring Sacred Heart Church. The exact date is unknown, since parish records for that period have been lost. It is assumed he was confirmed on the same day.

Joe proudly presents his sons as altar boys, Joe (l.) and Bud (r.)

Bud wears the black tie he earned for completion of his first six years in seminary.

Seminary, Ordination, First Assignments

Edwin finished grade school at Sacred Heart and entered St. Joseph Seminary in Grand Rapids on September 11, 1939. He was active in music and sports during his time there and graduated *cum laude* in January 1945. At his graduation, he earned a black necktie, signifying the completion of two years of study in philosophy, as the first phase of his seminary training.

The second phase of his vocational training was at Sacred Heart Seminary, in Detroit. He entered there on February 10, 1945, and earned his Bachelor's degree in philosophy, before entering the Grand Séminaire de Montréal in September

Dear Lord, bless my mother, father, brother, sisters, relatives and friends whose prayers and sacrifices have made possible this joyful occasion.

✠

Remembrance
of my
Ordination
June 3
of the Holy Year, 1950
and
First Solemn Mass
Sacred Heart Church
June 4, 1950
Rev. Edwin J. Frederick

✠

Immaculate Queen of the Holy Priesthood, pray for us.

Card to commemorate Fr. Frederick's ordination and first Mass.

Fr. Fred's ordination portrait.

Ceremony of Fr. Fred becoming a deacon.

1946. On June 11, 1949, he became a deacon, and a year later he graduated after completing his studies in theology.

Father Fred was ordained on June 3, 1950, at St. Andrew's Cathedral in Grand Rapids by Bishop Francis J. Haas. He gave both his parents the traditional blessing at his first Mass in his home parish on Sunday, June 4. Several photos of the family celebration show the very proud Joe and Anna and their son, Buddy, in the yard of the house on Watson Street.

Fr. Edwin Frederick was immediately assigned to serve as assistant pastor at Sacred Heart Parish in Mount Pleasant, Michigan. He served there until June 1951, when he was re-assigned to St. Joseph Parish in Manistee, Michigan. In April 1953, he joined Fr. Andrew Sikorski as assistant pastor at St. Michael in Muskegon, Michigan, where he remained for over six years, until June 1959.

Bishop Rose Remembers Father Fred

Young Robert Rose entered St. Joseph Seminary in Grand Rapids in September 1944. A talented pianist, he made a name for himself playing at the seminary. He remembers his friend, Ed Frederick:

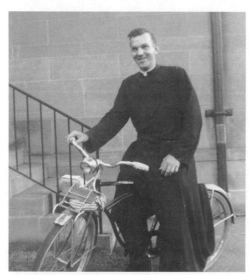

Fr. Fred in Muskegon, c. 1956.

As a freshman at St. Joseph Seminary in Grand Rapids, in 1944, I played the piano in the school music program. Ed was in his sixth year and ready to graduate. He and his brother, Joe, both played in the orchestra. Ed played violin. I have great memories of putting on the annual Christmas musical. Graduation was accelerated to February, that year, because of the war. So, Ed graduated and left for Sacred Heart Seminary in Detroit before I got to know him better.

Later, in October 1981, Fr. Rose was appointed the second bishop of the Diocese of Gaylord, the same diocese in which Fr. Fred worked during the last forty years of his life.

St. Michael Parish, Muskegon

It was in Muskegon where Fr. Fred began to mature as a priest. He immediately settled into a comfortable working relationship with the elder Fr. Andrew Sikorski, who was the pastor at St. Michael. They enjoyed lots of friendly banter and had a fierce cribbage rivalry. Parishioners fondly remember many stories that portray Fr. Sikorski as a stern mentor and a warm friend to the capable and popular young priest. Fr. Fred also connected effectively with the youth of the parish.

At he beach in Muskegon with some high school kids.

Connection with Muskegon Youth

More than anything, he wanted the kids to be safe. He brought his characteristic sense of playfulness and impish humor to work with him every day and mixed it with the life lessons he wanted to get across to the young people of the parish.

Loraine Anderson (Piotrowski), a student at St. Michael's in the 1950s, can recall when Fr. Frederick would come to school to teach religion to her grade school class. "One day," she tells, all these years later, "he came into the classroom, dancing and singing 'You Ain't Nothin' But a Hound Dog' by Elvis Presley."

Fifty-two years after he left his assignment in Muskegon, memories of Fr. Fred are just as sharp and immediate as if the people sharing them had seen him last week. Marilyn Mapes giggled like a teenager in remembering when Fr. Fred arrived in Muskegon; the back bumper of his old, black car playfully sported the letters: "KWITCHERBITCHIN." She also remembers that soon after the stern pastor, Fr. Sikorski, saw this, the lettering disappeared without discussion.

Ed Nowak, a parishioner, recalls how Fr. Fred related to the grade school kids at St. Michael's. "When the weather was good, he'd go out and play ball or a game of tag with the kids at noon in the schoolyard. He was quite an athletic guy and really loved the kids."

It was unusual for a priest, in those days, to take equal interest in organizing activities with the girls, as well as the boys. He was interested in and popular with all the young people. He wanted them to have fun, learn what he was there to teach them, and do some kind of service. "These would become the hallmarks of what we were supposed to be," remarks one of the girls, over fifty years later. "And he always had an innate sense of propriety."

As the assistant pastor, he had to offer Mass at the mission parish in the nearby town of Rothbury. He would leave Muskegon at dawn and take an altar boy or two as well as one or two of the girls to help with the singing. "The car never went under ninety." says Marilyn. "We thought it was great. He always took two of us, because he had a notion of what was right and how it looked. We knew he genuinely liked us."

It was common practice for the assistant pastor to train altar boys, plan athletic events with them, and put on an annual school picnic at the end of the year to thank them for their service. It was uncharacteristic, however, for a priest to organize activities for the girls. Parents just assumed that the Catholic school and the nuns were "taking care of all this," teaching the girls the risks of teenage behavior. Fr. Fred realized all kids needed more outlets, and he didn't think "everything was taken care of." The Sisters of Mercy had a strict schedule and could not be available to the kids after school was out for the day. He interacted on a spiritual as well as practical basis with the young people, making it fun. Even though he was a priest, many of the kids saw him also as a great friend. No priest had done that before in that parish.

The Sodality

Marilyn Rajewski and Annie Goggin were best girlfriends. Along with their friend, Karen Josefowicz, they were known to Fr. Fred as his "Three Stooges." They were the core of a sodality[3] group that Fr. Fred organized for them. The "Fighting 69ers" Sodality was based on the sixth and ninth commandments with the intention to keep the Catholic high school girls pure and chaste. For this group, however, it was much, much more. They were (and still are) a group of tightly bonded friends, influenced by the caring and charismatic young priest. Other parishes didn't have anything like this for girls.

---

3   A sorority-like social and devotional or charitable organization for Roman Catholic girls, based on Christian spiritual teaching.

Father helped the girls organize social, religious, and service activities. Beach parties on the shore of Lake Michigan were summertime favorites. At every event, there was devotional prayer and a short lesson. Marilyn remembers: "Father Fred didn't have to tell you something. He just showed you. He was so sincere in wanting you to be a good person. He brought out the good in everybody. We just had fun and learned so much from the way he lived his life."

Annie Goggin remembers:

> *It would not have occurred to us to fight with our parents, so we never had to go talk with the priest with our problems. We all had warm, loving families, where parents were parents.*

> *There were dances at the armory downtown—big public dances. Parents would not let the girls go, so we went to Father Fred to ask if he would intercede on our behalf and convince our parents it would be okay to go. He answered with: "I agree with your parents and don't think you should go." We all knew that was the end of the conversation.*

> *I knew both he and my parents must have seen something I didn't see. I respected their perspective and decision. I was surprised, because I thought he was a good guy and believed in fun and would surely advocate for us. Later, we learned there had been some rough stuff at those dances. It turns out he was not worried as much about our morality as our safety.*

> *In that time, whoever talked about the sixth and ninth commandments? He totally understood us as teenagers. He knew we were pretty responsible. It was different then. The sodality taught us responsible behavior. If you play with fire, you're going to get burned. His messages were always clear.*

Annie entered a religious order shortly after college graduation. Marilyn married, moved away, and raised a family. Karen Jo stayed in Muskegon and raised a family. Even from this abbreviated look at his "Three Stooges," we can assume that Fr. Fred's sodality lessons of the 1950s were effective, based on the lifelong commitments these women made.

Annie, who became Sister Ann, stayed in correspondence with Fr. Fred for the rest of his life, often discussing theological questions. She wrote this to her friend, Marilyn shortly after Fr. Fred's funeral:

> *I remember his talking about building the house with his dad and how much he loved it. And I sure wish I had kept the stack of letters I had from those first years as he grew into the work at the hospital. I think he used every disappointment to go deeper into the core of the Gospel and the heart of his vocation... It's wonderful to meet the genuine article when you're young.*

A Vocation Story

Ann Goggin initially attended the public school but found the high school religion classes dull, so she went to Fr. Fred's adult conversion classes. They were much more interesting, and she heard religion from an adult point of view. She also was in the habit of going to daily Mass to pray for her very sick mother.

One day, after Mass, she pointed out another girl to Fr. Fred and said, "I heard she is going to be a nun." She had never known anyone who was going to be a nun. He looked at her and said, "Yes, she is. Have you ever thought about it?" And in all honesty, she knew that her life had just changed, forever. She had never given it a moment's thought. "I knew I had not heard the end of it [from God]. I knew instantly. I even know exactly where we were and the exact moment, by the sacristy door of the church."

Her parents were furious, especially her mother. They insisted she go to college and get a degree first and by then, she would be able to make up her own mind. Fr. Fred encouraged that plan and quietly and confidently supported her. The two of them began a conversation about what order would best suit her personality.

Annie attended Marquette University in Milwaukee, studying with the Jesuits. She finished her undergraduate studies in theology and English prior to joining the Cenacle, a Catholic religious congregation devoted to making Jesus known and loved through prayer, community life, and spiritual ministries.

By the time she took her final vows, her mother had died, but her parents had forgiven both Ann and Fr. Fred by then. She asked him to be the main celebrant at that Mass. Her religious sisters wondered why she didn't ask some of the famous Jesuits she had studied and worked with. She was as loyal to Fr. Fred as he would have been to her. He was thrilled to be asked (though he admitted he was a little nervous) and relished being on the altar, concelebrating with ten Jesuits.

Very few of Fr. Fred's written homilies remain, yet we have a copy of the one he read from that day. He made these remarks about the difficult decision she made:

> *Ann... the whisper and gentle call of Jesus brought you through to where you are today—convinced that what you're doing is His will—what God wants. Pain, conflict, stress, discouragement have been conquered. Romans 8:39—"Neither death nor life will be able to separate us from the love of God that comes to us in Christ Jesus."*

> *I congratulate you. I am happy for you. Your seriousness of choice, your quality of determination, seems to me could probably stem from your individual personality, but then God had a hand in this, too. He clothed you with faith and courage and His presence.*

He expressed more thoughts about her decision with:

> *... For us, today, things aren't so clear-cut. There is more danger, not so much in making the wrong choice, as in making no choice at all. You, Annie, made a choice. You committed yourself, and you grew more strong (sic) as your doubts and discouraging moments dissipated. To think that one could commit one's self once and absolutely for a lifetime, and hope that this is it, would be kinda fatal and naïve. It was and is necessary to re-consider, to re-new, to re-examine, to rest in order to grow and fill God's order—God's want.*

Problems and doubts will continue to sprinkle your life.
That's normal, but look at them positively. They come to
strengthen you, the loved and chosen one of God.

Later, Ann earned a Master of Divinity and Doctor of Ministry from Weston Jesuit School of Theology in Boston. She taught at Regis University in Denver, several diocesan pastoral programs, and five years (Spirituality and Theology) at the University of Notre Dame. As a member of the Order, she lives, teaches, and works with Christian lay ministers in Houston, Texas.

Additional Assets to St. Michael

There is one St. Michael story that characterizes Fr. Fred as well as any other. As the assistant pastor, he was put in charge of a landscaping project at the parish. It involved some construction, some serious landscaping, and maybe even a new church sign and some sidewalk paving. The exact nature of the work to be done is, today, less important than the way it was handled. He was put in charge of the bidding process and selection of the contractor, since he had grown up in the construction business, with his dad. The project was described and the specifications published for bidding.

When all the bids were opened, he read them all and recommended one of the contractors. There was just one small problem—a contractor, who was a member of the parish, was not recommended, because his price was considerably higher than the one who was not a Catholic and it would take longer. Fr. Fred explained to Fr. Sikorski that he could not, in good conscience, recommend the parish member. The other guy got the job, and there were some bruised feelings, but Fr. Fred, with a fair and ecumenical practicality, went with the bid he knew would be the better deal for the parish. It was simply the right thing to do.

He was also put in charge of overseeing the installation of the new carillon bell system at St. Michaels. Called the "Basilican," the new instrument was equivalent to six tons of English bells. Speakers were installed on the school building that sat adjacent to the church. The Basilican could be programmed for many different uses, before Mass, or to ring the Angelus[4], on a daily basis. Made by Schulmerich Carillons, Inc., the automatic bell-ringing instrument was a duplicate of bells that had been recently installed in the new North American College in Vatican City.

---

4 The devotion was traditionally recited in Roman Catholic churches, convents, and monasteries three times daily: 6:00 am, noon, and 6:00 pm. The Angelus is usually accompanied by the ringing of the Angelus bell, which is a call to prayer.

Fr. Sikorski let Fr. Fred represent the parish when the new system was featured in a photo article about the new parish asset in *The Muskegon Chronicle*.

Always an Advocate

Another story is about Ed Nowak, a Polish kid who lived in Muskegon. He was fourteen when his dad died in 1940, and he had to go to work with his mom in the family market as a meat cutter.

Life was not easy for this lifelong parishioner of St. Michael Parish, now in his mid-eighties. In school, he was just one year ahead of Eddie Szoka, who later went to the seminary, became the first bishop of the Diocese of Gaylord, Michigan, then became Archbishop of Detroit, and was

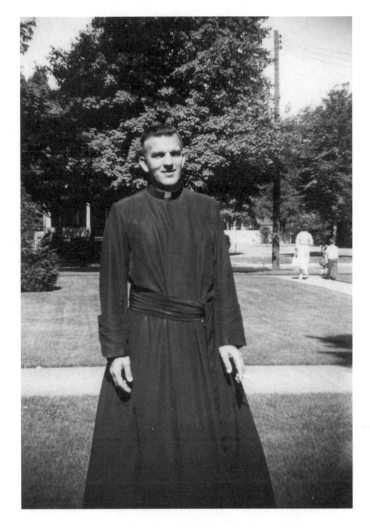

later appointed as a cardinal. "Oh, he got to be a big deal in the Church," Ed remembers. "He went to Rome and worked with the Pope."

After Ed married Georgiana, a Muskegon girl, the children they hoped for didn't come along, and they decided to adopt. Their adoption efforts with the local Catholic Services agency were met with stalling, red tape, and a frustrating lack of success. In her desperation, Georgiana called Fr. Fred and asked him to intervene.

While Ed recalls that "Father Fred called them up at the agency and chewed them out," the couple really didn't know what happened. However, the first interview came soon after the call and their first child, Michael, was adopted less than a year later. Marianne and Ed Jr. followed Michael at approximately one-year intervals—all adopted through the same agency. "I just can't thank Father Fred enough," Ed says. "I owe him so much. He was such a great priest, but [he] was just like an ordinary guy. He did so much for us."

Zdrowaś Maryjo, łaski pełna
Pan z Tobą,
błogosławionas Ty miedzy niewiastami
błogoslawiony owoc żywota Twojego, Jezus.
Święta Maryjo, Matko Boża,
módl się za nami grzesznymi
teraz i w godzinę śmierci naszej.
Amen.

-- Hail Mary (Polish)

Ed also recalls that Fr. Fred would occasionally attempt to deliver a sermon in Polish. "His Polish wasn't that good and he knew it. He'd get up and read his sermon, and the Polish members in the congregation did their best to keep from chuckling. But you know what? He still got up and did it. He was great."

Time to Move On

During the time he served at St. Michael, Fr. Fred developed in his vocation and came of age as a priest. He maintained an excellent relationship with his pastor and won the hearts of parishioners of all ages, especially the young people. He served the parish well and his record of service distinguished him as an ascending star in the Diocese of Grand Rapids. After serving St. Michael for just over six years, he was probably not surprised to be reassigned. Could this be the time for his

His parents join Fr. Fred at his going-away party in Muskegon.

first position as a pastor? Instead, he was stunned to learn that the bishop assigned him to be the chaplain at the psychiatric hospital in Traverse City. Plans moved swiftly, and before he could totally process this powerful shift in his expectations, it was time for him to say good-bye.

Leaving St. Michael was difficult for the popular thirty-four-year-old priest. He had made many friends in Muskegon, and there was a huge and tearful farewell party for him. His mom and dad were there to see the loving send-off the parishioners gave him. The "Three Stooges" were there, with the rest of the sodality girls, and made a scrapbook of the occasion that they presented to him. When he died, the scrapbook was returned to Marilyn Rajewski Mapes, who still cherishes the collection of those memories.

**Hail Mary, full of grace,
the Lord is with thee.
Blessed art thou among women,
and blessed is the fruit of thy womb, Jesus.
Holy Mary, Mother of God,
pray for us sinners,
now and at the hour of our death.
Amen.**

He was surprised, puzzled, and discouraged about his appointment to the Traverse City State Hospital. For the up-and-coming, bright, young priest, it was an unwelcome diversion from his vision of parish pastoral service. "What could I have done that was so bad," he asked a friend, "that I was banished to the insane asylum?" Yet, because of his vow of obedience to the bishop, he dutifully responded to his assignment orders. On June 16, 1959, he simultaneously became the part-time Catholic chaplain at the Traverse City State Hospital and at the Carmelite Monastery in Traverse City, Michigan.

He and his huge German shepherd, Jett, headed north. Thus began the unusual, thirty-year, unexpected continuation in the development of his priesthood.

ALL FAITHS

*Whatever you did for one of these
least brothers of mine, you did for me.*

(Matthew 25:40)

D an Deering, owner and manager of a multi-generational grocery chain in the Traverse City area, was one of the first people Father Fred met when he came to town. Fr. Fred stopped Dan on the steps of the post office, one morning, with, "Hey, mister, that dog's going to jump out of your truck." Being new in northern Michigan, he didn't realize that dogs and pickup trucks go together and that owners trained their dogs to not leave the bed of the truck, when it was parked. Fr. Fred had left his dog, Jett, locked in the backseat of his car.

"That dog isn't going anywhere." Dan replied, and that simple exchange began a friendship that lasted for more than four decades. The conversation continued with a comparison of the two German shepherds: Jett was about twice the size of Dan's dog. Fr. Fred told him about his new assignment as chaplain at the State Hospital, and how he was finding his way around Traverse City.

Original concept drawing for All Faiths Chapel

All Faiths Chapel

Soon, they got to know each other, because Fr. Fred would come into the store and buy groceries. He invited Dan up to the hospital and Dan would drop by and see him. He would come into Fr. Fred's office and be greeted with, "Boy, am I glad you stopped by. I need to talk with someone like you today." Little did Dan know, in those early days, how much he would be donating through his new friend during the next fifty years.

Traverse City Regional Psychiatric Hospital

In April 1883, construction began in Traverse City on the third insane asylum in Michigan, under the auspices of the state legislature. It was designed to serve thirty-nine counties in northern and western Michigan and all of the Upper Peninsula. The Michigan Asylum for the Insane had opened in Kalamazoo in 1859, followed by, in 1878, the opening of the Eastern Michigan Asylum for the Insane, in Pontiac. On November 11, 1885, while construction was still in progress, the first residents were transferred to the new Northern Michigan Asylum for the Insane. Housing was later to be in "cottages," according to the mental health culture of the time. However, the first building occupied was the Asylum Building, now known as Building 50. The first medical superintendant for the facility was Dr. James Decker Munson.[5]

From a *Traverse City Record-Eagle* review supplement in 1981, we see that even in the beginning, the hospital was a warehousing facility. Some of the early diagnoses set the patterns of how the mentally ill were viewed and treated:

> *The first patients were admitted for a variety of reasons that today often sound like archaic, unlikely tickets to a mental institution: isolation, overwork, vicious habits and indulgences, sun strokes, epilepsy, religious excitement, grief, over-study, nervous prostration, senility, morphine habits, hysteria, nostalgia, and something called pubescence.*

> *Many of the elderly patients were in their late 30s and 40s, people who were not tolerated and could no longer function in 1880 America. Many were immigrants [who], according to the register, never left the asylum.*

---

5 For an excellent history of the Traverse City State Hospital, see *Northern Michigan Asylum*, by Dr. Wm. A. Decker, M.D., and other texts, noted in the bibliography. Much of the material in this section is drawn from the diligent work of Dr. Decker.

... Unlike modern mental institutions, which are trying to de-institutionalize, the asylums of that time became catch-alls for the unwanted people, including the elderly, alcoholics, homosexuals, and even unwed mothers.

In the first half of the twentieth century, the Traverse City State Hospital, like most mental health facilities, was a scary and forbidding place for the outsider. It was shrouded in a mystique of horror, shame, misunderstanding, and what we call "urban legend." Some of this impression held by locals and visitors was earned by the behavior of some of the residents. In some cases, patients were heard screaming from caged porches on the cottages, where they were assigned to be for the day in attempts to

Fr. Fred celebrates Mass in the old chapel, in the basement of Building 50, 1960.

provide them some fresh air. In other parts of the hospital campus, they were seen acting out their strange and pathological behavior. This misunderstanding, when combined with the Kirkbride architecture of the facility, provided fodder for myth and spooky folk tales.

Kirkbride buildings have long been relics of an obsolete therapeutic method known as "moral treatment." In the latter half of the nineteenth century, these massive structures were conceived as ideal sanctuaries for the mentally ill and as an active participant in their recovery. The originator of this concept was Dr. Thomas Story Kirkbride, a founding member of the Association of Medical Superintendents of American Institutions for the Insane (AMSAII)—forerunner of the American Psychiatric Association. Through this association and in his writings, Kirkbride promoted a standardized method of asylum construction and mental health treatment, popularly known as the Kirkbride Plan, which significantly influenced the entire American asylum community during his lifetime. This architecture was also widely characteristic of sanatoriums, state training schools, reform schools, orphanages, and prisons. It is no wonder, in that prevailing environment, that Fr. Fred would be concerned about his assignment to that facility.

In the 104 years of its operation, major changes occurred in the treatment of mental illness; the state of Michigan's approach to funding the treatment; and social norms surrounding the issues of mental illness. Evidence of the changes begins with nomenclature. Originally, "lunatics, imbeciles, morons, feeble-minded, and idiots" were moved from almshouses, jails, and poorhouses and admitted as "inmates." Later, they became "patients." Insanity morphed into mental illness. A cottage became known as a building number; and asylums became hospitals, implying medical care and treatment, rather than warehousing. The name of the institution changed over the years to reflect the changing environment. In 1923, Public Act 151 changed the name to Traverse City State Hospital, and in 1978, the name was again altered to be the Traverse City Regional Psychiatric Hospital.

Dr. Munson held the beliefs that "beauty is therapy" and "work is therapy." Consequently, the ambience and grounds of the facility were made welcoming and pleasant and attempted to provide a family-like (as normal as possible) atmosphere.

The hospital also had a chapel on site. The first one held 318 people and was located in the back and to the west of the asylum building on the first floor, above the kitchens. The space was also used for amusement purposes, concerts, dances, and socials. By 1963, the chapel space had been replaced by the canteen and an "emporium," or patient store. The chapel moved downstairs, to be shared with the patient library and music practice rooms.

A chaplaincy program was part of the culture at the facility from the beginning. Dr. Munson, himself, took an active part in Sunday Protestant services. Dr. Decker writes about early religious services:

> *During those days, employees lived at the asylum and services were open to patient and employee alike. Patients were escorted to the chapel by nursing employees whose seating was arranged so that they sat in a separate section, facing the patients. Male patients sat on one side of the chapel and female patients on the opposite side. Services were on a strict schedule, and when the appointed hour arrived, every patient and every employee was in his place. Precisely at the hour of service, the Medical Superintendant, Dr. Munson,*

would walk down the aisle to his appointed place, seating
himself in the front row, in front of the pulpit, and with a flip
of the tails of his morning coat, would sit down, and at that
instant, services would begin.

The first chaplain was Reverend W. G. Puddefoot, who served from the opening of the hospital, in 1885, for two years. Eight more Protestant chaplains followed, until the facility closed in 1989. Fr. Fred was the only resident Catholic chaplain to serve the facility. On June 26, 1959, he started in a part-time capacity, having just been reassigned from St. Michael Parish. On November 10, 1960, he assumed the full time position of Catholic chaplain at the State Hospital.

Prior to Fr. Fred becoming a permanent presence, local priests from St. Francis of Assisi and Immaculate Conception parishes in Traverse City made visits to the hospital as part of their parish duties. Masses were held in the Chapel on Wednesday mornings, until 1955, when they were changed to Sunday mornings. Christian Science services were held every other Thursday, and Jewish services each Saturday when a rabbi was available.

In the 1950s, the advancement of psychotropic drugs and their ameliorative effects on the symptoms of the mentally ill allowed patients to be discharged and returned home or to other community facilities. Other changes in the treatment protocols for mental illness, including State funding made additional changes imminent. The population of the facility reached its highest in 1960—3,600. In 1963, the state of Michigan established Community Mental Health programs, and the population dwindled quickly. By 1973, the original asylum building, Building 50, was vacant. In August of 1989, the last patient left the hospital and the last services held at All Faiths Chapel. A couple months later, the hospital was officially closed.

Fr. Fred's thirty years at the Traverse City State Hospital are marked with countless expressions of his theology and the application of his pastoral profession. There are a few characteristics, however, that stand out. One is that he was ecumenically ahead of his time, since he served anyone who came to him, Catholic or not. The other is that he treated the patients with the dignity they deserved but were rarely afforded in the insane asylum setting. His effort to get the All Faiths Chapel built is the perfect conjunction of those two concepts.

The other significant manifestation of his unwavering theology, during those years, is the attraction of the townspeople who came to worship. Between 1965 when the Chapel opened, and 1989, when it closed, a pseudo-parish took shape on the grounds of the facility. By the time the hospital closed, there were about 150 regular visitors at the Chapel. His charismatic personality welcomed them, even though he never explicitly solicited their participation or attendance.

All Faiths Chapel

For his first few years at the hospital, Fr. Fred celebrated Mass and met with patients in a makeshift space that was shared with a library in the basement of Building 50, the hospital's main administration building. Each Wednesday afternoon, he would offer Mass in the Geriatric Ward in Building 41 for patients who were not capable of going to the chapel. He, and others who saw the chaplaincy program as a more integral part of patient therapy and care, began working toward a separate ecumenical facility on campus. There were a number of forces working against the establishment of such a facility. Money was just one of them.

John Parsons, a Traverse City businessman, entrepreneur, and good friend of Fr. Fred, led the effort to raise the money needed to build the facility. "He was not a particularly religious man," his son Grant recalls. "Yet, he cared for the people who were suffering. Like Father Fred, Dad was a big dreamer." Grant remembers, as a kid, riding along with his dad to visit homebound and shut-in people in the community. Often, they were folks John didn't know that well, but he felt they would benefit from a caring visit.

The funds were raised in the thirty-nine counties served by the hospital. The Council of Churches in each community was a leading force to raise the $300,000 needed to provide a "church home" for the 3,000 residents then at the hospital. In a 1989 article, when the hospital was closing, Joseph Neiman writes: "It was viewed as the 'chapel that couldn't be built,' due more to the perception of historic tensions among the Protestant, Catholic, and Jewish communities, than to any structural or budgetary constraints."

At the time of the fundraising for All Faiths Chapel, Dennis Goggin told his daughter, Ann, that his employer, Continental Motors in Muskegon, matched employees' contributions to such campaigns on a one to one basis. When they matched the donations to All Faiths Chapel, it was the largest such match in the company's history. Everyone, it seemed, had a relative or someone they knew who was being treated at the State Hospital.

One of the reasons the Chapel was built was so visiting family members could pray together with patients. So, the Chapel had a traditional church ambiance. The final construction was a model for ministering to the needs of the mentally ill and designed to accommodate "all faiths" that consisted of three chapels: Protestant, Catholic, and Jewish. It also included office space for the chaplains and a large multi-purpose room. Even though the building was a secular facility, owned by the state, the Chapel had to have a designated name according to Canon Law. It is a little-known fact that the official designation of the Catholic chapel was Christ The King Chapel, affiliated with Immaculate Conception Parish in Traverse City.

The Chapel was located near the edge of the hospital campus, not far from the main administration building and easily accessible for patients and staff. While most of the hospital was within the city limits of Traverse City, Division Avenue separated it from mainstream town activities. This made the Chapel accessible to the locals, but just enough out of the way to make it a conscious decision to worship there.

Traverse City architect Gordon Cornwell was commissioned to design the structure. With a nod toward the then-popular A-frame, the building stood out, in the 1960s, from the rest of the buildings on the campus. "There were a couple reasons for this," remarks Gordon's son, Bob, also an architect. "In today's age of historic preservation and adaptation, some wonder why this building was not designed to more closely resemble the existing surrounding buildings. The first reason is that urban renewal and modernism were the current norms. The second reason was the high cost of mimicking the existing architecture."

Gordon, now in his mid-nineties, recalls working with Fr. Fred and characterizes him as a really great guy. "The contrast in architectural styles was very intentional," he explains. He felt that this chapel should hold a clear distinction from the daily lives of the patients and be that special place of escape. He wanted it well-lit and open with high ceilinged spaces to uplift the spirits of those attending services, to give them a feeling of freedom in contrast to their daily living conditions. At the same time, the location was ideal for the greater community to feel welcome as well. The intent was to integrate the entire community and all faiths.

While there were some variations from the original concept, the Chapel was built as an ecumenical expression of service to the patients and staff of the hospital, and a welcoming, inclusive retreat for members of the community.

As All Faiths Chapel was being designed, in 1963, Paul Welch was teaching art at Northwestern Michigan College near downtown Traverse City. He, along with several other artists, submitted some ideas for the stained glass windows in the building. It was a competition that included glass companies and artists from around the country, and at least one artist from France. Paul had done some stand-alone pieces as a student at Michigan State University, but never a commission like this. His design ideas won the competition, and he was awarded the job.

Members of the final design committee included Fr. Fred, John Parsons, Gordon Cornwell, and Dr. M. Duane Sommerness, Superintendant of the State Hospital. The committee settled on designs for fourteen windows: Twelve were side windows for the two main chapels, Protestant and Catholic, and two twenty-four-foot-high windows were for the ends of the building above each altar. Themes included images of the Madonna and Child, the descent of the Holy Spirit, a chalice, an orb to represent eternity, and some Old Testament based stories. The end pieces, above each altar, were similar but not identical.

Paul worked on the commission for a year and a half, using a variety of glass from different sources. Some came from Blenko Glass in Milton, West Virginia; some from Kokomo Glassworks in Kokomo, Indiana; and some came from local, Traverse City demolition sites. When the pieces were finished, a moving company was hired to transport them. On that very nervous day of installation, Paul brought his art students to watch. The installation was completed without a single problem.

Fr. Fred was very much involved with the design of the windows, and Paul appreciated that. "He had an uncanny ability to work with the patients" he tells. "He had the great sense of humor anyone would need to have in his position, yet he was the most empathetic man I've ever known." Welch attributes this to the fact that, in all the years he worked there, Fr. Fred developed unique skills in working with the mentally ill and brought those skills to his work among "regular" people.

Paul observed that the patients were drawn to the windows that brought some beauty and colored light into their lives. He was so touched, a few years later, on a visit to the Chapel, when he saw a patient lying prostrate on the floor, praying before the Madonna and Child image in one of the side windows. He also chuckles, as he tells the story of how, on a visit to the Chapel, his conversation with Fr. Fred was interrupted by a man leading a group through the Chapel, explaining very eloquently and in great detail the significance of the design in each window. He wondered who this docent was, leading the tour. "He's a patient," Fr. Fred said with a smile. "So are all the people in his group."

Fr. Fred appreciated Paul's artwork, and liked to share it with the community. Twenty or thirty years after the installation, Paul met a woman who had only recently discovered he had done the windows in the Chapel. "One of my best grade school memories," she told him, "was when we went over to the Chapel as a school art project and we drew pictures of the windows. Father Fred was so proud of them."

Then-Michigan governor George Romney joined local officials for the groundbreaking ceremonies. All Faiths Chapel was dedicated on May 18, 1965, in an ecumenical service led by the Right Reverend Archie H. Crowley, Suffragan Bishop of the Episcopal Diocese of Michigan and then-president of the Michigan Council of Churches; the Most Reverend Allen J. Babcock, Bishop of the Roman Catholic Diocese of Grand Rapids; and Rabbi Philip Rosenberg, spiritual leader of Temple B'Nai Israel in Muskegon.

At the time of the dedication, Reverend Robert Bell was the hospital's Protestant chaplain. He held services in the largest of the chapel spaces. Fr. Fred was the Catholic chaplain, and established his "parish" in the slightly smaller of the two main spaces. He referred to his chapel as "The Little Vatican." There were occasional visits by rabbis, who used the smaller facility designated for them between the two main chapels. In the architectural planning of the facility, the space was divided according to the relative sizes of the religious populations, as stated on patient intake forms.

In 1978, Rev. James Brammer was named the ninth Protestant chaplain at All Faiths Chapel. He and Fr. Fred had a collegial working relationship until the hospital closed.

Ecumenical Ministry

Right from the beginning, Fr. Fred was involved in the ecumenical movement that was characteristic and growing throughout the country in the 1960s. He helped initiate and remained active in the Grand Traverse Area Council of Churches. One article, in the *Traverse City Record-Eagle* (October 28, 1965), features a photo of him and five other clergy at their sixth annual dinner, held at the First Congregational Church. Fr. Fred and Reverend Robert Bell, the Protestant chaplain, joined over 300 at the dinner where Father Michael Beahan of Grand Rapids spoke about the current ecumenical movement.

While Fr. Fred was committed to the concept of ecumenism in his work at the hospital, he did so in strong defense of his vocation as a Catholic priest. His Roman collar was always worn comfortably, in all situations. He also used an ecumenical approach to define and defend the role of chaplain.

By March of 1978, *The Catholic Weekly* and others reported that Rev. Bell was preparing to retire from the Protestant chaplaincy at the hospital. Superintendant Dr. Philip Smith announced to the Traverse Area Ministerial Association that, because of budgetary reasons, he would not be replaced. Fr. Fred would be the sole chaplain at the facility. He told the group that he "expected Fr. Fred to coordinate a multi-faith approach for meeting the religious needs of the patients utilizing Protestant clergy on a volunteer basis."

This sparked a debate about the role of the chaplaincy. Dr. Smith's position: "Chaplaincy as such is blind to the parent church. The job description in the civil service regulations does not designate the religion but the duties of the chaplain." The official position of the State was that a chaplain could serve the needs of the patients and staff, but could not do anything to proselytize or convert patients to a particular denomination.

Fr. Fred's response, built on nineteen years of experience in the role, was, "A lot of people still think the chaplain simply carries on liturgical services for the people, but the role involves much more than that." He had pulled together the shared experiences of the other chaplains from a 1976 study for the Michigan Department of Mental Health. In that report, he documented the work he was doing with psychiatrist Dr. Seuk Soon (Luke) Im, MD, Clinical Director; and Dr. Edward Hayes, PhD, Chief Psychologist. The three of them showed there was clinical progress for patients by introducing a spiritual component to the treatment protocol, along with the more traditional pharmaceuticals and other treatment options. While this approach may have been frowned on, it was often effective.

His written response was profound, in that it addressed ecumenism not just among denominations, but among the people living inside the hospital and those living outside. In it, we see a wonderful explanation of his understanding of the needs of the patients as people of God:

> *The chaplain's job is one with many parts. It's a spiritual job, a clinical job, community job, and an administrative job. It is spiritual insofar as the chaplain is trained and has skills to help make persons whole; that is, useful, dignified, and producing individuals. We respect, in other words, the whole person, not just his appetite for food, but his appetite for a friendship with God.*

He went on to explain the clinical and administrative parts of the job and finished his statement of strong conviction about the community aspect of a chaplain with this explanation:

> *I think I would summarize it with the sentence which the superintendant, Dr. Duane Sommerness, implanted in our brains a long time ago: "These people living here are a little more like us than different from us." I do this by allowing people from downtown to come and participate in services at the Chapel. The patients love this because they experience somebody accepting them. The people from downtown learn in this that the patients can sing and pray and touch just like anybody else. It's surprising, by the way, how many people are afraid to touch or be touched by someone who is sick.*

When the chairman of the Traverse Area Ministerial Association asked Fr. Fred if he could meet the needs of Protestant patients as a Catholic priest, he replied, "You cannot divest me of my priesthood, so I cannot lie that aside. However, I respond to all who seek help, regardless of their persuasion."

Fr. Fred loved bringing the "people from downtown" together with the patients living at the hospital. At Christmastime, 1978, he arranged a Christmas party after Sunday Mass at All Faiths Chapel. He wrote about it for *The Catholic Weekly*. About 200 people met in the social hall at the Chapel for coffee, soft drinks, cookies, and a visit from Santa. There was a Christmas tree, green centerpieces, and a Christmas greeting in Polish from Pope John Paul II: *"Wesolych Swiat Bezogo Narodzenia."* A literal translation is "Joyous World, God's Birth," or "Joy to the World, Christ is Born."

While the event and its description seem very simple, it is a classic orchestration by Fr. Fred to incorporate his ministry into the community. Not only did he bring

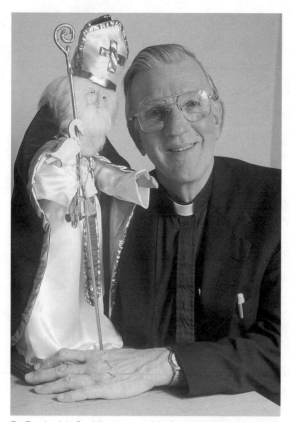

Fr. Fred with St. Nicolaus, at his favorite time of year.

community leaders and visitors together with the patients, he wrote an article it to make sure people knew about it. The article brought attention to the ecumenical work being done by the two chaplains at the State Hospital. It also demonstrated how the celebration brought the members of the community together with the patients.

Even the way Fr. Fred wrote the article was inclusive at multiple levels. He included quotes from community leaders, patients, and other visitors from the community. Bernie Sobczak, who played Santa Claus, said, "I had more fun than the kids. The party—it was great. That's the way it should be all the time!" Dan Deering was quoted in the article as saying, "I think it was fun. Everyone was happy… these people get tired of talking to themselves or to each other. They like someone else to talk to." Fr. Fred was certain to include a quote from the wife of legendary, well-liked Traverse City football coach, Jim Ooley: "I sit by these people every Sunday but never introduced myself to them," she said. "I enjoyed talking with them. They are very enjoyable and real." He included this touching quote from a patient, identified as Emily B., "I took some cookies to the ward so my friends could have some and not choke on them." A longtime friend and supporter of Fr. Fred, Lorna Ameel, said in the article, "The Christmas spirit is so elusive. I felt I experienced it for a few brief minutes, as I saw the proud and the humble shaking hands and greeting each other with love."

Patient Dignity

Fr. Fred truly loved the patients and was as much a therapist for them as he was chaplain. He believed that if the patients were "re-humanized," after being stripped of their dignity, their behavior and their mental health would get better. He was not alone in his belief that the improvement resulting from elevated dignity was not restricted to treatment protocols in the wards. The entire campus was a place for healing, and every element should be considered.

His thinking paralleled that of Earle Steele, who served as superintendant of the Grounds Department. Earle describes, in his book *Beauty is Therapy*, that an integration of work and therapy benefitted the patients. This was taken from the early concepts described by Dr. Munson, the first superintendant of the Northern Michigan Asylum.

Earle was nine years old when he moved to the campus of the Traverse City Regional Psychiatric Hospital in 1922, when his father, Edgar, took the position as the Florist-Gardener Supervisor in charge of the greenhouses and gardens. Earle grew up on the hospital grounds, working with his dad, and saw first-hand the benefit the patients derived from working with them. It provided them with some dignity and got them out of the dayrooms and wards, where they would otherwise spend their days. Their dignity was further elevated when, outside, they were referred to as "residents" rather than patients.

> **"Our work is about giving people their dignity. Everyone has a right to that."**
>
> *Father Fred*

Residents worked in the gardens, on the farm, and assisted hospital employees with construction and maintenance projects. "It was a sad day," Earle recalls, "when the State told us we could no longer use unpaid patient labor." He notes that the decline in attitude was immediate, that the patients were deeply saddened and depressed when they could no longer work on the grounds or in the greenhouse. Earle also writes that Dr. Munson's vision included an additional requirement. He was adamant that all residents who were capable of attending church were required to do so. Over time, that concept also faded.

Dignity, for many patients, came in the similar integration of spirituality, grooming, and daily life at the hospital. Looking back over the thirty years he worked at the hospital, Fr. Fred recalls his early days and some of the ways patients were dehumanized by the engrained institutional attitudes:

> *... and when you look at the state hospital almost thirty years ago, one wonders how did everyone endure life then? Today, I can tell a resident, "You look awful" and he/she*

can look in a mirror, see himself/herself and fix up. But so many years ago, there were no mirrors—just the glass in the windows that reflected the person's image. After all, the hospital did not want to be a contributor to someone trying to self-destruct or to mutilate himself with a mirror? Heaven forbid!

And then, how could anyone look respectable or beautiful in state clothes? Cotton dresses and cotton socks for the girls and ladies. All the same—and the dark, drab overalls or pants, probably discards from big outfits for the men. It seemed that when anyone was committed to the state hospital, they had to disrobe, suitcase their own clothes, and put on a patient's wardrobe. Wouldn't that make anyone sicker? Well, at that time nobody thought of it that way. You were mentally ill and had to be put away.

It was always his conviction that if patients were allowed to groom and dress better, they would feel and act better, and this, he theorized, would lead to improved mental health.

The best expression of this theory was in All Faiths Chapel, at Sunday Mass. Typically, there had been a handful of patients in attendance. Fr. Fred said they told him they were nuts, didn't have to go to church (weren't welcomed anyway in the local churches), and didn't have to keep the commandments. And when the few church devotees attended Mass, they had to sit with men on one side and women on the other. As the congregation grew, the men sat by wards on one side and the women by wards on the other. This arrangement was dictated by the culture of the institution and by the superintendant.

After a considerable amount of wrangling and arguing with the superintendent, Fr. Fred convinced him that a simple experiment would be worth a try. They agreed that if the experiment caused more confusion and trouble, it would be immediately cancelled. The experiment was to let the men and women come to Mass and sit wherever they wanted. This was apparently some scary and dangerous territory for the superintendant and the staff. The announcement was made and the new seating policy would be in effect the following week.

The congregation grew immediately and dramatically, and Catholics and Protestants alike came to Mass, just so they could be next to the opposite sex. Fr. Fred reminisces in his writing:

> *And to everyone's amazement, the boys and men started to keep themselves clean and better dressed and so did the femmes—girls and ladies began to look halfway human, beautiful and seductive. Of course, that made more work for the psychiatrists and attendants because, they figured those people were not all with it, so why should they act normal. But normalcy began to pervade the institution and somehow or another, frowns, grimaces, aloneness, blossomed out in smiles, jokes, associations, dance, and good times—for patients and employees.*

It is no surprise that the new policy stayed in effect, as everyone, including the superintendant, could see the improved behavior among the patients. The same theory of providing dignity through dressing and grooming was seen in the wards.

His sister, Theresa (Sister Agnes of God), wrote of this in her memories that were preserved in the Carmelite Monastery where she lived, in Jefferson City, Missouri. Fr. Fred had visited her at the monastery on the occasion of the twenty-fifth anniversary of her religious profession. She recalled how he shared stories of his work with the patients and how beautiful and inspiring it was to hear him speak of his ministry. She could see how much he loved the people with whom he worked. She told this story:

> *He told us about how things were when he first went there. When patients were admitted, they were deprived of their clothing and all other personal items, such as jewelry, etc. In place of these, they were given a loose gown. Doubtless, this policy reflected concern for patients' safety, but Father felt this deprived them of their dignity. Reforms were eventually made, after which patients were permitted to retain use of their own clothing.*

He told of one young woman who, made to wear a hospital gown, would run screaming to the shower room and turn on the water each time she saw him approaching. After the changes were instated, Father noticed how differently she behaved towards him. When Father walked in, he found her all dressed up and swinging her feet so that he would notice her new shoes. Father said to her, "Oh, that's a nice pair of new shoes you've got on." And she replied, still swinging her feet, "Yes, all God's children have nice shoes." Oh, so beautiful!

Fr. Fred observed the same effect on the men who were allowed to work on the grounds, dressed in white coveralls. Whether they were mowing the lawn in groups or assisting with a painting crew, they took pride in the fact they looked professional in their distinctive white uniforms. They enjoyed the attention from their fellow patients and the adulation from the hospital staff.

Simple dignity was established by these small acts of self-expression and the effects were palpable. It was a classic example of a Fr. Fred mechanism and his understanding of human nature. When someone asked him where this came from, he quoted a Gillette razor blade commercial that ran during TV boxing matches in the 1950s and '60s: "Look Sharp" - *Ding* - "Feel Sharp" - *Ding* - "Be Sharp" - *Ding*. He loved that expression and used it many times, even years later, at The Father Fred Foundation. The biggest thing he could do for clients, he thought, was to help them look sharp, feel sharp, and be sharp.

His unique position and special training allowed him to serve on patient treatment teams and have contact with patients in a capacity other than as a chaplain. His studies earned him the designation of Certified Mental Health Chaplain Supervisor from the U.S. Catholic Conference, Washington, D.C. This is "... to certify the competence of clergy serving in psychiatric, Community Mental Health Centers, and facilities for the mentally retarded and to help set standards for ministers in these fields."

Among the doctors with whom he studied was his Korean frined, Dr. Im, another believer in patient dignity. They became good friends as well as working associates.

Listening

One of the most memorable Fr. Fred sayings of all time is "Listen, Care, and Share." While he was working in the office of the State Hospital or, later, at The Foundation, everyone was impressed with his ability and capacity for listening.

His writings provide some definition and articulation of this concept and can be traced to some training he received while working at the State Hospital. He talked and wrote about a Polish doctor, Dr. P., to whom he was very close. He could tell when Fr. Fred was under stress, just by the tone of his voice. Likewise, Dr. P. was highly regarded by his friend, the chaplain. Fr. Fred's own words describe a piece of advice Dr. P. gave him:

> *When you're listening to someone and you think you have the answer, listen some more; and then when you think you have the problem arranged in your mind, listen some more, and then when you think you have a solution, listen some more!*

> *I have never forgotten that advice to this day because I get impetuous sometimes and feel that I have all the answers. But thru my mistakes, I have learned. This Dr. P. was the first one of whom I know that referred to the brain as a computer years before Apple and the rest of them came on the market. "Put that in your computer and see what you come up with," he would advise. And I always did. I still do.*

Countless people have benefited from the advice given to Fr. Fred by Dr. P. over the years. One such beneficiary is the unnamed patient in this story, told by Father Dennis Morrow, archivist in the Diocese of Grand Rapids, as told to him by Fr. Fred: *Marty*[6] had slipped into a total catatonic state. He sat in a chair, staring at the wall or through a room during all his waking hours — hour after hour, day after day, month after month. Therapists and psychiatrists tried to interact with Marty to see if they could bring him out of his condition and back into an engagement with reality. Nothing happened.

One day, Fr. Fred was in Marty's ward and took a seat next to him. He simply sat with Marty for a while. He didn't touch him and didn't say anything, then got up and left. On another day, he did the same thing. Over time, Fr. Fred sat with

---

6 Throughout the book, when a name is presented in italics, it is fictitious. This is to protect the privacy of certain individuals for a variety of reasons.

him quite often, sometimes for a few minutes, sometime for as long as an hour, but never saying anything. Then, he would just quietly get up and walk away.

Eventually, as this went on, therapists began to communicate with Marty. Once started, his progress grew to the point where he could communicate quite effectively. Fr. Fred observed his progress, and asked him about his condition. "What made the difference, Marty?"

"Father Fred," the man said, "during that time I was having that trouble, you were the only one who could understand me. You were the only one who listened."

All Faiths Chapel as a Parish

The chaplaincy program was in place to serve the needs of the patients, and the chaplain was a civil servant employee of the State of Michigan. However, because of the nature of the campus environment, with so many employees living and working on site, the work of the chaplain spread to serve more than just the patients. Once All Faiths Chapel was opened and working, more and more Catholics from the Traverse City parishes began to discover the interesting congregation with the charismatic priest. Regular attendance at Sunday Mass continued to climb as more and more townspeople considered this their church home.

Attendees enjoyed the non-traditional services as much as they enjoyed the Gospel message Fr. Fred served up each week. Fr. Fred was pleased that he could introduce the local Catholics to the patients. He felt that each would benefit from knowing and worshiping with the other. Patients were exposed to a more "normal" parish life, and visitors were taught compassion as they lost their natural fear of the mentally ill. It was a good *quid pro quo*.

Dr. Vince Prusick, a Traverse City orthopedic surgeon, and his wife Paula were regulars at All Faiths Chapel. "Father Fred was an extraordinary man," Vince tells. "I think he would have done what he did, even if he weren't a priest. He was as much a psychologist as a priest. He could have been a psychiatrist at the State Hospital without a religious role. He could operate this unique little congregation in this unique way, since he didn't have to follow the same dictum as a parish priest."

Dan Deering agrees: "If he were not a priest, he would have been doing something very similar, something sensitive. He was certainly the right guy for the job. He cared about everyone. He really took his patients to heart and we had great talks." He then goes on to tell this story:

> *On several occasions, I shared with Father how Vickie*
> *and I desired to be married in the Catholic Church, as we*
> *were both raised in Catholic families and had been married*
> *before. On one such occasion, Father said, "Dan, with your*
> *permission, I would like to provide you and Vickie with the*
> *necessary documents to start the process where you could be*
> *married in the Church." He took the bull by the horns and*
> *approximately one year later, our wish was granted. Fr. Fred*
> *married us at All Faiths Chapel after the ten o'clock Mass,*
> *with our cousins standing up for us. It was a great day!*

Townspeople, patients, and staff were all part of the congregation. They didn't just come for Mass at scheduled times, they'd come when they needed him. Fr. Fred was unique at helping people when they were having stressful times in their lives and he had a way of dealing with that. His love for people seemed to be returned to him many times over. He was a "people magnet" whom everyone loved.

Many of the hospital employees would drop by for visits during the day for some "sanity amid the insanity." One nurse, Caryn Cleland, tells of the comfort of having a "parish" right on campus. She had been raised in Roscommon, Michigan, and at age nineteen was away from home for the first time to attend the resident nursing program at the hospital and living on campus. She saw her faith as the constant in her life and needed the personal touch of religion in her life. Visits to Fr. Fred during the week and attending Mass on Sunday in the Chapel might result in a hug and some reassurance. "He helped me face the fears and insecurities of living alone in Traverse City."

Lorraine Laird met Fr. Fred at the Chapel on Elmwood when she moved to Traverse City in 1985. Shortly after she began to attend Mass there, a good friend of hers was diagnosed with AIDS. Her friend was hoping to receive Holy Communion even though his health no longer permitted him to leave his home. She went to Fr. Fred and asked if she could bring her friend Communion at his home. Typically, she would have had to submit her name to a higher authority than a parish priest for approval before she could become a Eucharistic minister. "Because my friend was so ill, Father Fred agreed to allow me to bring him Communion those last few weeks of his life," she tells. "I remember so well Father telling me that there was 'man's law' and there was 'God's Law' and having to submit my name for approval was man's law."

Bill Maxbauer met Fr. Fred when his family started attending the All Faiths Chapel. He remembers:

> *He had a way of making you feel important, like talking to you was going to be the highlight of his day. I began being an altar server at his Sunday Masses. That was a real cattle call! Unlike a conventional parish, which might schedule two servers at a Mass, Father Fred had a philosophy of "the more the merrier." So, you might be the only altar server, or you might be one of six, but that was part of the specialness of his Masses.*

> *I remember forgetting about a wedding I was supposed to serve for Father Fred, until the only way I could make it in time was to come as I was —dressed in blue jeans and wearing orange high-top Converse All-Star tennis shoes. Father Frederick naturally accepted me for who I was. I am sure the bride and groom thought I was a patient at the State Hospital!*

Then, there is the story of *Billy*. Billy was mildly impaired and considered a low-functioning patient. For years, he became known and accepted around town. He fell in love with and married *Bonney*, also a patient, who was bound to a wheelchair. Fr. Fred married them at All Faiths Chapel and made arrangements for a reception. Bonney had been "stashed" at the State Hospital at age eleven for some odd behavior and a physical impairment. Late in her life, her diagnosis of mental illness was reversed, but her fifty-year institutionalization left her without normal life-coping skills. She and Billy made a great pair.

Billy was able to hold a job as a crossing guard. Jerry Martineau, who was an altar boy for Fr. Fred at All Faiths Chapel and at the Carmelite Monastery in Traverse City, tells of how Billy, at Fr. Fred's encouragement, would hang around with the high school football team. It was good for the students, and good as a team builder. It also provided Billy with a measure of dignity and belonging.

Dennis Carney remembers:

> *There were also regulars at All Faiths, like "Bonney the greeter,' who positioned her wheelchair at the corner of*

*the first pew during Communion and would ambush each
person returning from Communion and greet them with a
handshake or a hug. Somehow this sharing of the limelight
and holiness of the moment seemed perfectly in the spirit
of the Last Supper."*

The lessons continued, even after the hospital closed and Fr. Fred moved to St. Joseph Parish, in Mapleton. Billy and Bonney followed him there, yet they could not drive. In his direct way, Fr. Fred would often ask Dennis Carney's family or another family to give them a lift home from church. This would invariably also result in a short stop at the grocery store or wherever else Bonney would ask to stop, and subsequently, the need for a little money to pay for all the items.

This became a source of amusement to Dennis's children and wife but also a great lesson in charity and recognizing the needs of others. Eventually, Billy and Bonney asked for themselves without the intervention of Fr. Fred. This system worked well, as several families were recipients of these requests over time. However, it was easy to sense when any of these families had some pressing business after church: They managed to give Billy and Bonney a wide berth throughout Mass and made sure to receive Communion on the opposite side of church from where Bonney set up shop.

A Funeral Story

Fr. Fred loved the patients, staff, and visitors in the All Faiths Chapel pseudo-parish, even after they died. Several touching stories circulate about funerals he conducted and what a source of loving comfort he was for grieving families. Nothing, however, describes his commitment and dedication to deceased patients more than how he treated their lonely funerals when there was no attendant, no grieving family.

Nick deBoer was working as a funeral director in Traverse City and witnessed several desolate funerals at All Faiths Chapel when Fr. Fred would celebrate the Mass of Christian Burial for a deceased Catholic patient. There were no family members present, only a small handful of patients, an assistant from the funeral home, and himself. Years later, Nick is still touched by how Fr. Fred would quietly and graciously guide an adult patient altar boy through the funeral Mass, conducted with as much dignity as if it were for the town's mayor. Nick says, "Father Fred had incredible patience and always showed compassion and respect for all the souls at the hospital, right through to their entry into the afterlife."

Altar Boys and Girls

Fr. Fred knew he had an effect on young people. He loved kids. Once, at All Faiths Chapel, he had no altar boys, so he enlisted second grader, Jamie Shirley. "You're an altar boy," he said to the young boy. Jamie had no clue what to do, so Father coached him at every move. He was so short that his eyes were just at the level of the altar. Later, Fr. Fred asked for an older boy, and Jamie's older brother, Patrick, stepped up. Patrick was nearly as tall as Fr. Fred and said, "When I'm taller than Father Fred, I'm done being an altar boy." On the altar, from behind where Fr. Fred couldn't see him, he'd make comparing gestures of measuring his height and Fr. Fred's. People in the congregation snickered, and Patrick's mother, Alice, was in the congregation ready to throttle him.

In keeping with his approach to his faith, Fr. Fred was inclusive of all the people he met. He had the first girl altar server in Traverse City, and later, a boy with Down syndrome was asked to serve. Serving for Fr. Fred meant a lot to those kids. They learned to see him as a man—as human as any other—not simply as a priest, who is often seen as someone separate from "regular" people. They learned gentleness, acceptance, and dignity from him.

Patients at Mass

There are as many stories about the patients and their unique behavior as there are people who attended Mass at All Faiths Chapel. They are more than simply amusing, they also point to the loving care and acceptance that was characteristic of Fr. Fred. Often, during Mass, a patient at the hospital would walk onto the altar and begin to talk with Fr. Fred. Gently and reverently, he would ask the patient to have a seat and wait until Mass was over, using the event as a not-so-subtle lesson in compassion and tolerance before the gathered congregation. Following are a few of the hundreds of stories of patients at Mass:

On weekdays, when Fr. Fred would open the Chapel at 9:00 a.m., one of the patients with grounds privileges would march down Elmwood like a drum major in great ceremony to help him open the Chapel.

Charlie Hoxie, a longtime hospital employee says patients would sometimes act out in Mass at All Faiths Chapel. Fr. Fred would kindly walk them back to their seats. "The sicker they were," he says, "the more he loved them."

Dennis Carney says, "I have many recollections of Father Fred nearly every week managing an unplanned disruption during Mass at All Faiths and turning the moment into a lesson in humor, tolerance, and dignity for all involved. This included visits up to the altar during the middle of Mass by patients and former patients who were gently recognized then calmly redirected by Fr. Fred after their cameo moment."

> **"Each one of them is Jesus in disguise."**
>
> *Mother Teresa*

Many patients would simply wander up to the altar for a hug from Fr. Fred, or want to talk with him. He was never upset by this and always treated that behavior with dignity, respect, and love. Observers say, "That's the way Christianity was meant to be," as they learned acceptance of the mentally ill.

One patient came into Mass wearing a fur coat that had been hung in the back by one of the "townies." She came up to the altar, and asked Fr. Fred to help her find the owner. He asked her, "Why don't you model it for us?" So, she put on a show for a couple minutes before he told her to go hang it up where she found it. She did.

Mike Shirley tells about how one woman got the nickname of the "Blessed Virgin." One of the well-known patients was often disruptive during Mass. When this occurred, Fr. Fred would simply stop Mass and gesture to the congregation with his oversized hands outstretched, palms down in a calming motion, and say something like, "Let's stop for a moment and listen." On one particular Sunday, this woman walked up to the side altar, where there was an image of the Blessed Virgin Mary and began shouting, "I hate you and I'm pissed off at you!" Fr. Fred made his usual calming gesture, took control of the situation, and had her take her seat again. Thereafter, that particular patient was known as the Blessed Virgin.

Vince and Paula Prusick remember a few patients who would come through the Chapel during Mass and ask Fr. Fred for a quarter for the cigarette machine. Without breaking stride in the rhythm of the Mass, Fr. Fred would reach in his pocket, pull out a quarter, give it to them, and they'd leave.

Bill Kildee remembered the patient who would purposely fart loudly and ask Father if he heard it. "Yes, I heard it, but these people aren't interested in that," he'd reply, as he calmly proceeded with Mass.

Dolly Cataldo remembers the patient who crawled up the center aisle. A subtle look from Fr. Fred and a little shake of his head, and the patient returned to her seat.

Bill Maxbauer remembers:

> *Father Fred always accepted people as they came to him. He seemed utterly unflappable, whether it was somebody interrupting a part of the Mass, or somebody praying aloud when the priest was supposed to be leading a prayer, it was all in a day's work to him. I remember a patient at the hospital named Maggie, who was the sweetest old lady. Father Fred used to say that if "there wasn't room in Heaven for Maggie, then there was no hope for the rest of us."*

One Sunday, a patient walked up onto the altar and said, "I'm Jesus Christ." Without missing a beat, Fr. Fred replied, "Yup, and I'm Father Fred. Now sit down." The Mass continued on.

Fr. Ron Gronowski was the pastor at St. Francis Parish and decided to check out what was going on over at the State Hospital:

> *One Sunday, I went to Mass at the Chapel. It was a most enlightening experience for me. During the liturgy some of the congregation would shout out Alleluias and phrases like, "That's right, Father. Amen." Also, during the Mass, several of the patients came up to the pulpit to "assist" him. Through it all, Father Fred was not disturbed one iota. He was patient, kind, gentle, and compassionate. I recognized, without a doubt, that I saw Jesus in the presence of Father Fred at that altar. I also knew that not in a million years could I emulate Father Fred. What I saw confirmed all that I had heard: "Father Fred was a living saint."*

Occasionally, there were patients who could not be calmed. In these cases, Fr. Fred would have to ask the staff to remove them. He might be the first to hold the person with his strong and firm, yet gentle and loving hands. "Having someone removed from Mass is the hardest thing I have to do, whether it's here in the chapel or up in the ward," he told Charlie Hoxie. "I really hate to see them removed from the Eucharistic experience."

Christmas at All Faiths Chapel

Fr. Fred liked the fact that Jesus was the attention for a lot of people at Christmastime. He felt the Christmas displays were a way of drawing local attention to the work going on at the hospital:

> *We had crèche scenes on all the wards and even on the front lawn of the administration building. Trees—those large, full Xmas tree kind, were illuminated by colored lights. The grounds were simply beautiful. The townspeople used to cruise along Green, Orange, and Red Drives on campus just to say: "Ooh and ah, isn't that pretty?" That was a nice way of getting the attention of the city folk.*

It seems Christmas Eve was Fr. Fred's favorite day at All Faiths Chapel, when he would personally assign each child at Mass a role in the Christmas story. He had a few makeshift costumes, and then would march with the kids around the jam-packed Chapel in a singing procession. The smile on his face was the best part of the evening. One year, he told Vikki Hardley and Barb Bonham he needed a lot of angel costumes, since not everyone could be a shepherd or a king. Vikki recalls:

> *Ted and I pleaded with the State Hospital and Munson for old used sheets, and two other ladies and I sewed angel*

You will share a special remembrance in my Christmas Masses celebrated at Christ the King Chapel. Traverse City, Michigan

Father Frederic

Chaplain

Christmas card, 1966, offering Mass in All Faiths Chapel.

*costumes and trimmed them up with shiny garland. We
worked right up to Mass time so each kid had a costume.
Father Fred acted like we had given him the world. He was
so excited, just like the kids, and I never forgot that.*

Mass on the Grass

Summertime at All Faiths Chapel brought a new tradition to the growing *ad
hoc* congregation. Fr. Fred would offer Mass outside on the lawn, behind the Chapel.
On pleasant summer Sundays, Fr. Fred would announce that he had talked with
God and arranged another beautiful day—nice enough to have Mass outside. Even
after so many years, people who went to Mass there, recall: "Did you ever go to
Mass on the Grass?"

Vikki Hardley tells how Fr. Fred would stop over at their house across from the
Chapel, have coffee and coerce her husband, Ted, into mowing the grass for outdoor
services or doing some other favor for him. Ted always said Fr. Fred could always get
one up on him, and he would be scratching his head trying to figure out how he had
been "bamboozled by that guy." The first time this happened, he wandered into their
yard, and Ted, seeing the Roman collar, announced, "Well, I'm a Baptist, sir, born
and bred." Fr. Fred's reply instantly made a friend with Ted, when he said, without
missing a beat: "We won't hold that against you, Ted." Vikki recalls Mass on the Grass:

> *It was truly a family spirited event. We had picnics after
> Mass and it was not unusual to have a patient or two wander
> over (to the picnic table) and help themselves to food. Once,
> during Mass, a man made a sandwich and strolled up to
> Father smiling and eating his treat, Father gently asked him
> if he was enjoying it and the man with big eyes sparkling
> nodded. In his typical calm manner, Father said that was
> great, and to be certain to get a soda, too, then continued
> the Mass. He was such a compassionate man.*

Bill Maxbauer recalls: "During the summers, Father Fred used to enjoy saying
his Sunday Masses outdoors. I don't know whether the bishop ever signed off
on that, or whether it was ecclesiastically correct, but it was a setting that the
congregation enjoyed, and that Father Frederick used to relish."

Their Good Shepherd

Patients truly loved Fr. Fred, and he returned that love on a daily basis. They wanted to be with him as much as possible. Consequently, there was a stream of patients through his office every day, where he kept a pot of coffee and some doughnuts or cookies for them. This gave him a way of being hospitable while not allowing them to disrupt his daily business. They felt they were with him.

Bishop Robert Rose had been Fr. Fred's bishop, in Gaylord, for the last ten years of the Chapel's operation. He remembers:

> *Father Fred was always enjoyable to be with. His work with the patients at the Hospital had made him very sensitive to human quirks and foibles, including those of us who would qualify as "normal." He had lots of interesting stories to tell … His parishioners were the residents and staff at the Hospital, and he certainly provided them with the full pastoral service. He loved his people and they responded to his care.*

By 1979, when one woman first met Fr. Fred, his reputation had spread through the community and his outreach extended beyond the campus of the State Hospital. She was twenty-three years old, struggling with a relationship with her boyfriend, and felt depressed. She saw Fr. Fred a couple times, but the depression deepened when her sister got married. Finally, she asked her parents for help. After a lengthy conversation, they decided to call Fr. Fred on a Saturday, to see if he would do an emergency visit. He agreed to meet them at All Faiths Chapel.

> *When my parents and I arrived at his office at the chapel, he took one look at me and said, "You need more help than I can offer." To make a long story short, he asked me to admit myself to the State Hospital, to which I agreed. As horrible as that experience was, I learned very quickly the value of my life and learned how lucky I was to have two wonderful parents and a priest who cared enough to help me find the way out of my depression. Father Fred taught me a lesson about life that I hold to very tightly. He taught me the life I was headed for if I did not change my ways and attitude, and he showed me the wonderful life I could have if only I had faith*

> # "Laughter is the best medicine and we have a pharmacy that won't quit."
>
> *Father Fred*

in myself and in the Lord. I am eternally grateful for the awesome relationship that bloomed from that experience.

For years, patients, staff, and townspeople arrived at his office at All Faiths Chapel and placed their troubles in Father's capable hands. They knew he would help them, and he seldom failed. He had a nickname for nearly everyone, as part of his "Friendship Therapy." "Hey there, Gov'ner," might be a greeting for someone coming into his office. Other nicknames included "Chief," "Colonel," "Commander," and "Coach." Another part of Friendship Therapy was the distribution of cigars. At the end of his conversation with a male visitor, he might push a cigar into the visitor's hand, watch him light it up, and escort him to the door with a hearty, "Have a great day, Gov'ner," and the guy would walk away, feeling like a million bucks.

The same thing went on in the wards, in the early days. Attendants in the wards told stories about how Fr. Fred would breeze through a ward and offer candy to the women and cigars to the men. He'd walk away as the ward filled with thick, blue smoke. The staff hated this practice. The patients loved it. Joyce Weathers, who worked at the State Hospital, remembers:

> *Whenever anyone mentions the name Father Fred, I immediately think of the days when I worked in a men's ward and he would come to visit these elderly gentlemen. They may have been old, senile, mentally, or physically ill, but they sure associated Father Fred with a pocket full of fat cigars, a kind word, and a smile. After he made his rounds of the ward, talking and offering cigars, as well as lighting up a dozen or so, he would leave to go on to another ward. It was up to the staff to go around and make sure beds and clothing weren't on fire.*

Fr. Fred showed his insouciance when he wrote about how this custom got started. He told a priest friend about how a cigar had calmed a patient, and broke a catatonic episode, the first time he tried it:

> *... I related the incident to a priest friend of mine, Father Al, who said, "If a cigar brings lucidity, even for a moment, to one of those creatures, I'll supply you with ten boxes of King Edwards a month." To this day I still receive cigars. Father Al's dead, but a family who heard about this episode continues to supply me with the word-provoking cigars. Today, it is still talked around. Father Fred and his cigars. UGH! Whew! Phew! Good! You can't please 'em all.*

There are legendary stories about how Fr. Fred and the superintendant clashed over some issues like the distribution of candy and cigarettes. When the superintendant shut that practice down, Fr. Fred simply began handing out dollar bills, so the patients could go to the canteen and buy their own.

Longtime State Hospital employee, Charlie Hoxie, claims, "He should be canonized. He never said a cross word to any patient. He gave his all, because they were all God's creatures. He treated everybody the same."

On May 28, 1968, the U.S. Catholic Conference certified Fr. Fred as a Mental Health Chaplain Supervisor. Later, the National Standards and Accreditation Committee of the Association of Mental Health Clergy elected him to a leadership position.

Fr. Fred showed his love for the patients right up to when the hospital closed. As the staff and Community Mental Health employees started the difficult task of moving patients out of the hospital, transitioning them to foster homes or group homes, the patients were scared. They showed their fright when they were being taken from the wards and would yell out, "Father Fred. I want Father Fred. I have to see Father Fred." The more the staff struggled with each patient, the more the patient would act out in fear of what was happening. They were being taken from the safe, predictable environment into the "unknown." Their panic was visible, understandable, and painful.

Fr. Fred was summoned, and arriving at the scene, would offer a warm, strong, calming hand and put his arm around the patient. Immediately, the situation altered and settled. Knowing the patient's life was about to change, and understanding the trust they held in him, he'd then clap the patient on the back and say, "It's okay. Go with these nice people, it'll be okay." Comforted, they would comply, once they heard him say it was all right.

Those patients never saw the inside of the Hospital again.

Staff Friendships

Fr. Fred didn't limit his work or attention at the State Hospital to the patients. Many of the employees he worked with on a daily basis tell of friendships they developed with him. Because of who he was and how he operated, anyone who walked through his door was eligible to be a friend. Some sought his listening ear, others would stop by to simply share a good joke with him, and not just a few would come to the chapel for a visit with Fr. Fred simply to get "out of the line of fire" for a few minutes. He had the same charismatic effect on these friends as he had on the patients and the visitors to All Faiths Chapel.

Several of these friendships grew to be deep and lasting. Years after his death, these relationships are still cherished and tenderly recalled. From the hundreds of stories that have been told by his friends, and the statements made about these friendships, none is more succinct than that of Leon Hayes, a longtime State employee and longtime friend: "If I live to be a thousand, I'll never find a better, truer friend than Father Fred."

Fr. Fred was, in many ways, "one of the guys." He socialized with these friends, traveled with them, attended sporting events, went fishing, and even bowled with them on the staff bowling team. His clinical work with Dr. Im and Dr. Hayes led to close personal friendships, as well. Fr. Fred traveled with Dr. Im and his family several times to the national American Psychiatric Association

Fr. Fred and his friend, Dr. Im, on their way to an APA conference in California, 1980.

meetings. One memorable trip for Peter, Dr. Im's son, is the time Fr. Fred joined their family on a car ride from San Francisco to Los Angeles: Three adults and three kids for three days in one car.

Dr. Im's daughter, Susan, remembers during the holidays when her mother would give Father generous amounts of her Korean cuisine, especially a spicy beef specialty called *bulgoki*, thin strips of sirloin marinated in soy sauce, garlic, ginger, green

Fr. Fred and his friend, Dr. Im, in San Francisco, 1980.

onion, sugar, and sesame oil. Other Korean dishes included *mandoo* dumplings, *japche* stir-fry, and the Korean spicy cabbage staple, *kimche*. Fr. Fred had made the point of telling her how much he enjoyed the original sampling, so every year, the gift grew until she would give him so much, he couldn't eat it all. He'd share it with his neighbors and take plenty to his relatives in Grand Rapids.

Just as with the patients, he was a "soft touch" for a loan of a couple bucks until payday. The only difference is, with the patients, he didn't expect to be repaid. He usually got it back from staff.

Carl Bauer was a painter on the maintenance staff. He and Fr. Fred had something in common with a lot of the staff: they disagreed with much of what the superintendant had to say. "You gotta do this or that," they would hear from the "Southeast Corner," then they'd do what they knew "really needed to be done."

One Sunday in the fall, Carl and one of his buddies went deer hunting near Kalkaska, Michigan, about thirty miles from the hospital. Unknown to them, Fr. Fred was also in Kalkaska, substituting for the absent priest. When the hunters arrived at Mass, hoping to be unnoticed, because of their hangovers, they took a seat in the back of the church and during the sermon, fell asleep. They were surprised when Fr. Fred loudly announced to the congregation, "I'd like those two guys in the back to wake up."

Nancy, a fellow employee at the State Hospital, tells about the time she was being released from the hospital, after surgery. As her husband was pushing her to the car in a wheelchair, Fr. Fred recognized her, came up to the back of the wheelchair and told him, "I'll put her in the car." "He just seemed to be everywhere," she claims. "It was so good to see him, and he certainly didn't have to push me to the car. He just appeared—like an angel."

"God bless you," said Fr. Fred, after he gently helped her into the car. Then he closed the door and disappeared.

Ursula had been baptized as a Lutheran and worked at the hospital for years with Fr. Fred. Because she was married to a Catholic, he would ask her: "When are you going to turn Catholic, Ursula?"

"When they get rid of confession, Father," was her standard reply. This happened nearly every time he saw her, and it went on for years. It became a real connection between them. Eventually, at one of her kids' baptism, at All Faiths Chapel, he told her: "Okay, Ursula, you don't need confession. Come over here." Then he baptized her, right there, along with her child, as a Catholic. "That's just the way he was," says Ursula. "He knew I was ready, and it was the right thing to do."

Bill Kildee, who died in 2010, was a painter on the maintenance staff at the State Hospital for twenty years, up until 1988, just a year before the hospital closed. Interviewed just three weeks before he died, his memories were clear and immediate as he talked about the priest who had become a friend so many years earlier. "He was well-liked, right from the beginning." Bill remembered. "Some of the other employees and I would put together work crews and help him and his dad, on our own time, when they were building his house on the Boardman." Bill continued:

> *The thing about Father Fred, is that he was a regular guy who happened to be a really good priest. A lot of Catholics, especially in the old days, were brought up thinking Catholicism was fear-based. He made us feel as though we had some redemption. We were not just in the hands of an angry God. I think that's what made him so approachable. I think that's why people liked him. He was always patient with the residents, never cross.*

Bill and Fr. Fred had both been involved in the movement known as Cursillos in Christianity (in Spanish: *Cursillos de Cristiandad*, short course in Christian living). It is a ministry that began in the Roman Catholic Church and has since spread to other Christian denominations. It was founded in Majorca, Spain, by a group of laymen in 1944 when they were refining a technique to train pilgrimage leaders. The *cursillo* method focuses on training lay people to become effective leaders over the course of a three-day weekend. The weekend includes fifteen talks, some given by priests and some by lay people.

Bill and Fr. Fred had been to Muskegon on a Sunday afternoon for the closing day of a *cursillo* as part of their continuing service to the movement. They were on their way back north, with Fr. Fred at the wheel "driving to beat Hell." When a Lake County Sheriff's Deputy pulled them over, he walked up to the car and asked Fr. Fred for his driver's license and registration. When he noticed the Roman collar on Fr. Fred, he apologetically said, "Well, Father, how are you this evening?" After some conversation about how nice it was to see him and how fast he had been going, the sheriff let him off with a warning asking him to keep the speed down a little.

Back on the road, Bill asked him, "Did you know that guy, Father?"

"No, I didn't, but that was a close one, don't you think?"

Employee friendship stories about Fr. Fred will go on for years and most will probably get better with each re-telling. His caring friendship will last in the hearts of everyone who knew him until the last of those people are gone.

Charlie Hoxie, a longtime employee and friend says this: "A good Father Fred story? Hell, any story about Father Fred is a good story!"

In His Own Words

Who can tell the story about Fr. Fred and his interaction with the patients more effectively than Fr. Fred, himself? During his thirty years at the State Hospital, he did so much and learned so much. He met and worked with and touched the lives of thousands of people. After the hospital closed, he began writing some stories he had gathered during those years. Perhaps, he was intending to write a book about his experiences with the patients, there.

In the next few pages, we see a selected few of these stories. They are presented, almost totally unedited[7] as they were found.

---

7 While these stories are presented as they were found, the author has obscured the names of patients with regard to their privacy.

And then how could anyone look respectable or beautiful in state clothes. Cotton dresses and cotton socks for the girls and ladies. All the same - and the dark, drab overalls or pants, probably discards from big outfits for the men. It seemed that when anyone was committed to the state hospital, they had to disrobe, suitcase their own clothes and put on a patient's wardrobe. Wouldn't that make anyone sicker? Well, at that time nobody thought of it that way. You were mentally ill and had to be put away. Boy! Stalag 19 was no prize but neither was the dress code 30 years ago. And what about the marital privileges for the husbands who came to visit their wives or vice versa. Unheard of - and maybe a loss of privileges for even thinking about that precious item. I remember one of the doctors to whom I made a suggestion for a family visiting room, saying, "What are you trying to make of this place? A whorehouse?" I couldn't understand that at all. And you know when I had Sunday services, there was only a handful - (12) people at Mass. The patients told me they were nuts, didn't have to go to church (weren't welcomed anyway in the local churches) - didn't have to keep the commandments. And when the few church devotees attended Mass they had to sit - men on one side, women on the other. And as the congregation grew the men sat by wards on the other. I changed all that and told them to sit where they wanted. Would you believe that my congregation grew by leaps and bounds. Catholics and Protestants came to Mass, just so they could be next to the opposite sex. And to everyone's amazement, the boys and men started to keep themselves clean and better dressed and so did the femmes - girls and ladies began to look halfway human, beautiful and seductive. Of course, that made more work for the psychiatrists and attendants because, they figured those people were not all with it, so why should they act normal. But normalcy began to pervade the institution and somehow or another, frowns, grimaces, aloneness, blossomed out in smiles, jokes, associations, dance, and good times - for patients and employees.

Psychiatrists, psychologists, nurses, and everyone was present when a staff doctor presented a patient for learning from them or else to accept from others a better way to treat the complicated case. I knew very little about paranoids, schizophrenics, psychotics, catatonics, and the whole dictionary; so when this interviewed patient talked about seeing the devil, communication with the devil, talking with the devil, etc., I confidently (after all, I was a smart priest?) questioned, "And how did the devil look?" She glared at me, pointed a finger and said convincingly, "Like you!" Needless to say, I crawled into my space and felt foolish for the question I gave her. But I learned something that day; and I kept learning something everyday hence.

And y'know, talking about the chapel services in the library reminded me of ▆▆▆ the organist. He pumped the old relic full of air to produce some ecclesiastical music, like you never heard. He never said a word. Once in awhile he smiled at me, but now I recall, he never said "good morning" or "good day." He was a perfectionist and sat at the keyboard like he was prepared for a concert in New York. So prim and proper (tho he dressed sloppily and carried his music in his pockets and in his arms all the time). I liked him, because he played so well and was so compliant to directions, but some wave lengths got crossed one Sunday morning, because instead of the liturgical entrance hymn, he tickled the ivory keyboard to play "How Much is that Doggie in the Window?" Even amidst the smiles of the audience I let him finish, and then we began all over again. That day, the congregation left quite happily and greeted the organist/artist with compliments —and "play some more for us." Since there were not too many TVs around in those years, a real live performer was a premium to behold. Even my friend and ▆▆▆ friend, ▆▆▆▆▆, who always thought that I was part of the Inquisition, tee-heed quite a bit that day and never forgot that service.

It was new for these people to go to confession and to attend Sunday Mass. After all, they were "different" or the Church made them different by celebrating Mass on Wednesday instead of Sunday until I got here in '59. I roamed the several wards where people sat along the walls all day, rocking back and forth, staring and glaring in silence or watching the hallways, and I asked why they do not attend church. One toothless wonder gave me a smile and said, "Oh, Father I love you but I don't have any money."

Little did I realize that in her early life, she was programmed to give something when she went to church and today, she had nothing—until she found a nickel in a bin at the laundry where she worked. To my surprise, I saw her one Sunday in church, all smiles and as being exited from the chapel she held up the line, pulled out her handkerchief. In one corner she had tied up, the nickel she found in the laundry become visible. She pressed it into my hand with a wink, with a smile, and with "I love you, Father". The extra hug she gave me made my eyes water. In a split second, I came up with the idea to send the nickel back to the laundry where an employee would be sure that she found it again. And you guessed the rest. That nickel made it from laundry to chapel and back to laundry and back to chapel for a long time. And ▧▧▧ came with it until she was discharged form the hospital. Where she went, I do not know, but she left the hospital a lot happier than when she came here, years before I met her.

Those words, "tenderly care," bring me to another incident in the chapel. Before my "reign" at the chapel, few people brought their children to the hospital. The old fear about the kids catching a mental disease was quite prevalent. But like time, the ole hang-up fell by the wayside when young mothers began to bring their young ones to Sunday service. One time, a young mother brought her baby who cried, screamed, and fussed from the onset of Mass. Then ▧▧▧ arrived. She was a gal who had a few children previously to her admittance to the hospital. Her frame measured about four feet high and 3 feet in diameter—a short gal, but with a heart as big as her body—full of motherly love. She asked the young mother for the baby. With relief in her face, the mother gave her baby to ▧▧▧ who fondled it, cuddled it, kissed it, hugged it, and held it close to her breasts all the while Mass continued. Up and down the side aisle, ▧▧▧ walked slowly patting the baby on its bottom—and the church was quiet. No baby shrieks, cries, or embarrassed mother. Mother attended services with devotion and thanks. ▧▧▧ pampered the child, who became quiet and sleepy. ▧▧▧ was thankful and happy to have a baby in her arms. And one would have to say peace reigned in everyone's heart. What love these people have! What love everyone is capable of. A real true gift of God.

O – and when I say He works, I mean sometimes He uses things, persons, and even babies to help to reintegrate people into society. I can't remember this fella's name, but he spoke very, very little. He sat on the right side, in back of the chapel, and remained motionless. One time he was in chapel when I was baptizing an infant. Usually I encourage all the people to kiss, love, and bless the little one. Occasionally, a patient would arm the baby, hug it, kiss it, and pass it along. This happened this Saturday. ███████ loved the little tyke to pieces and then handed the little creature to let's call him ████. "Here. Hold him!" she suggested. ████ broke his rigidness and received the baby. As quickly as he accepted it, he passed the little one back to the mother—and then couple days later, ████ came to my office and CONVERSED. Yes, he did. Before that little incident, he would say nothing—just look at me, drink coffee, and pack a donut in his mouth. But this time he had it. "I think it's time I get out of here and go back to Muskegon." He convinced me and the staff. It wasn't too long afterwards that the short, pot-bellied ████ returned to his native town.

Speaking above there, about someone not speaking, there was a fella on the custodial unit who never said a word. He was inappropriate. He slobbered, mumbled, and smiled as he sat all day almost, on a portable toilet seat. I never heard him say a word, except "son of a bitch," under his breath. He looked alive and friendly, but he certainly mumbled a detectable word flawlessly and clearly. On the medical ward, where he was getting some extra loving care, I met ████. With me, I had some cigars that someone gave to distribute to the patients. Thinking that I might help ████ overcome his "S-O-B" expression, I offered a peace offering/ a King Edward cigar. The attendant warned me not to give it to ████—saying, "He doesn't know what to do with one." Well, let's see, I thought. ████ took it, examined it, carefully unwrapped the cellophane. Then with two fingers and his thumb he held the end of the stogie and injected it into his mouth. Then he pulled it out, grabbed the wet end with the same three digits and inserted the dry end into his mouth. All the while, smilingly. Who said he did not know what to do with a cigar.

███ was an ole cigar-smoking pro. Thought I, let's light him up. To all the negatives that the attendant threw and me like, "He'll burn the place down," I gave some positives. "With you and me here, how can he? We'll watch him," I commented. A strike of the match put flame at the end of the cigar, which ███ held in his lips and fingers. He inhaled and exhaled, and as he moved his head to the left and to the right blowing smoke, he bellered out in some very clean, audible words, "Jesus Christ, it IS a cigar."

The idea of death and dying brings to mind ███. He was so sick—he fell into a coma and nobody believed that he would regain consciousness, especially his wife. She would visit frequently, talk about ███, and his money. About what she was going to do with it when Arthur died. "Do you think he will die soon?" I remember distinctly saying. "I dunno!" Good thing, because one day I walked onto D-2 and ███ had his eyes opened, and he responded to "Comment allez vous?" with "Bien." But then he frowned and showed anger about his wife. He had heard, in his coma (?) state all that his wife talked about for days.

Then there was ███ on D-2 who was seriously ill with no hopes of getting better. He was dying, and one evening (I was called many a time in the nite for people who were critically ill) the nurse requested that I come to comfort ███. He was afraid to die. During the hours I sat with ███, we talked; he talked about remorse, guilt, and fearing God for the way he behaved in life. It was a sad tale that he had to speak, but I listened. In that dimly lit room, ███ became a little less tense and frightened. "What was death like?" I really never went through physical death so I couldn't tell him. But I did tell him about my dad, who was a bricklayer, just like he was. The more I talked, the more he talked, and gradually the depressing look faded into a smile. "'This day you will be with in paradise,'" I quoted Jesus as saying before He died. "And when you get to Heaven, give my regards to my dad." Later contemplating on what I had said, I realized that this was a quick way to get a message to Pop... ███ smiled and fell asleep. And the next morning, only his body remained. ███'s spirit returned to God.

Speaking of the sacraments and their importance, I recall how many times I was called from home in the middle of the nite to anoint some critically ill person. "Prepare them for death," one attendant called it, but that was not too far from wrong. One nite there were two critically ill people in Building 41. I responded to the call. Because there was bedlam on the ward—noise and patients scurrying here and there, the attendants shouted the number of the room in which the sick man lay. Interestingly enough, I found four people in the same room. Two looked like they were at death's door, so I anointed the both of them. "Can't hurt them," I thought. After I finished I recorded my action on the charts, smoked a Camel cigarette, and chatted with the attendants. "You anointed a Jew and a Catholic," they told me. They were not kidding. Well, I couldn't tell which one was which. They were so sick and unresponsive and like I said above, it wouldn't have hurt them. The next morning, as I came on duty, the attendant told me that the Catholic died—but the Jewish person resurrected and was causing "all kinds of hell." He got out of bed, played hide and seek with the staff, pounded everyone's door, broke a door, snapped the lights on and off, wrestled with an attendant, pounded him until he was finally subdued with a little injection in the butt. "Holy hell," exclaimed, the nurse. "What kind of powerful stuff do you have in that holy oil?" I can't remember how long the wrongly anointed person lived, but the fact of what I did still lives on in the memories of quite a few people.

One other time, I believe that the sacrament of the anointing needs to be mentioned and regarded, as I always regard it, as a powerful source of healing and curing. This could be flippancy/casualness on my part, but I believe the age of miracles is not dead. Take for instance the case of ▮▮▮▮, who was diagnosed as having cancer of the larynx. Tests and x-rays showed a diseased voice box. It must be removed—according to the doctor... everything was prepared. A room at the hospital was secured and surgery was scheduled almost immediately.

The nite before the operation, ▮▮▮▮ called to request the sacrament of the anointing. She figured that it would be her last time to speak with her voice. Believe me, that nite visit with her was sad for [redacted] —like going to the executioner's room. I sat and listened to [redacted], gave her the sacrament of Communion and anointed her. After a couple of hours I left for home. The next day I prayed hard, especially at the hour of surgery. I calculated my time very carefully and called the hospital. I wanted to find out from [redacted]'s relatives, how the patient was doing. Dialing the room directly, and letting the ding-ding ding a couple of times, I heard this "Hell-lo?" - thinking the person on the receiver was a relative, I said, "You sound just like [redacted], how is she doing??" "THIS IS [redacted], Father Fred, and I'm doing fine. I didn't need surgery! It's a MIRACLE!" I was flabbergasted, but listened to [redacted]'s explanation of the miraculous episode. It seemed that the doctor wanted another picture of the larynx before surgery. When the negatives were scrutinized, there was no sign of cancer. Nothing detectable. Talk about jubilation!!! Excitement!! And tears of joy??!! There was a plenty of each—and [redacted]'s voice, of course.

[redacted] still has her larynx/voice, but I haven't seen her much since she retired from the hospital. But, as I ponder on the sacraments, I wonder how many unrecorded miracles there are, God knows—more and more I am convinced in the power of the Almighty and the signs He left us to guarantee His statement, "I will be with you till the end of time." Every year I make a trip to Gaylord for the Chrism Mass on Holy Thursday and listen to the Bishop and forty priests and eight hundred people who promise to pray for the individuals anointed with the newly consecrated oil.

Something that most patients did know when they came on scene was card playing. Everyone had a deck or two. What else was there to do?? Televisions were not so full of diverse programs as they are now, so game playing was it. On the medical ward, which was always full, the patients would wait for me to play cards with them. Sacraments came second; cards first. On purpose I would lose games. On purpose I would cheat just to see how sharp they were, and you guessed it. The blood flow to their brains increased expansively every time they said, "You can't do that, Father! You cheated." Well it was all in fun and the laughter amongst all those sick ones certainly added to their recovery. Good thing we never played for money. I would still be paying my debts.

Lots of free things seemed good for the patients. There was one enterprising fella who dug worms and scoured the green grass at nite looking for nite crawlers. He found lots of them. This ole fella would small-carton the worms and fish bait and sell them cheaper than the bait shops downtown. Local fisherman and tourists would drive up to Hall 2, buy some worms and go fishing. Talk about bargains and happiness. These guys loved to get such a discount on fresh worms or crawlers, and ▬, the baitman, smilingly counted the dollars he made during the day. Week-ends were doubly rewarding for Andy. He made money and he made friends. I really do not know what happened to my baitman (sure, I bought some, too) but he left the hospital after awhile. Maybe it was when the superintendent enforced some edict forwarded from Lansing that the patients could not be enterprising and make money on State property. Hmm—now that I recall that situation, I should have told ▬ to go across the street on private land. But like they say, too late smart, too soon old—or something like that.

I have to divert from the memories of the past and tell you of a recent episode that really brought me a warm smile.

Every Sunday morning after the ten o'clock Mass; five, six and sometimes ten little tykes approach the communion rail, with the eagerness of latching on to one of my fingers and leading me out of church. They look so cute. All of them stand on each side of the center aisle like an honor guard, and when the last verse oft he recessional starts, down the aisle I go, supported and led out by these holy kids. Be mindful that these young'uns will be tomorrow's honor guard for Christ. Last Sunday, as we approached the exit to the chapel, one very small girl gave me a round sort of heart shaped orange piece of paper with lots of black scribbling. Evidently, it was a note understandable only to her. As she handed it to me, she said, "Will you give this to God?" I assured her that I would. Ah! That was sweet!

They never bothered lil' ole ▬ though. This fella had a face and stature like Danny DeVito. He wasn't a comedian per se. ▬ liked to fish, whether he had permission to leave the grounds or not. ███went fishing down at the creek. I rarely saw him smile or converse. When he was being reprimanded by the superintendent for leaving the grounds, he would feign deafness and walk away. That frustrated the M.D. —but so what, I got a lot of nice trout from ███.

I remember another lady who had the faith of the staunchest of Irish people. Poor ███ was plagued with scrupulosity, fear, anxieties, and the whole bit. She would exhaust herself trying to breathe. She gasped for air and she looked so heavily medicated. The doctors and nurses tried to calm her agitation with meds, but the poor lady got worse. She thought she was going to die in sin. She needed and screamed for repentance and absolution. I made it to the ward may a time to hear ███'s confession and give her Communion. The grace didn't last long. Before I left the ward, ███ was agitated restless, pulling her hair and gasping for aid. She paced the hall, but in such a manner that her knees touched each other at every step. What could I do?? Just bless her, counsel her, comfort her and pray, pray, pray for some calm. Funny thing, during this period, I was invited to an AMHC (Association of Mental Health Chaplains) convention in Detroit. At one breakfast time, I sat next to Dr. ███ (I hope he let's me use his name) and we talked about peoples' behavior and more generally about hospital folks whom he thought were possessed "Vhy don't you prrriests do summthink?" Like what? I asked. "EXORCISE them." Well I didn't discuss or argue with him anymore, but after the convention I drove home pondering what he said—that there could be a little diabolical possession in people. I thought of Marie, who was not affected by any medicines; she was a walking pharmacy. So a few days after my Detroit convention, I told ███ what the doctor said and prepared her for the event. I knew that for a formal exorcism a priest needed a delegation from the bishop and he needed to fast and do penance for quite awhile, but I thought, why can't I use the prayer of exorcise that I used when I baptized babies (in the old ritual). So I arranged for a day to cast the devil out of ███. I was younger than I am now, rule-less and reckless with the church's power—and confident too that it would help. I met ███ in a visiting room. She was near, clean, well dressed, and well combed; but her disposition was the same as before. As she sat before me, she disheveled her permanent, pulled on her dress, breathed and gasped for air distressfully, and repeatedly crossed her legs—right over left and then left over right until the was almost falling off the chair. She was pleading for so much help! I read the prayer of exorcism from the ritual of baptizing infants, and I must confess, I really trembled when I confidently exclaimed, "Then, accursed one, depart from this temple of the Holy Spirit." Heaven and Hell clashed—███████ was tranquilized, sat calmly, neated up her clothes and tried to arrange her hair and gave me a soft grateful smile. She was cured (?)!! Thanks to Dr. ███████. I kinda figure that this time God showed His hand because ██████ never needed a PRN again. She participated in a lot of activities and even graduated to a family care home in the community. She didn't have to come back to the hospital except for a cure and brief hospitalization of pneumonia. But right after that she returned to the community where she lived happily and contentedly until she died. The miraculous power of Jesus Christ. He works.

The hospital with 3,000 patients was a little city with its own water supply, electric supply, safety officers, and fire station. You should have seen that ole red pumper we had in the middle of the campus to protect the property. The engine was started every day to make sure the plugs did not corrode, the lube job was done regularly, and weekly our fire marshal would putt-putt around the hospital lanes to blow out the black carbon stuff. I can't remember whether they dinged the "dong-dong" of the highly polished bell or not, but that ole relic looked nice in its own crib in the back of the hospital. Good thing we never had a fire; I had my doubts whether enough water could be pumped up fast enough to put out a match flame.

If that sounds amusing, you should have known ███████. There was a gal who knew every funny story, and she knew how to tell each one. I believe that she picked them up working as a waitress in one of the bigger cities on the east side of Michigan. One story that still sticks with me is the one she told repeatedly about the girl walking into church, topless. Her pride and joy (bosom) were exposed for everyone to behold. The priest stopped the girl and told her that she couldn't come into church like that. ▬▬▬▬ related the story thusly. "But I have a divine right," the girl confided. And the priest responded "You have a divine left too, but you have to wear something." Ha! Ha! Ha!—that's what you would hear from ▬▬▬▬afterwards. Every story broke her up. She thrived at story telling, and making people laugh. I'm glad that she was a participant in the daily and the Sunday Masses. She did much to popularize the "Kiss of Peace" at Mass. Literally, she would go through the pews of the church shaking hands, smiling and greeting everyone with "Peace be with you." She would even kiss a few individuals. I sure miss that gal in church. I hope that she is spreading her cheer to all the saints in Heaven. That darn emphysema, which plagued her most of the years I had known her, finally conquered her life. We buried her from the chapel in the presence of a lot of people.

Interesting is the exact word because as I roamed the campus, I could see the screened-in porches and all the people pacing back and forth like caged animals. Oh, they would holler a "good morning" "good afternoon" or a "hi," but it was sad to see people so confined. However, at that time years ago, it was the only way to get some of the folks to breathe some fresh air and to be sure that they would not run away. Boy, am I glad that some advancements have been made in treating the mentally ill! After all, whether they are mixed up or not, they are all creatures of God and are destined for the same place as you and I.

What was it about this chubby little fella who knew all the prayers of the Mass, who loved to go to the confessional, who performed like the ideal acolyte and was perfection personified in church. But, on the ward he was a terror. Hall six was his home, his recreational spot, his work place, and he was always in trouble or mouthing off to someone—not to mention fight with someone. Ah! But he confessed to (Father) attendant. Every Sunday after Mass, and while putting the paraments and vessels away, he nipped on the bottle of altar wine. I wondered why my supply was depleting. Never did I figure my acolyte, especially this one, would imbibe. But he did—until I began to lock up the cupboard—and then we were back to normal—and I lost an acolyte.

Work therapy was always beneficial in the recovery of patients committed to the hospital. The laundry employed so many of the residents. Some strong men unloaded the trucks laden with tons of dirty laundry (imagine laundry and bed linens for 3,000 patients). Others placed the goods in larger washers, then the dryers, then the ironing machines. What came out of the exit door was nice, clean linen and laundry; folded, wrapped, marked, and ready for shipment back to the wards. The patients loved working at the laundry despite the smell at the entrance and heat inside, but they could compliment each other on a work well done and especially themselves for being so worthwhile and productive.

Besides the job at the laundry gave individuals the chance to get off their wards and see other folks, socialize and strike up an occasional emotional friendship. I gotta remind you that all this work was gratis. There was no pay-for-work program in those days—just an occasional bottle of pop provided with money from the patient's benefit fund.

I got a lot of attention from the city folk and patients by introducing a story with my homilies. One that brought the house (oops, chapel) down was the one about two other priests and I going to heaven for our rewards. God showed the first priest a barren room with a table in the middle—at the table sat a wrinkly sad old hag. God said, "Son, you have led a wicked and immoral life. For the rest of eternity you will live here." Then God took the second priest and showed him his reward. It was an empty room with bare walls and only a table in the middle at which sat another wrinkled up old hag. "Son, you had led a wicked and immoral life. For the rest of eternity you will live here." Then—God came to me and took me to a room almost barren, too, except for a velvet curtain on the back wall. From the folds of the veiling came a beautiful, voluptuous Bo Derek. Then God said, "Bo! You have led a wicked and immoral life. This will be your reward for eternity." O - I got a million of them, if I had time to write them all down. But maybe somewhere else in the book you can find another gem.

A Sad Farewell

By mid-1980s, there were fewer than 400 patients left at the hospital due to changes in the approach to treating the mentally ill. There were two main factors: new therapeutic protocols and the development of new psychotropic drugs; and changes in the funding environment at the state level. These changes led to the eventual closing of the entire facility. Along with that closing arose the question: What was to be done with All Faiths Chapel?

The new State of Michigan Mental Health Code of 1974 moved the responsibility of providing mental health services from the State to the counties, with the establishment of Community Mental Health (CMH) facilities. This approach facilitated the mainstreaming of patients into the community, justifying the eventual closing of the state psychiatric hospitals. It also shifted the expenses out of the State budget. CMH didn't hire chaplains. Along with the concept of mainstreaming, they preferred to have patients find a church home in the community, rather than belong to a special congregation.

The prospect of closing the Chapel led local Protestant leaders to separate the future of chaplaincy facilities from the building. Catholics, however, had been drawn into the All Faiths congregation by the charismatic Fr. Fred. About 150 Traverse City Catholics now called the chapel their "church home," along with the dwindling number of regularly attending patients. Fr. Fred had not specifically recruited the local Catholics, but recognized it as a way to provide the patients with a more normal parish community.

Fr. Fred's ministry at the hospital had been carried out in three parts. For those too sick to visit the Chapel, he would hold services and visit patients in their wards. Others would come for Mass and counseling at All Faiths Chapel, where they were introduced to a quasi-normal parish setting. Third, was the benefit of introducing the members of the community to the patients and to the mental health environment. They would take this experience with them back to their own parishes and into the community and into their daily lives. This last part was an essential part of his community-based initiative.

By mid-summer 1989, plans were being finalized to close the State Hospital. In the eyes of the state of Michigan, All Faiths Chapel was just another building along with the others and had become surplus. Local support began to push for a way to keep the cherished community-centered facility open. In an article in the *Traverse*

City Record-Eagle, Fr. Fred commented on the unique importance of the Chapel:

> *The people who come here are a special congregation. The community people come here. The patients come here. The discharged patients come here...For years, the people who have come here have proven the fact that they are not afraid of the mentally ill and they have taught their kids that they should not be afraid of the mentally ill. I call them my "co-therapists." It is a caring center. It is a training center. It is a crisis center.*

> *I would like to keep my fingers in All Faiths Chapel after the hospital closes. In the seminary, they don't teach you how to deal with these people. I had an education right here on the campus. This is the priesthood to me. I feel God has given me the charisma to take care of the less fortunate than I.*

The Chapel was truly an important community center. Not only had members of the Catholic community established a small congregation there, it was used in a number of other ways. Local community mental health workers held monthly meetings there to train foster care givers. State police used it for educational programs, and there were regular meetings of Alcoholics Anonymous.

Most Reverend Robert Rose, Bishop of Grand Rapids, recalls the struggle to keep the Chapel open:

> *Eventually, he lost the battle and the residents had to leave, supposedly to their hometowns. Actually, many of them had no "hometown" and they stayed on in the Traverse City area—and maintained their contact with Father Fred. He was the one stable factor in many of their lives. I presume that is what led to the establishment of The Foundation. He needed a steady income for "his" folks.*

Dan Deering and other community leaders sought assistance from Governor James Blanchard and U.S. Senator Carl Levin to keep All Faiths Chapel open. There was a local letter-writing campaign to State and U.S. lawmakers. A local task force was established, with the idea of preserving the facility as a non-profit corporation that could take control of it and lease it to churches and other groups. Despite all this and the growing local passion to preserve the facility, plans moved forward for closing All Faiths Chapel, along with the rest of the hospital. High maintenance and operating costs were cited, along with the serious need for roof repair estimated at $200,000.

There was also a legal barrier to saving the Chapel that had been such a haven for so many, for so long. When the facility was built, twenty-five years earlier, there was a lot of excitement and passion to raise the money to build it. However, in the rush to get it established, designed, and built, there was no separate deed created for the property. A separate ownership of that piece of the hospital campus was never established, so it was just another redundant building on a redundant piece of State history. There was no interest in Lansing to even consider such a proposal as the State was trying to "clean-up" their books and dispose of the property.

On August 20, 1989, Fr. Fred celebrated Mass at All Faiths Chapel for the last time. The sad, emotional, standing-room-only congregation was packed with patients, former patients, and townspeople. According to an article in the *Traverse City Record-Eagle* the next day, Fr. Fred's final sermon there included words of encouragement. He urged members to "have the strength, determination, and willpower to do instead of just pray. We have the power to bring hope to families. Your world is important to God. What you make of it is your gift to God." In his interview, he told the reporter:

> I give them a little bit of love and they throw 1,000 percent back. They like humor and humanness. Sometime I let the humanness cloud over the theology. I give 'em all I got. I feel like the good shepherd—mine know me and I know mine. Now, they feel disbanded and powerless. I'm going to miss them... Patients respond to me because I follow the Golden Rule. I treat them as I would like to be treated.

At the time during the Mass when Fr. Fred distributed the Holy Eucharist to the faithful, the Communion hymn was "I Am The Bread of Life." As the last line of that hymn was being sung, tears choked Alice Shirley's voice. She stopped singing, lowered her head, and wept as nearly 300 voices sang, "...I will raise you up on the last day." Her tears spoke for so many people in the community.

By the following week, All Faiths Chapel had been padlocked by the State of Michigan, and Fr. Fred was helping out at St. Francis of Assisi in Traverse City, at the invitation of the pastor, Fr. Ron Gronowski.

A few weeks later, as a way of saying goodbye, on Sunday, September 24, a group of about 200 people held hands and formed a ring around the building and prayed. Led by Fr. Fred, they sang "How Great Thou Art" and "America the Beautiful," and recited the Lord's Prayer. Fr. Fred offered a prayer that lasted about ten minutes. The crowd stayed gathered for a little while, sadly reminiscing. Among the attendees that day were a couple of former patients who had been married in All Faiths Chapel by Fr. Fred. "It was really a heartbreaking situation," the husband recalls, "to see all those people there and the church closed and locked."

The Traverse City State Hospital closed on September 29, 1989.

In the Name of the Father

A broken, wounded heart, O Lord, you will not spurn.

(Psalm 51:19)

An *ad hoc* local group was organized to try and save All Faiths Chapel. Young attorney, Dan Dingeman, felt indebted to Father Fred because of the way he had helped in some earlier family matters. "The community was in an uproar," explains Dingeman. "All Faiths would close unless we could prove it didn't belong to the State." "Don't worry, Counselor," Fr. Fred said to him back then. "You'll figure it out." Dan was immediately soothed by this reassurance and Fr. Fred's use of the characteristic nickname.

The effort was sadly unsuccessful. In the end, it mostly came down to one little detail: Twenty-five years earlier, there had been no effort to define any community ownership of the Chapel. The $300,000 raised by the local group, from the thirty-nine counties served by the hospital, ended up being a donation to the State of Michigan. The general sentiment in the community was that the State was insensitive in the way the hospital was shut down,

Fr. Fred is amazed at the community's response to an appeal for food donations.

> ## "If I have it and you need it, it's yours."
>
> *Father Fred*

especially when it came to the disposition of All Faiths Chapel.

As the last few patients were moved from the State Hospital, there was a general fuss in the community, from a number of different sources. The most severely affected patients were moved to other inpatient facilities around the state. Others were moved into foster housing in the area; and a few made their way to the streets of Traverse City, significantly increasing the previously small homeless population. The concomitant closing of All Faiths Chapel was disturbing to the regular congregants: both patients and townspeople. Most disturbing, to some, was the confusion and sense of loss on the part of the patients who had been drawn to Fr. Fred and had benefitted so long by his guidance, wisdom, and handouts. He was simply no longer available to them.

Fr. Fred accepted Fr. Gronowski's invitation to be of assistance at St. Francis of Assisi and began saying Masses there, as well as assisting with funerals, etc. Dutifully, he preached as he always had, and the All Faiths congregants followed him to St. Francis. His charismatic personality, his popularity, and "his people" arrived at St. Francis with him, which was problematic for both the parish staff and congregation.

Not all the parishioners at St. Francis held the same joy Fr. Fred did for helping "his people." The former patients soon became "those people." When some vandals broke into the church, did some damage, and stole some things, the inference was: "This sort of thing didn't happen before 'those people' started coming here." A small bit of that sentiment lingered, even after police found the kids who did it and they were successfully prosecuted.

Another incident that reminded the congregation of "those people" was when a former patient came to St. Francis after the State Hospital closed. Fr. Fred was celebrating Mass and the man threw handfuls of condoms at him, screaming about teachings of the Church. Fr. Fred recognized the man as a former patient, and remained calm, although the congregation was upset. He never lost his composure, but afterwards talked briefly to the man—who then listened to him—and left the church.

The assignment at St. Francis lasted only a few months, and Fr. Fred was assigned by the recently appointed Bishop Patrick Cooney to St. Joseph, the oldest Catholic church in the Traverse City area. There, Fr. Fred was the assistant, helper, and friend to the aging pastor, Fr. Denay. True to form, many of the former patients and other All Faiths congregants followed him. The small parish on the Old Mission Peninsula endured the boost in attendance. By March 1990, Fr. Fred was named pastor at St. Joseph Parish.

Through all this, the former patients were encountering aspects of life they hadn't needed to face before and were being forced into new responsibilities they weren't prepared for. Survival was now their issue, and Fr. Fred was worried about them. Winter was coming to northern Michigan. His thirty-year infrastructure had also evaporated, but not his concern for these distressed and needy friends. Fr. Fred voiced his concerns for the newly dispossessed to his associates and the men he had breakfast with every Tuesday morning.

A small group still fought to keep All Faiths Chapel alive. Their vision was the continuation of a community-owned, inter-faith facility that would give Fr. Fred a place to continue working with those he had cared for so long.

In September 1989, just prior to the closing, Jim Lizenby asked Fr. Fred if he had ever considered a foundation. "With your connections and energy, it would surely be a success," he said. Fr. Fred appeared not to hear the idea, since he was so totally focused on saving the chapel. Their strategy meetings were preparing them for the final audience with the state's twenty-three-member task force, set up to decide on the disposition of the buildings.

During the last week in November, coming out of the City Hall with his small team of fighters, after the final "No" was spoken by the State of Michigan, Fr. Fred turned to Jim and asked: "Why don't you tell them about your idea, Jim?" What followed for those few men standing there, as Jim laid out his idea, was the realization that they had just witnessed the moment of conception for The Father Fred Foundation. They decided to follow up on the idea, form a steering committee, and get started.

Dan Dingeman says he felt like the pup among the others, all older than he, when he was called to the formation meeting in Dan Deering's office above the grocery store on Fourteenth Street. Nonetheless, he joined Jim Lizenby, Dr. Carl Madion, Maurie Dennis, Dan Deering, and Fr. Fred. Dan was nervous, knowing he was going to be taking on the legal end of the formation of whatever was about to happen. "Don't worry, Counselor, you'll figure it out," Fr. Fred told him, once again.

"How can you keep on doing what you've been doing for these people once All Faiths Chapel is gone?" Lizenby asked Fr. Fred. "Well, the patients will be gone," Fr.

Fred explained. "They've been set free. We've got to act fast." So, the small group went into action. "We'll raise $50,000 and rent you a place to work from," the men assured him. Their next thought was, *How, in hell, are we going to do that*?

Spouses of the core group of supporters, the very first Father Fred Foundation volunteers, worked on assembling a list of 1,200 names for a mailing. They wrote a letter explaining the idea and asking for support and launched the campaign to raise the $50,000. The mailing went out on December 10, and by year-end they had met their goal. They found and rented a small office suite adjacent to a dentist's office on Fourteenth Street in Traverse City, about twelve blocks from All Faiths Chapel.

Branding the alliterative name and character of The Father Fred Foundation came early, when a graphic designer, the wife of a board member, scribbled out an image of a broken heart to use as the logo for the organization. The "wounded heart" image became the trademark for The Father Fred Foundation and has often been paired with one of Fr. Fred's favorite scriptural passages, from Psalm 51: "A wounded, broken heart, O Lord, you will not spurn."

Meanwhile, the core leadership group kept on having regular breakfast meetings every Tuesday. These became their informal "board meetings" where the attendees conducted business, addressed problems, and made decisions. Each breakfast started with a Gospel reading, a prayer, and a pep talk by Fr. Fred.

The Father Fred Foundation, a domestic nonprofit corporation, was incorporated and registered in the State of Michigan on December 6, 1989. The Articles of Incorporation show the stated purposes for which the corporation is organized:

> *To receive contributions, grants, endowments, and the like, to be administered in assisting the mentally distressed, physically diseased, poor, hungry, and suffering; to use the funds raised by such efforts in any charitable or public welfare manner which will aid and assist the mentally distressed, physically diseased, poor hungry, and suffering; to manage and acquire real and personal property, and to do any and all related acts which are lawful and proper in meeting such charitable purposes and goals.*

The original leaders were simply a group of friends of Fr. Fred from the All Faiths Chapel days. Original board members were Dan Deering, Dan Dingeman, Carl

Madion, and Jim Lizenby. Operations began immediately in the Fourteenth Street location, as a small facility for drop-ins. Former patients soon began arriving. Carl Madion smiles as he remembers the first visitors coming out of the winter cold:

> *They were living in foster care facilities and on the streets.*
> *They gravitated toward Father Fred, because he took care of*
> *them. They were always so happy when they saw him, and*
> *each other, again. It was like a little club. They would greet*
> *each other in the lobby and have a hot cup of coffee and a*
> *doughnut. They were with Father Fred again.*

Donations began arriving about the same time as the visitors. A small group of volunteers—LaVerne O'Neil, Barb Lehnhard, Pat Cloutier, some spouses of the leadership group, and a few others—began helping Fr. Fred in his new enterprise. The board started attracting other community leaders and givers. Money started coming in, along with boots, sweaters, jackets, and food.

It wasn't long before the original $50,000, raised by 400 donors, doubled to $100,000 raised by nearly 800 donors. Other local businessmen joined the group, like Jerry Carlson, who had been a longtime friend of Father's, and Arnie Ochs. Arnie, who describes himself as a Muskegon Heights Catholic School kid, perhaps says it best:

> *...giving back is just the right thing to do. It was very clear*
> *to me from my Catholic upbringing we have an obligation*
> *to give it back. Not everybody is built that way, but we all*
> *should be. Father Fred preached that. That was just part of*
> *his ballgame.*

All were well connected and committed to helping Fr. Fred and the new Foundation. Their initial premise was tenuous, but Fr. Fred invested it with a calm and confident authority. He knew how to motivate the men on his board. His ideas always seemed to prevail. He'd listen to what the others had to say, always interested in their answers; and then, in the end, do it his way. For much of the time, Fr. Fred treated his board members like his acolytes.

One thing Fr. Fred wanted to do, but never did, was to get into low-income housing. That is where his board drew the line. "There were no airs in him, in any way, shape, or form," tells Arnie Ochs. "His humor helped us all get along, especially in the heavy discussions about finances. He didn't tell a lot of jokes; he would just re-state the truth in a way that made it humorous. Sometimes the board would have to rein him in because he was giving money away faster than we could bring it in."

Administrative details of running an organization were something for which Fr. Fred had little patience. No meeting with him lasted more than fifty-nine minutes. "If we can't get done what we need to do in an hour," he'd say, "we aren't working together well. We have other work to do." Many times, people were surprised when he'd simply get up and walk out of a meeting after the hour was up.

In March of 1990, just a few months after the formation of The Foundation, Fr. Fred wrote to a friend:

> *...Since Christmas, the community, under the direction of four creative persons, has put together the Father Fred Foundation. The purpose of the organization is to help patients and ex-patients, the people with heavy hearts, the folks who need food and electricity and fuel and prescriptions and all the basics of life. We all know and realize that there are a lot of those folks out there. So far, we have been doing nicely, getting money and food and all sorts of things for our Foundation. What a blessing some people are. I like this work and it is no different from what I have been doing for the last thirty years. Never did I think that I would be doing this since I retired from Civil Service. But God must have a hand in it.*

The Early Days of The Foundation

Fr. Fred's work at The Foundation was not, strictly, a pastoral assignment, even though there were many incidents of pastoral activity. The ecumenical spirit of the State Hospital continued at the new foundation. In the first newsletter, Spring 1990, Fr. Fred wrote about the charter: "The charter was carefully drafted, separating the Foundation completely from Father Fred's religious responsibilities. The Foundation was to serve all, regardless of religious affiliation."

From a 1992 article in the *Detroit News*:

> *Father Fred meets as many people as possible. Sometimes he'll write a small check, arrange for someone to get gasoline from a nearby service station, make a call to another social agency.*

> *And sometimes, through the window of the office, he and a visitor will be seen with their heads bowed. After one such incident, an elderly woman came out, smiling. "I got what I needed," she said, to no one in particular as she left.*

The pace at The Foundation quickened, and it didn't take long for things to start falling into place. Volunteers were added, and a routine of assistance was established. There were four essential components that made the project work: the visitors (clients), volunteers, donors, and Fr. Fred. Sally Suprenant, one of the early volunteers describes the very early days:

> *When Father Fred was there, people from the State Hospital would come over. We had a table there and sometimes they'd come for cookies and coffee. They didn't really want anything, but they would come just to see Father Fred. "Father Fred," they'd ask, "could you give me a blessing today?" Welcoming them into his office, he would bless them. He was always concerned about the people. His quietness and gentleness would relax a lot of those people when they came in. They felt like they could sit and talk with us. It was an extension of the State Hospital, after it closed. The transition was so difficult for them—they just wanted to be with him. He was their rock.*

Fr. Fred was the constant they missed when things shut down at the hospital. He was still available, so they found him. The Foundation's new drop-in center gave them a place to go. Sometimes the visitors didn't really need anything; they were simply reconnecting with Fr. Fred.

The concept was really quite simple and Fr. Fred wanted to keep it that way. Donations were coming in and his philosophy was: "If we have it and you need it, it's yours." If he didn't have something, it would soon come in. He fixed up what was broken with his people and sent them on their way. At first, the people would simply help themselves to what was available. Later, the volunteers made up bags for them, based on their needs. Some days, bags and boxes of food lined the walls and filled the space. Other days, they might run short. "God will send us what we need," he'd say.

The Father Fred Foundation was not conceived as a Catholic organization, even though many, if not all, of the original core group were Catholics. That was because they knew him from worshipping at All Faiths Chapel. It has remained that way throughout its history. Nor is there a formal affiliation with the Diocese of Gaylord, in which the organization resides. By 1992, Fr. Fred identified that The Foundation was serving fewer Catholics than other denominations. There was a decision not to accept any state or federal money because of the accompanying restrictions. From the beginning, it was all donations that came in: food, clothing, and maybe some money for their bills.

Fr. Fred had a small office space and met with every visitor that came to him on a one-on-one basis. The volunteers crafted a working system—work either pantry or clothing. If a client's problems were particularly private or thorny, Fr. Fred might step outside for the interview because there was so little space. When someone came by with a donation, he was sure to say, "Come back when you can and volunteer."

One extraordinary aspect of the success of the organization, right from the beginning, was Fr. Fred's ability to make connections in the community. Depending on the need of the client before him, he could pick up the phone and call someone he knew and get help for that person. This worked with doctors, lawyers, dentists, the gas company, the electric company, and even the police and Sheriff. All he had to do was identify himself and he'd get what he needed for the client.

In the ascendant days of The Foundation, for record keeping, there was a little Underwood manual typewriter. Volunteers began making up cards for each client or family. They kept little information—just enough to keep track of how often folks were coming by for help. A simple intake process was set up and the clients would talk to Fr. Fred and tell him what they needed. If he had it, he'd give it to them. The office was open from 10:00 a.m. to 2:00 p.m., Tuesday through Friday. Fr. Fred was simply focused on helping people and had little patience for the structures of record keeping or accounting. One volunteer claimed she didn't know much about what was going on, but she felt Fr. Fred knew even less. He kept five-dollar bills in his desk drawer and if there was a need, he'd pull one out and hand it over with, "Here's enough gas money to get your kid to the hospital."

The Foundation outgrew the space on Fourteenth Street within a few months. Clients were often lined up out the door, and there were so many donations the little office could hardly contain them all. Additionally, all the daily activity with clients and donors coming and going was disruptive to the dental practice that had leased them the space. Word had spread about the nascent foundation. Father and his board began looking around for a larger facility. They found some empty space less than a block away on the corner of Griffin and Cass Streets. On August 8, 1991, The Father Fred Foundation moved to the new location.

The new larger space gave The Foundation the capability to store and handle food differently, and be more efficient with their food expenditures. They had room to add a newly donated refrigerator and freezer. More advancement came with the addition of a computer to keep records. George Kuhn, a retired physics and math instructor from the local college, had some computer skills and worked with Fr. Fred and LaVerne O'Neil to devise the first computerized client database to track donors as well as clients.

> "If they take advantage of me once in a while, well that's going to happen. People are going to do what people do. We'll give them the benefit of the doubt, because we are on God's side. It is on them, and they will have to answer to Him for it."
>
> *Father Fred*

George watched Fr. Fred's fascination as the possibilities for helping more people improved. "He certainly wasn't afraid to jump in and work on the computer," says George. "When LaVerne was not there, he would sit down at the computer and enter data himself. He never really got very good at it, but he appreciated what the technology would do for the organization." One early application Fr. Fred was interested in was tracking clothing distribution to spot abuse of the system. While he was never judgmental, Fr. Fred would limit clothing to two bags of clothes, twice each month. That original system is the basis for some of the software still in place at The Foundation.

Rick Coates had been a regular visitor at All Faiths Chapel. As the days of the State Hospital were winding down, Rick watched the early formation of The Foundation, and later, volunteered at the original facility. He remembers:

> *I'd be working over there, and Father would be interviewing someone who was pouring her heart out to him with her troubles. I'd move toward the door, to give her some privacy, and Father would say, "That's okay. You don't have to leave." I would stay and hear the stories. If that had been a State agency, there is no way I could have been in there, and some of the stories just tore your heart out. I'll bet I sat in on sixty or eighty interviews and not one client ever asked who I was. I guess they figured if it was okay with Father Fred, it must be okay. He had a built-in BS meter. He could tell if someone was lying to him.*

Rick also tells the story about a woman with four kids who had no job, no husband, and little dignity. Fr. Fred gave her enough money to go get a new outfit and a makeover for her hair and make-up. In a return to his mantra, he told her, "If you're going to get a good job, you gotta be sharp. In order to do that, you gotta feel sharp. In order to do that, you gotta look sharp." The woman got the new outfit and makeover, and after a few months she had a driver's license, a new steady job, and her high school GED certificate.

Another story is about a widower who had five or six kids. He had never learned to cook. When Fr. Fred heard that, he called into his office a woman volunteer who had a reputation as a pretty good cook. He re-assigned her as a volunteer to cook at the man's home, teach him how to cook, and share her recipes with him. A year later, he was employed—as a cook.

Some of the volunteers expressed concern about visitors scamming Fr. Fred. "We're not here to judge," he would tell them. "I'm pretty good at knowing when people aren't telling me the truth, yet people are going to do what people do, and if we are right ninety-five percent of the time, we are doing well. Besides, God is on our side, and they are the ones who will have to answer for that."

Carol remembers the first time she met Fr. Fred and how surprised and impressed she was with what he had to say. A friend of hers had heard the story of a certain poor family that had been beset with one problem after another. The two of them decided to approach Fr. Fred and see if he could help. He listened to the two women as they told him about the unfortunate family. When they finished, Fr. Fred said, "I know that family, and they have been in here several times already and we've helped them." With that, Fr. Fred explained how he had helped and why he was not going to do more for them at this time. There were some limits, and not even Fr. Fred could help everyone. So, he set up a referral system to other agencies that might be able to do a better job. His philosophy was "teach them how to fish," and nothing was more pleasing to him than to see someone turn their life around after getting some help. Often, he'd simply tell someone to go find a job and was known to draw the line if he thought people weren't really working to help themselves. He showed his disappointment when he had to say no to anyone. It was rare, but it happened. He kept a mental database, and often referred to it as the computer in his head.

One man presented his case for help to Father for the fourth or fifth time before Fr. Fred realized the man's problem was alcohol based. "Okay," he told him, "if you're going to get any more help from me, here are the things you will need to do in the next ninety days: go and get a job, any job; go to AA and bring me a note from your sponsor..." and he laid out a plan for the man. Hearing this, the man replied, "Well, Father, what am I going to do in the meantime?" "Oh, God will help you figure that out," Father replied. "You've gotten this far in life without Father Fred. You can get through the next ninety days just fine."

There was one condition where he never refused help, and that was when someone said they were hungry. When he was asked, "How many times can I come back to The Foundation?" He would say, "How many times do you get hungry?"

Daily Dignity at The Foundation

Volunteers could see that Fr. Fred was brilliant at human psychology, and even though he carried the burdens of all his clients, he did it easily and comfortably. Everyone who came in contact with Fr. Fred appreciated his positive mental attitude, and whether he gave them a cigar, a coupon for food, or assistance with the rent or the utilities, he was always searching for a way to ease peoples' burdens. Bill Maxbauer, who grew up in Traverse City serving Mass for Fr. Fred at All Faiths Chapel and at the Carmelite Monastery, fondly looks back: "People knew that he was a person who could help them through rough patches in their lives. Did he ever get taken advantage of? Of course he did. While he could be a shrewd judge of character, he always wanted to err on the side of generosity, not stinginess."

In a 1992 article in the *Detroit News*, Fr. Fred talks about his philosophy and mission: "Poor people hate to say they're poor. It takes a lot of courage to come here and ask for help. We try to help them maintain their dignity." Paula Prusick, an early volunteer, tells, "If visitors were willing to ask for it, he thought they probably deserved help. If you came forward, you got it. You had to be honest." Fr. Fred sat down and talked with every visitor and got to know the recipient very well.

Dan Deering remembers Fr. Fred's generosity and how it affected his own giving patterns: "When The Foundation got low on food, he'd come over to the store and fill up. One Christmas, he called and said he needed a few hams. 'How many?' I asked him, thinking, maybe six or eight. 'Forty,' he told me. 'And, we're going to need some turkeys, too. How about thirty?'"

According to Fr. Fred, taken from a status report to the board:

> *The foundation is more things than food, we have soaps, detergents, paper products, (something that other agencies don't bother with) because our aim and slogan is, "Look sharp! Feel sharp! Be sharp!" With all the things we take for granted, soaps, deodorants, diapers, hair spray, toothbrushes and paste, are essential… we figure that gives them dignity.*

Volunteers were treated with equal dignity, since Fr. Fred understood the significance of their contribution and the effects on their lives. As with the clients, there were two types of response to the volunteers when issues arose. Most common was the response of guidance and gratitude for the time they spent helping the needy and vulnerable visitors. There was also a response that meant "deal with it." If one volunteer didn't like the way another volunteer was doing something, he'd tell them: "Well, maybe you just need to pray a little harder for that person."

If someone felt something was wrong and complained to him, he'd ask, "Aren't you happy here?" "Yes, of course I'm happy here," he'd get back. "Good, that's what we want—for everyone here to be happy. Now, how about if we get back to work."

There were only a few things that angered Fr. Fred. Most significant among them was if the children of the visiting families were suffering. He had real empathy for them and worked constantly to protect them. Another was alcohol and drug addiction. There are many compassionate stories of how he helped people face their addictions, yet if the client didn't cooperate, there was little Fr. Fred would do to enable the behavior, especially if there were children involved.

Very few got away with lying to Fr. Fred about their needs, yet there were a few times it did happen. One year, after the distribution of Thanksgiving baskets had been completed, there was one in the office that had not been delivered. So, before they wrapped up for the day, Fr. Fred and Matt Myers got in the car and went to the home of the recipient. They arrived at an upscale home, with two late model cars in the driveway, and could see they had been duped. Matt tells that he had never seen Fr. Fred more upset that he did that evening. How could someone like that take Thanksgiving dinner out of the mouths of the poor?

Volunteers

Right from the beginning, there were two essential elements that worked well in serving visitors: Fr. Fred and the volunteers. Just as he was the Pied Piper for the former patients and the needy, his magnetism attracted volunteer help.

Fr. Fred and Matt Myers work on the Hastings Street renovation, 1999.

Barb Lehnhard and Jerry Carlson in the pantry on Hastings Street.

For many years, the organization was entirely volunteer-run, except for part-time payment for an office staff person. Volunteers worked out all the details of the day-to-day business. The board of directors was in place to simply facilitate and manage at a higher level.

In the early days, on Fourteenth Street, volunteers defined the mission and processes of The Foundation. They stacked a few shelving units they called the pantry with food donations. They sorted clothes and other donations. They brought what little order there was to the growing inventory at the meager facility, and they gathered and stored client information. Originally, the information was on simple index cards, kept alphabetically. Later, they were data entry clerks, using the first rudimentary computer system. Volunteer assistance allowed Fr. Fred to spend time doing what he did best: interviewing and assessing the needs of the clients who came to him for help.

A few of the volunteers who were there in the beginning still work regularly on a weekly schedule. Others had more of a commitment to Fr. Fred than to the organization and were there because he was there. When he died, they left the organization. Fr. Fred's incredible memory for names and faces helped him know every one of the volunteers, the names of their children, and facts about their lives. Even after a period of not seeing someone, he might greet a volunteer with, "Hey, *Jan*, it's so good to see you. How's your mom doing after her stroke?" or "How's that baseball team doing that your son, *Jason*, is playing on?"

Volunteers marveled at Fr. Fred's capacity to help the visitors. Because of the small facility they were in, volunteers often overheard the stories of the clients, wondering how he could listen so empathetically all day. For Fr. Fred, it seemed so effortless, yet one volunteer, Sally Suprenant, said she had to often get up and walk away because the stories were overwhelming to her. Sometimes, Fr. Fred would tell her to stay. "You need to hear this," he'd tell her.

Every day was inspirational for the volunteers. They were extensions of his strong and capable hands. The organization evolved as it grew, and roles changed and settled into a working routine. Early on, Barb Lehnhard managed the volunteers' schedules and activities while Matt Myers oversaw the operations, enabling Fr. Fred to simply be free to be Fr. Fred. These three good friends ran the day-to-day activities for the first few years. Barb paused one day to exclaim, "There's a miracle going on here—a new one every day. This is Christ at work." She remembers a time when she realized the shelves were scarce of beans, and at the same moment a donor dropped off two or three cases of beans. Fr. Fred saw these as spiritual transactions.

Pat Lizenby and Fr. Fred enjoying some cake and company.

Fr. Fred after Sunday Mass in the conference room on Hastings Street.

For every volunteer, there was a connection with Fr. Fred and a connection with the people coming in for help. Everyone got something out of it. Those who volunteered became as close as family. They ate and socialized together, supported one another, and became close working friends.

Fr. Fred would start each day with a prayer with the volunteers. After the move to Hastings Street in 1994, he offered Mass upstairs in the meeting room. It was a carryover from the days

at All Faiths Chapel, when Catholics found him in a non-traditional, non-parish setting. The meeting room was always full, the Mass intimate and personal. And then, as if the sacred liturgy was being extended, members in the group would go out to brunch. It was an easy transition from one celebration to the next. Many of the attendees say they felt this was the way it must have been like with Christ in the Upper Room.

The upstairs room was also the site of other celebrations. Finish a Garage Sale? Celebrate. Reach a certain milestone? Have a celebration. Haven't had a gathering in a while? Have one. This socializing with the volunteers and friends of The Foundation was merely an extension of the liturgical celebration of the Mass—in the same setting. It didn't matter if the wine was sacramental or celebratory; he connected with his friends truthfully and effectively, and on a regular and very personal, undisguised level, celebrated life.

Spiritual Transactions

It is still the case, today. The volunteers' dedication was inspired by the same spiritual mechanism Fr. Fred identified in himself and others who offered assistance: There are two sides to every giving transaction. Certainly, the person receiving the aid (food, money, clothing, furniture) got something from it. As important, the person doing the giving got at least as much (sometimes more) from the same transaction.

One such transaction story is about Matt Myers. While Matt was the first paid employee of The Father Fred Foundation, he started as a volunteer in 1991 and left just after Fr. Fred died. His relationship with Fr. Fred stands out as a wonderful, redemptive, classic example of how Fr. Fred helped re-build people's lives.

Matt was raised as a Lutheran. His wife, Mary, was a Catholic who knew Fr. Fred through church. While Matt was away for five years, paying his debt to society for some problems he'd gotten himself into earlier in his life, Fr. Fred was a source of comfort for Mary and their two boys. When Matt returned home, he got to know Fr. Fred better. Then his troubles returned, on the heels of a parole problem, and he had to re-appear in federal court in Grand Rapids, about 150 miles from Traverse City.

Who showed up and spoke at the hearing, unsolicited and unannounced? Fr. Fred. Matt's case was reviewed and he was sentenced to do some more time. As he was being led out of the courtroom, he asked the federal marshals if he could stop and say something to the kind priest who had helped him through his ordeal and had appeared on his behalf. "Fr. Fred," he began, "thank you for your help. What can I do for you?" Fr. Fred told him, "When you get out, Matt, come and see me. We'll need your help at The Foundation."

While Matt was away, at the federal prison in West Virginia, he met a priest named Fr. Frederick Annie. Matt called him "Father Annie," since he already knew a Fr. Fred. He worked in the prison chapel and converted to Catholicism. When he got out, he pondered how he was going to put the pieces of his life back together. His first stop was The Foundation, where he began his work as a volunteer. "Father Fred was one of the only guys who stood by me earlier," he says. "I felt as though I owed him a lot." It wasn't long before the members of The Foundation board asked him to work full time, and together, they structured the first paid position at The Foundation.

It was classic Fr. Fred behavior to reach out to someone who needed a hand and help him. For that, Fr. Fred knew Matt would dedicate himself on behalf of The Foundation. During his time there, Matt was instrumental in many of the initiatives still in place. He worked side-by-side with Fr. Fred to organize the growing volunteer base and the warehouse operations. He was a prime mover in the Frostbite Food Drive and the annual Thanksgiving Dinners. He also worked with the local school system administration to have student hours counted as community service. Along the way, he developed a close, personal, and symbiotic relationship with Fr. Fred. When Fr. Fred died, Matt lost a very close friend and mentor.

The story of Matt illustrates the two halves of the spiritual transaction Fr. Fred employed so effectively in countless other situations. In an undated, mid-1990s piece titled "The Need," Fr. Fred writes about the transaction between the volunteer and the experience.

> *...Amidst all this activity, a volunteer may stop and stop to think, "Where do I fit in here? What do I possess, what abilities do I have to give and to offer to this organization? Furthermore, what can I give, and what can I receive and learn by serving?"*

> *Initially, from the very beginning, a volunteer owns two extremely precious gifts which he or she can donate... his/her*

> # "The miracle is not that we do this work, but that we are happy to do it."
>
> *Mother Teresa*

self and time. These are the two essential components to all service. In volunteering for a few hour shift, there are a variety of jobs that may be undertaken. A volunteer may assist in sorting clothes and hanging them upon racks, move furniture into a pick-up truck, or shelve canned goods in the pantry. But, as more than eighty volunteers will testify, these tasks are not what they will solely remember about their service at Father Fred's; their lives will forever be influenced by the lessons they were taught about themselves in their interactions with the clients and other volunteers.

In that same piece, Matt Myers writes:

Working with The Father Fred Foundation is special to me because I am dealing with both sides of the need. There are people in this community who need to help other people ... they have a sense of duty and the Foundation helps to fulfill that. Others discover the value of helping people, I watch them do it every day. They can additionally realize that there is incredible poverty, even in the community like Traverse City, and that has to be dealt with.

Fr. Fred's effect on volunteers and donors was neither casual nor accidental. His innate understanding of human nature led him to realize the effect he and The Foundation activities had on their lives. While he knew he had a following and that he was important to so many people, he didn't often verbalize it. The work of the volunteers was inspired by his calm, straightforward, uncomplicated approach of helping others. Some claim he knew more about them than they knew themselves. He inspired volunteers by teaching them how to give, recognizing the spiritual transaction that occurred when one person gives and another receives. It is axiomatic: There is a *quid pro quo* in every transaction.

Jim Lizenby, one of the founding board members of The Foundation says:

> *Father Fred knew everyone wants to help other people,*
> *myself included, yet most of us have to make a conscious*
> *decision to do it. Not Father Fred, for him it was as natural as*
> *breathing. He never had to think about it. The only time I ever*
> *heard him talk about giving to others, from his perspective,*
> *was when he would talk about wanting to be more like Mother*
> *Teresa. He mentioned that to me several times.*

The volunteer spirit at The Father Fred Foundation is stronger now than ever. With over 150 people registered as volunteers, they participate on a weekly and monthly schedule. There are so many, some don't even know some of the others. "Oh, I'm on Wednesday afternoon. I think she might work on Fridays," you might hear. Volunteers wear their blue t-shirts with pride. A few are still serving who were with Fr. Fred at his earliest Fourteenth Street location. It is inspirational and amazing.

Fr. Fred certainly led by example. He seemed to have an insatiable appetite for helping the people who came to him. Often, he would exhaust himself meeting their needs. Barb and Matt both tell about how, at the end of the day, he would seem to be totally spent—worn out in his office, elbows on the desk, with his head in his hands—and the phone would ring. It would not be unusual for someone to call with a request to have him get over to the hospital and administer Last Rites to a relative or friend. "No problem," he'd reassure the person on the other end of the line, "I'll be right over." That's probably why, Barb explains, he had such an emphasis on breakfast:

> *The reason he liked to go out to breakfast so much is that*
> *it might be his only meal that day. Foundation hours were*
> *from ten to two and he'd work right through lunchtime. We*
> *had to get after him to eat. He didn't take very good care of*
> *himself, sometimes.*

Fundraising

By 1996, The Foundation was able to report that ninety-four cents of every dollar of cash or in-kind goods received was distributed to the needy. The cash and in-kind donations, that year, totaled $985,000. Some say that Fr. Fred never asked for money—it just came to him. That is difficult to believe in concept, and there may be a case to be made that he was a very effective fundraiser. He simply did it his way.

As soon as The Foundation was established, he began issuing a quarterly newsletter. In each issue, sent to every donor and others on The Foundation mailing list, he would include updates on the organization and colloquially tell stories about the recipients of the good work being done. The stories told the reader: "This is how *you* helped a family in need." It was dramatically more effective than simply asking for money.

Here is a sampling of stories from these quarterly newsletters, as is from an existing, alphabetical index of ways clients were helped:

Alcoholism

Appliances

> *Would you believe that W.J., way up there in the U.P. called and told me the whereabouts of a practically new refrigerator in an unoccupied cabin? "Give it to someone who can use it," he declared. During the summer heat, a poor family, who were using Styrofoam coolers to keep food from spoiling, became the recipients of this big gift. Visualize, if you can, the radiant happiness of the faces of mother and kids. I can't describe it accurately enough to do it justice, but I can tell you it spelled, thanks a million, and no more spoiled milk.*

Coats

Dental care

> *When a woman came into the Foundation recently needing to pay for a root canal costing over $1,000, we found $100 to help begin payments. "I always figure if I can help a little at first, maybe they will be able to provide the rest."*

Dignity

Divorce

Fuel

Gratitude

Halloween costumes

Homelessness

> *To come by car from Acme to the Foundation office takes about 20 minutes, I think. How long it might take by foot, I don't know, but a slim, thin, thirty-year old woman told me she walked that distance. She was exhausted and desperate for a room—somewhere. It was cold, too. With the assistance of the Bell invention to several motels, a vacancy was found. On that sad face, there was no ecstasy, only a sigh of relief. The human creature left the office, sadly saying a friend would share a meal with her. But three days later, almost stuporous, this same unfortunate leaned on the counter of the office. She hadn't eaten a thing in three days. Sue and I gulped in amazement. When we closed our mouths, we gave the hungry lass a voucher for food, plus a lunch/dinner at the La Senorita.*

Jackets

Job loss

Kids

> *Each time we see little kids respond with glee and happiness as they latch on to some gift that they never figured they would own, we are reminded of why the Foundation exists. Recently, there was a four-year old girl who came by and spied a small stuffed white and black-eared puppy dog. Pat, the manager of the food section, gave it to her. She oozed love all over. She hugged the animal and for all the while she was with mother at the office she followed Pat. All over the place. She did not let him out of her sight. Giving time, giving talents, and yes, giving a stuffed animal away is all part of volunteering and sharing at the Foundation.*

Living in cars

Meat

Talk about a windfall, providence, or whatever makes us believe that someone is watching over the poor folks—a gentleman with the initials J.N. approached me with an offer of two steers (about 1,500 pounds). "I'll get them butchered into quarters, and deliver them wherever you want. Then you can have them cut up into steaks, roasts, ribs, or hamburger or whatever and distribute them to those who aren't able to buy meat." Can you imagine how much each bite will be savored? Bless you, J.N.!

Moving on

Pregnancy

Poverty

Redemption

Bill Marsh, Jr. presents Fr. Fred with the keys to a new van.

Religion
Prescriptions
Sharing

> *I gulped a couple times when I read this letter:*
>
> *"Hi Fr. Fred,*
>
> *I have been out of work for 3 years and no unemployment. Got a check today that was not expected ever to come. I just get by each month. Can pay my bills and food, no frills. Yet I feel to share with someone who has nothing. Thank you for what you have done."*
>
> *The gentleman had enclosed a cash donation to The Foundation.*

Shoes
Volunteers
Widows

Gifts from a Friend

Fr. Fred had a way of attracting and inspiring generous friends. When the original core group of supporters told Fr. Fred they'd raise $50,000 and rent him some space to get started, donors stepped up and funded the first year. A year later, with the impressive growth of The Foundation, the operation had outgrown the Fourteenth Street facility. An anonymous donor came forward and helped find the new quarters on Griffin and Cass, with a commitment to continue paying the rent. By 1994, there was a need to expand again, and once more, the same donor appeared. He led the search for new facilities and bought the warehouse on 826 Hastings Street that became the new rent-free home for The Foundation in November 1994.

In a covenant deed, dated December 26, 1995, a year after the move to Hastings Street, this same anonymous angel transferred the ownership to The Father Fred Foundation "for the sum of: NO CONSIDERATION." The only conditional limitation on the deed is shown as one that transfers ownership of the property to the Grand Traverse Area Catholic Schools in the event The Father Fred Foundation ceases to actively use it for the currently intended purpose.

Board Expansion

The original founding board of directors continued working with Fr. Fred, and in 1991 a businessman friend of Fr. Fred, Jerry Carlson, was added to the board. It was also at this time that Fr. Fred was first listed as a board member.

By the time The Foundation moved to Hastings Street, Fr. Fred realized he needed to expand the original group even more, and simultaneously realized he needed to add women. In May of 1994, Arnie Ochs, who had been a part of the Tuesday breakfast group for some time, was added. So were Ed Mende, Amanda Girard, and longtime volunteers Barb Lehnard and Sally Suprenant. Another longtime volunteer, Paula Prusick, was elected to the board in June 1997. Notwithstanding these additions to the board, however, before the meetings were moved to the boardroom, Tuesday morning breakfast meetings still included only the men.

In the Summer 1994 newsletter, Fr. Fred wrote, in his own style:

> *"Give it some depth and some youth" was the cry. So, the seasoned organization of the Foundation voted Arnie Ochs, Barb Lehnhard, Sally Suprenant, and Ed Mende into the organizational setup of the Foundation. Now, one cannot deny that we have youth, wisdom, looks, and personality. A beautiful blend.*

However, Fr. Fred's appetite for administrative detail or any other "distraction" other than serving his people never increased. He really didn't want to deal with the business side of the work. To this end, he effectively managed the board and their activities, positioning them as supporters, while he and the volunteers got the day-to-day work done, out on the floor of The Foundation. He never got ruffled about it; he merely kept moving in a straight path. He saw the board as something to be tolerated.

You might not have wanted to play poker with Fr. Fred. He was hard to bluff. Jim Lizenby tells of the commitment Fr. Fred had toward the basic mission, yet Jim felt there was a need for more direction from the board. Jim admits that Fr. Fred had a vision to help people physically as well as spiritually and would do anything to do more for his people. Jim felt a need, as a responsible board member, to draw the line. "I wanted a five-year plan and make it visible," Jim tells, "so we could attract bigger donations through estate planning and planned giving. Father Fred resisted it so I bluffed him and said I can't do it if we don't have a plan." Jim felt so strongly about it he told Fr. Fred if he didn't go along with it, Jim didn't know how he could continue on the board.

Fr. Fred acknowledged the sentiment as a serious one and told Jim he'd think about it. A week later, he told Jim, "I thought it over and have decided to accept your resignation from the board. I have already found someone to replace you." Jim was flabbergasted, since he never thought Fr. Fred would call his bluff. "Who is it?" he asked. "It's your son, Scott." So, in January 1999, Scott Lizenby, at Fr. Fred's invitation, replaced his father on the board of directors.

Early Mission Statement

At some time, the following Mission Statement found its way into the culture of the organization:

> *The Father Fred Foundation endeavors to enrich the lives of members of the community by providing support for individuals and families in need.*
>
> *Through the thoughtful administration of contributions and the dedication of volunteers the Foundation will share its resources and care for the mentally and physically distressed, poor, hungry, and suffering in a loving and respectful manner.*

In 2008, the Mission Statement was updated as part of a comprehensive strategic planning process that included the board, staff, volunteers, and members of the community.

In His Own Words

Once again, as in the earlier chapter on the State Hospital, we see that Fr. Fred is the best one to tell us about some of the clients in the early days of The Foundation. These excerpts were taken from the same writing he had done earlier about his recollections of patient stories from the State Hospital. In the next few pages, we see a selected few of these stories in his words and writing. They are presented, almost totally unedited[8] as they were found. To change the grammar, spelling, or syntax would be to move these thoughts and impressions further away from his actual hand.

---

8 While these stories are presented as they were found, the author has obscured the names of clients with regard to their privacy.

In preparation for the Easter event, most everyone is familiar with doing something extra during Lent... like maybe denying oneself of favorite foods/snacks, or like performing some extraordinary task. This early kindergarten girl came with mom and younger brother to present me with one can each of Spaghetti-O's and baked beans, "for the needs." The little princess spent her own allowance money, she told me, to choose the items, and she insisted on delivering the goods in person. A very commendable act... my thought—the nation's future looks promising when such babies do their bit for others.

On occasion, depression and loss of dignity of job and of self confidence prompt God's creatures to come to the Foundation. Today, two desperate maidens came with a little more than the usual distressing facts. They had an urgent desire to get a job. All they hoped for from me, was 5 gallons of gasoline for their run down auto, reasoning that if gas could be obtained, they would be able to keep their appointments tomorrow for an interview. And wouldn't you know it?? Tomorrow came! The interview was had! The girls were rewarded for their efforts. They got the jobs... Why did they return on Ground Hog Day? To say thanks and to give me a hug! Happiness is...getting a job (I must tell you too, that these two girls devoured a lot of donut holes, imbibed cup after cup of coffee and danced to the trendy music on the radio. They were so happy!

Winter fires ate away a lot of people's property this year. One fella lost his car and camper, with this description... "An explosion, then flames, and then smoke" —a big "O' my gosh!" and a loss. But, (let's call this man, ███) he visited with me to say he "got a job," that he's getting his "bills paid" and that the insurance company will pay for the loss of camper—not the car, for some extraneous reason. "Things are looking up" he commented. "I just need some food."

And responsible parents will do anything to help educate their kids. In Kalkaska, parents were forced to drive their "young'uns" to and from school. Daily! Quite a responsibility especially if you live 15 miles out of town. This winter which gripped everyone with its Arctic snowy arms made things worse. Mom could get her kids to school only 10 days in the last month. (Jan) Travel was made impossible—do you remember? Don't you? So this mom arranged to move to an area where schools were open and where bus transportation was provided and wouldn't you know it, this proud responsible soul finished our conference with, "I want to get off D.S.S. and welfare" with such determination, I'm sure she will!

You don't want to be shy, but if you are, be determined. One day a quiet young fella, entered the lobby, dressed in shirt sleeves. What he was doing out in the sub-zero weather without a coat boggled my mind. As I pondered the situation the secretary prompted me to see him quickly. "We have a few down-filled coats, " I offered. "Try one and keep it," I suggested. Amongst all the navy blue and khaki down-filled merchandise recently. A red jacket caught his eye. It was a medium size and he really needed a large size but he was intent on trying on the red, classy covering. "It fits!" he cried. Really, in my opinion it didn't. It was a bit too snug. But he insisted, that it fit. "See! I can raise my arms." Well, at that point there was no changing his mind. He wanted the red jacket... with it zipped up on his frame he stalked thru the lobby with an ever wide smile and with a heart full of joy—and my I add, with a body, too, protected against the cold.

I'll let you add up and solve this crisis situation. "The mice ate the insulation in the cook stove!" "My husband got fired from his job, I have five kids." "The refrigeration stopped." "The car wouldn't start." "We need formula for the baby." "We need food for the family." etc., etc. And all this brave woman could add to this litany was, "I never got this low before... please help me." Talk about predicaments and difficulties!

If after you visit Mayo Brothers in Rochester, Minnesota, where the diagnosis of a diseased liver is given you and the doctor suggests that you go to the U of M hospital for surgeries, (two of them) you would think that you wouldn't be ready for any celebration, on Christmas day, especially. And, then if your wife is to spend time in the same hospital for her surgeries you would begin to wonder what's there to celebrate? But not these two people. They wrote in their Christmas card, "I ask you humbly for your prayers. Someone gave us a turkey for Christmas. So, like every year, we invited three people for Christmas dinner who otherwise would not have Christmas dinner and they would be alone. This makes us very happy that we at least can do that. We want to pay back some. It is so little, but it sure makes our harts (her spelling) feel good about it. God has been so good to us so many times!? Nuff said?!

And as I look at these down-filled coats again, I am reminded of the young couple who came to the office on a very cold, cold morning covered only by thin veil-like coats (more like smocks). She was very, many months pregnant. He was quite sober-looking—and desperately in search for a job; but for now the two of them needed food and strength enough for three. Plus, some warm coats. Luckily, the sizes they needed, we had; the colors appealed to them. It was a sight to behold; to see the two of them promenade out of the Foundation with a fullness of joy and warmth. Too Bad my thinking computer was not acute, I could have presented them with a layette—for their first born.

A true story is stranger than a soap opera. I recall a young lass in her middle 20s who had lived with her husband for eleven years, ever since she was 14. It was (past tense) a good relationship. She worked and helped her "hubby" build up his business; she bore his children and supported him in hundreds of ways like a good wife should. Then—the other day he just up and left. Not unwittingly though. He planned it so he signed everything, home, bank accounts, etc., in someone else's name. What a shattering experience. She was afraid but she was much aware that she was without a home. She nervously showed me a handful of bills, one for a down payment on a mobile home, others for utilities' hook-up, for lawyer's fees, for doctor fees (she was pregnant, 6 months). Most of us can thank our luck stars (God especially) that we have security, love, and support. Would that we could wave a magic wand and blow away all obstacles and tribulations that stand in the way of harmony and peace and joy.

"Will you thank Santa Claus for the crayons, markers and paints that my 8 year old received for Christmas? They were the most ideal gifts. My daughters, to release anger, go to coloring and painting. "She's gonna be an artist or gymnast some day" signed, a well pleased mom. Thanks to you, friends—and Santa!

To get my point across to forty first-graders in a public school, I dramatized, with the help of the teacher, the Legend of the Irish King. She played the beggar who later turned out to be THE KING. I played the boy who sought to rule the Kingdom after the King died. One requisite for Kingship was: one had to love people and to be compassionate. I brought all kinds of props with me. A duffel bag with bread and money in it, a change of clothes and a beat-up stocking cap, and a crutch. Needless to say, I captured the kids' attention immediately, and it held throughout the entire play. The kids were awed, and curious about The Foundation. I explained to them that The Father Fred Foundation cares and shares daily with the hungry, the homeless, the neglected and the unfortunates. (I used simpler words then those, tho). Money, which comes from individuals from all over, helps to pay for utility bills, for unexpected prescriptions and for unexpected crises. Nothing could have mesmerized them more. While they were still contemplating in their little minds what I conveyed to them the teacher asked them to thank me for coming. "Thank you Father Fred for being here!" And then like a dart in the blue, a little hand shot up. "Father Fred," he declared, "when you die, I'm gonna take your place, and I'm gonna do what you do!" You guess the rest of the story. Almost everyone of the other kids said, "Me too!"

Talk about good fortune and being in the right place at the right time with a determined disposition that was extremely commendable. A young, robust father confessed that he was never on welfare. He always managed to work. He was good at what he did and he did not want to change his manner of living. "I'm not afraid of work. What I do, I do well." However, due to the tough times all over the area, he lost his job. He sought another. He applied all over, and when he went to the

Employment Service Commission, it happened... He took his two little girls, 5 and 7 years old (the seven year old was somewhat handicapped) with him as he could not afford a babysitter. All three lingered for an hour in the building waiting for an appointment. The girls got restless, so papa and they went outside to play in the cold snow. This is the truth! Believe me! An employer happened by and asked if he were looking for a job. After an affirmative answer was made known. The seeker invited this young fella to come to his shop to apply. With gusto he did—and he was hired. Tomorrow he was to start the job, but he needed to fix his car to get there. It needed a hose for the power steering, plus a key for the ignition (someone stole his), and a little gas. Excitement and a chance to purchase the necessary parts to put his vehicle in motion prompted this energetic father to make a couple calls. His friends, who knew something about mechanics offered their help today to repair the auto so he could go to work tomorrow.

She had to be tiny—this little 4 month old delivered child—but she was alive. The hospital monitored but she was alive, and cared for her until she was 8 months old. Then she was released (still monitored) to join her family of three small siblings. Mom told me that all of the kids will be able to crawl around on the beautiful, used carpeting that we gave to her. And, more than that, she doesn't have to worry about her little ones catching colds from playing on the hard cement floors.

From the Southeast diagonally to the Northwest of Michigan came this young mum. With her 7 and 9-year-old children who had learning disabilities, she left what little security she had. "Family life just wasn't the best." "It was a rough life," she sighed. But up here, in Traverse City, she intended to start anew. She had no family except us, her adopted friends—and too, she insisted on continuing to attend college to graduate in business management.

Here's One For You: The Interview

For many years, Tom BeVier, a respected veteran journalist, wrote northern Michigan stories for the *Detroit Free Press*. Early in the history of The Father Fred Foundation, about the time Fr. Fred was named as one of George H. W. Bush's "Thousand Points of Light," Tom got a call from Detroit to go over and interview Fr. Fred and send in a 700-word story about the priest in Traverse City who had contacted Fr. Bill Cunningham in Detroit and started a foundation similar to the Focus: HOPE initiative.

Since 1968, Fr. Bill Cunningham and Focus: HOPE had been busy building and re-building people's lives in the inner city of post-riot Detroit. He and others had very lofty ideas about civil rights, job training programs, technology training programs, childcare, etc. Over the years they built a complex, multifaceted, and politically super-charged organization on Oakman Boulevard in Detroit. Yet, for all the inherent complexity their organization developed over the years, Fr. Cunningham could always bring everyone back down to earth with the simple stern reminder: "This whole damn thing is about a food program." The organization felt that their other goals would be unattainable if they couldn't help disadvantaged infants and children get the type of nutrition required to nurture them for cognitive development.

Like Focus: HOPE, filling a social services void precipitated Fr. Fred's work. Instead of riots, in Traverse City it was that the State Hospital had recently closed. While there are many differences between the programs, there are common themes between them. Each deals with basic human needs, and each was built within an envelope of spirituality.

Tom admits he wasn't very excited about writing the story and thought he'd go meet Fr. Fred, get the interview over quickly, and file his story by deadline. He set it up and arrived at the messy and crowded Foundation facility on Fourteenth Street.

Fr. Fred greeted him warmly as he cleared a place at his desk for Tom to make notes. Just as the interview got started, the phone rang and Fr. Fred excused himself to take the call. In no particular hurry to get back to the interview, Fr. Fred gave some advice and offered to help the caller. The interview started again with a, "Now, where were we?"

Just as things resumed, another client came to the door seeking assistance. Again, Fr. Fred excused himself and spent plenty of time giving food and clothing to the client. The interruptions continued and about two hours later, after watching Fr. Fred helping "his people" and getting nowhere with his story, Tom gave up on the idea of an interview and began packing up his things. He had witnessed two hours of this marvelous man at work, firsthand. "Where you going?" Fr. Fred asked Tom. "We are just getting started."

"I have everything I need for my story, Father." Tom told him. "Yup, everything I need."

Here's One For You: A Donation Story

Everyone knew Fr. Fred had little patience for details and recordkeeping, vyet he was practical about being able to attract donations and raise money for "his people."

Marsha Smith tells about a time in 1991 when she was working for the local Community Foundation and a donor wanted to make a sizeable contribution to the young Father Fred Foundation.

In doing the preparation for the donation, Marsha called Fr. Fred to get some recipient information—information that every non-profit organization is required to keep. "Fr. Fred, I need to get a copy of your Form 990 and your letter of tax exemption from the IRS," she explained. With a nod to his reluctance for detail and paperwork, his response was something like: "Oh, we don't really keep track of that sort of thing." She knew very well that The Foundation had these documents available, and maybe he simply didn't want to be bothered looking for them.

Marsha went on to explain that she was simply doing what she had to do in order to make the donation. "If we don't have that information, we cannot make this donation on behalf of our client, Father."

"Well, then," he responded, "I guess we'll have to do without that particular donation. We're too busy helping people to bother with details like that."

"Okay, Father. I just want you to know that the gift is $5,000 dollars."

Without pause, he shot back, "Oh, well, then you'd better call Jerry Carlson. He has all that."

Here's One For You: Giving Back

The most inspirational stories are those that include recipients turning their lives around. That was also the most rewarding thing for Fr. Fred to see. He was always happy when he heard of someone "making it." We end this chapter with a letter received by the author:

I personally went to The Father Fred Foundation for help with a gas bill six or seven years ago. I was met with respect and courtesy. They made me feel okay with asking for help. That was a very hard thing for me. It took me a lot of thinking about it and praying. I was so glad I did.

From that day on, I gave groceries once a month. To do my part in repaying the favor, helping someone else. I so enjoyed giving to this foundation. It helps families in need, and doesn't make them feel bad about needing help. I have now moved away, but when I am in town I still try to drop off whatever I can.

We are so indebted to this man. What a wonderful foundation, a great work to be memorialized about.

Thank you,

Shelia

COMMUNITY SUPPORT AND RECOGNITION

Well done, my good and faithful servant.
(Matthew 25:21)

In the thirty years he spent at the State Hospital, Fr. Fred was well-known to the patients and staff at that facility. He was part of their daily lives as chaplain, mentor, advisor, priest, and friend. Additionally, over the years, his charismatic and compassionate personality found its way into the community, and the congregation at All Faiths Chapel grew. The townspeople loved him and many local Catholics had made All Faiths Chapel their worship venue of choice. By the time the Chapel closed, there were about 150 regular attendees at Mass there each weekend.

When the hospital and Chapel closed and The Father Fred Foundation began to gain velocity, more and more people in town jumped on the "Fr. Fred Bandwagon." The Foundation grew quickly and effectively because of tremendous local support. He had put a face on one problem the community saw when the hospital closed: What will happen to the patients? To show

support, the residents of Traverse City honored him and his work in a number of significant ways. The original location for The Foundation was overflowing with donations within a few months, and yet served the need for about a year and a half. The second facility lasted only a few years before it, too, was jam-packed and bulging at the seams with donations from the community.

Before we look at a few examples of this wonderful community support, we need to recognize the countless ongoing initiatives seen every day. Hardly a day passes without a reference to The Father Fred Foundation in the local paper or other news media. The Cub Scouts, or Weight Watchers® franchise, or realtors, or a church group will be featured in an article about a food drive or fundraiser of some sort. Obituaries direct memorials to The Foundation, and school kids come up with programs of their own. It is certainly not a just local Catholic cause. Organizations of every stripe, and congregations of every denomination support this work in a unique and endless manner. There simply isn't space enough to list all the support, so we offer these few.

The Summer 2010 Foundation newsletter featured an article on the "Most Creative Fund Raiser of the Year Award."

> *Last summer, 12-year-old Anna Thorson and her neighborhood friends wrote and performed a play in their backyard. It was a benefit performance generating $27 to help the work of Father Fred. What a creative gift of vacation time and energy! Stay tuned ...* My Fair Lady *is planned for summer 2010.*

Following are a few other ways northern Michigan has supported and continues to support and recognize Fr. Fred and The Foundation.

A Charity Dinner Event Like No Other

It was quite the celebration at The Baywinds, one of the area's finest restaurants. Invitations had been sent to the attendees, including many prominent community members: Tim Quinn, President of Northwestern Michigan College; U.S. Congressman Bart Stupak; City Manager Richard Lewis; and Hal Van Sumeren, President of the Traverse City Area Chamber of Commerce. Doctors, attorneys, and business leaders joined them as guests filed in to be seated for their reservations. Live music filled the air, white linens covered the tables, and every female in attendance received a pink carnation boutonnière, pinned on by Doris and Bud Quick. Everyone was dressed in their finest, as a professional photographer snapped pictures to capture the joy on film. Was this a fancy, expensive outing, reserved for the well to do? No, it was the inaugural Father Fred Foundation free community dinner on Wednesday, November 25, 1992.

> **Bay Winds Restaurant**
> 1265 U.S. 31 North Across from State Park
> is proud to serve you, your family and friends
> Pre-Thanksgiving Dinner
>
> November 25, 1992   4:30-6:00 pm.
>
> Call 929-1044 to reserve your place at our table.
> This certificate will guarantee you Food,
> Friendship, and Fun.

Invitation to the first Community Thanksgiving Dinner, 1992.

The guests were single mothers and their children; unemployed men, treating their families to a nice Thanksgiving meal; singles without anyone else to be with; and others to whom life had been cruel and unkind. The guests were enjoying the rare visit to such a nice restaurant in dignity. The community leaders were the *maitre d'*, waiters, and servers. For this one evening, roles had been reversed, and the deserving, needy client-guests were being served by those of greater means.

In the next newsletter, Winter 1993, Fr. Fred wrote about the magical evening enjoyed by those unaccustomed to such events:

> *It allowed them to dine in style ... many had never been in a restaurant this nice. "Let Me Call you Sweetheart" brought tears to the eyes of a couple celebrating their 20th wedding anniversary. The evening was festive ... and everyone wore a smile. They played, talked, sang, and ate plenty of turkey, mashed potatoes, and pumpkin pie (all donated). It was a different world for a couple of hours. Every person and every being packed their minds with memories, which would sustain them during their usual everyday situations*

Judge Mike Haley, Fr. Fred, and Hal Van Sumeren serving at the Community Thanksgiving Dinner.

With U.S. Congressman Bart Stupak in 1999, Fr. Fred's last Community Thanksgiving Dinner at the Park Place Hotel.

of worry, doom, and gloom. Look at the number! Over 300 had the opportunity to come and attend this colossal event.

This was the first of seventeen such pre-Thanksgiving events hosted by The Foundation. Every year, the number of attendees climbed, and after a few years the event had to be moved to a larger venue, the Park Place Hotel, in downtown Traverse City. At its height, the event drew 600 diners at two seating times. Kids were given toys and coloring books, and the tables were decorated with balloons. Matt Myers arranged to have linen companies, florists, photographers, dairies, grocers, wholesalers, and restaurants donate everything for the dinner each year. No one enjoyed the event more than Fr. Fred, as he wandered from table to table, visiting with the guests. He greeted them each by name, and they returned the love with their smiles.

Paula Prusick claims it was in times like this that Fr. Fred was happiest: being among the client-guests and watching them smile and have fun. He loved any kind of social gathering, and this seemed to be a favorite. He would observe that he liked this event because all the guests were dressed in the finest clothes The Foundation had provided them. They were there in dignity. Guests could enjoy the fancy evening and a great dinner and not have to worry about the bill. Doris Quick remembers a woman at one dinner who was particularly touched by the flower-giving gesture: "She said no one ever gave her a flower before. That gets to you."

In 1999, just five weeks before he died, Fr. Fred allayed the fears of the community that wondered: Is he well enough to attend this year? "You bet," he told a reporter, "I'm feeling pretty good. I made darn sure that I could handle everything tonight and not get sick. I wouldn't miss it." With the help of a small group of his closest friends as a support team, he was delivered to the event and sat stationary, propped in a seat by the door, as he weakly and cheerfully greeted everyone upon arrival. The trusted support team of intimate friends never left his side. He did not feel well enough to eat, and his face appeared fatigued and swollen from his treatments. Attendees sat next to him to have their photos taken, as if with Santa Claus, as his weak, sweet smile barely masked his pain. It was his last public appearance.

Bring on the HOGs

Fr. Fred did a lot of things to help raise money and bring attention to the work of The Foundation. One of the most effective in meeting both of these goals, and also one of his favorites, is the annual motorcycle ride. It started in 1993 and has grown nearly every year since.

The Harley-Davidson Company celebrated its ninetieth anniversary in June 1993, with a huge gathering of motorcycles in Milwaukee, home of their classic American product. Estimates were that sixty to eighty thousand motorcycles filled the town for the event. Don Pishney, owner of Classic Motor Sports in Traverse City, was among the attendees. *Wouldn't if be great if we could bring some of this excitement to Traverse City?* He thought.

Pishney approached the local chapter of the Harley Owners' Group (HOG), which had recently been brought back to life by a small handful of riders after being inactive for many years. They thought it would be fun to organize a

fundraiser for a local charity. Some favored the Make-A-Wish Foundation, others wanted to do it for Fr. Fred. However, one of the HOG directors, Dan Free, was on the board of Make-A-Wish and didn't want to have it appear like a conflict of interest. For the first year, they decided to support Fr. Fred, and would rotate to a different charity each year, afterward. They wanted to have the money they raised stay local.

On July 25, just a few weeks after the idea was hatched, a group of about twenty-five motorcyclists gathered at the dealership for the *ad hoc* event, passed the hat for contributions, and hit the road. Others joined the procession along the way, and by the time they arrived at Union Street Station, a downtown bar in Traverse City, there were nearly a hundred bikers. They passed the hat a few more times, and at the end of the day had raised $999. At that point, the owner of the bar tossed in the last dollar to make it an even thousand. Fr. Fred told them that the gift was the largest single cash donation to The Foundation that year.

Bob Dohm had a pretty nice bike with a sidecar, so Fr. Fred, who was never one for riding a motorcycle, rode with him as they led the parade. At the end of the ride, Fr. Fred told him, "I'll do almost anything to raise money for 'my people,' but please don't make me do that, ever again." He was terrified in the sidecar, going at highway speeds, just inches off the ground. After that, Fr. Fred rode on the back of Garry Plane's motorcycle.

Fr. Fred loved the excitement of the motorcycles and the interaction with this interesting cross-section of people. He admitted later, that even though there was a lot of excitement, he was frightened by riding on a motorcycle. The most interesting part of that are the surviving legends about Fr. Fred. Some call him "the Harley-Davidson priest" or tell stories about seeing him "riding around town on his motorcycle." It's all myth.

One thing the event did was smash some existing stereotypes about the "bad boy bikers" image of motorcycle riders. Matt tells that as the riders were gathering for the post-ride celebration that first year, a woman watched from across the street and beckoned one of the motorcycle policemen who had escorted the ride. "Who are these people?" she asked, "and when are they going home?" "Well, Ma'am," the officer replied, "many of these people are the bankers, lawyers, and doctors in Traverse City, and they are home. Oh, by the way, there's Father Fred." She didn't say much more as she marched off down the street.

In the second year, the event grew to be a weekend-long event, with a poker run on Saturday and a motorcycle display on Front Street in Traverse City on Saturday evening. Motorcycle clubs from around the state participated. Each year, on the third weekend in July, the riders return to Traverse City to continue the rumbling tradition. Fr. Fred never preached about helping "his people," and made sure it was a non-denominational benefit for helping others. Seeing the great success of the event's ability to help The Father Fred Foundation, the organizers did not stick to the original plan of rotating the charity each year. Instead they chose to continue to support Fr. Fred.

Every year there is concern if the weather will cooperate with the event, and every year when he was alive, Fr. Fred would say: "Don't worry about the weather. It'll be okay." He always seemed to have a way of calming the fears and making people feel good. After a few years, the ride changed to a route that went to the end of Old Mission Peninsula, past Fr. Fred's parish in Mapleton. While the current route no longer goes past that church, the group continues to ride to the end of the Old Mission Peninsula as a tribute to him.

Garry Plane remembers how Fr. Fred related so well with the mixture of riders who came to support him:

> *It wasn't that he was a priest—he was just a friendly man who was just like everyone else. He looked forward to seeing them every year, and he would put his arm around them and ask how they were, making people feel at ease. He knew how to bring out the best in people. He was just so thankful that people were giving to his charity, through him. He never shared any fear, except when he was riding on the back of my bike and I could feel it in him. He was apprehensive, but he wanted to do it, because these people were doing so much for him and he wanted to be a part of it. "I'll do nearly anything for money once," he told me. "Riding on the back is the least I can do."*

Fr. Fred truly loved this event. He loved the people who came out for it and the thrill of being among all the rumbling motorcycles. The Harley-Davidson hats, shirts, jacket, and helmet the group presented him were always worn with pride. For a while each summer, he became an everyman, as he joined the riders in an effort to help the disadvantaged in the community.

In 1996, masking his fear of riding, he told the *Traverse City Record-Eagle*: "This is a nice bunch of guys. The money they raise stays locally, it doesn't go downstate or out of state. I just love to ride! I look forward to it every year. It is a real thrill. I hope they have something like this in Heaven; it is awesome!"

The ride in 1999 was a very special one. He had been out for a couple years, due to knee surgery. He was also becoming more ill. The question arose: Will

Fr. Fred has a laugh with Frank Carter at the 1999 HOG fundraiser.

Fr. Fred ride this year? He reassured the community by saying: "You better believe it. I'll be there. I've been waiting a long time. I like all the gals and guys. They are real nice professional people. They gave me a jacket and a helmet. It's real fun and games. It's going to be okay." That year he rode in a convertible.

The year before, in 1998, Frank Carter, a HOG member, had declared that if people would contribute $1,000 he would shave his beard. His beard was a distinguishing feature for Frank. In the fifteen years since he had been clean-shaven, his beard once reached his belly button. There were contributions of only $143, so he didn't do it. Frank extended the offer for the 1999 ride and even gave the cause credit for last year's contributions. If the group raised $857, he would cut off his beard. The group raised $2,023.79, and contributors began snipping until Frank's beard was gone. Fr. Fred looked on with great pleasure. Frank was the hero of the day.

When a reporter from the *Traverse City Record-Eagle* asked Fr. Fred about the excitement of the hundreds of motorcycles and the ride, he replied: "This is just wonderful. When I die, there'll be a Harley in Heaven for me."

In July 2000, the first ride after Fr. Fred died, over 700 motorcycles rode past St. Joseph in Mapleton in tribute to Fr. Fred and raised over $16,000. It was a beautiful day.

Cigar Dinner: Where There's Smoke, There's Money

A relationship with cigars goes way back in the life story of Fr. Fred. His mother and her sisters were employed as cigar rollers in Grand Rapids, before she married his father. Later, to the chagrin of the State Hospital staff, he discovered how to make male mental patients feel like a million dollars by giving them a cigar. "Here you go, Gov'ner. Have a cigar," he'd say, just before he walked out of a hazy, smoke-filled ward and headed to the next. That same stunt worked for him when clients at The Foundation looked for relief from their day-to-day hardships. He always had a pack of smokes in his desk drawer for his visitors and a growing stack of empty cigar boxes in the corner of his office. Consequently, he was in familiar territory whenever he walked into the most successful fundraising series in the history of The Foundation.

Rick Coates and Mike Shirley are members of the Bun Brady Division of The Ancient Order of Hibernians (AOH), a local organization dedicated to promoting friendship, unity, and Christian charity among its members and to foster the ideals and cultivate the history and traditions of the Irish race. Coates and Shirley were also part of the informal All Faiths Chapel congregation before it closed. They watched as Fr. Fred set up the nascent Foundation, and they saw the good that could be done with any money they could raise for the new enterprise.

In 1993, Rick and Mike invited Fr. Fred to a meeting of the AOH to discuss the possibility of a fundraising project. Mike had seen the success of the March of Dimes Lucky Shamrock program and hatched the idea of the Lucky Leprechaun, which was to be run in conjunction with St. Patrick's Day. When he presented the idea to the AOH, there was instant recognition of the benefit, and the new program was off and running. Through a network of gas stations, the group raised $2,500 by donations of a dollar per sheet of printed green paper that would then hang on the stations' walls and windows. In the second year, Rick's wife, Caroline,

designed a die-cut caricature of the Lucky Leprechaun. In the first seventeen years of this successful program, it has raised over $200,000 for The Foundation.

A few years later, Mike Shirley was in Chicago and saw the idea of a fundraising cigar dinner. It was another light bulb moment. He brought the idea to the AOH, at which it received a welcome reception. The inaugural Father Fred Cigar

Fr. Fred, Mike Nolan, and Tim Smith celebrate at the 1999 cigar dinner.

Dinner was held in the spring of 1996, in conjunction with a golf outing, attracting about 150 attendees. The organizers were Rick Coates, Mike Shirley, and Traverse City tobacconist Mike Nolan.

The dinner in 1996 featured six or seven of the area's best chefs and a selection of the most professional waiters and waitresses in the region. Everything was donated, aiming at a zero-overhead event. At the end of the evening, when the crowd passed the hat for tips for the wait staff, even they donated the amount collected for them to The Father Fred Foundation. The following year, the same organizational team enlarged the event, again with much success. In the third year, Mike and Rick turned the organization of the event over to Mike Nolan and Tim Smith, who, even at the time of this book's publication, are still running it. In 1999, the fourth event attracted over 250 attendees, and by then, had contributed over $60,000. A pattern of success had been set. In 2010, as in the past several years, the dinner was sold out, with 350 guests and a waiting list.

Each year, the black tie dinner reception features the world's finest cigars, the finest local chefs working together to present a six-course meal, samplings of single malt scotch, specially-blended bourbons, wines, and beers. There are also impressive live and silent auctions. "It's our way of supporting the work of Father Edwin Frederick," says Mike Nolan. "He was a great man with a big heart. It's a legacy and mission all Hibernians want to keep alive and thriving." After the fifteenth cigar dinner, in 2010, the AOH tallied that it has donated nearly a million dollars.

From the *Northern Express* newspaper:

> *The dinner is known nationally. Ashton Cigars annually donates $10,000 to the Foundation as a result of their participation. Woodford Reserve, the premium bourbon maker from Kentucky, sees the importance of the event. Each year they donate an auction prize that allows four people to come to the distillery to blend the bourbons that will become the next year's Father Fred Foundation Cigar Dinner Signature Blend. The special bottles are sold at the dinner with all proceeds benefitting the Foundation.*

In 2010, the fifteenth annual event was threatened by the new Michigan smoking ban. Through a close examination of the law, and by exploiting some of the vague definitions in the legislation, the attorney members of the Ancient Order of Hibernians were successful in getting a one-year exemption for the dinner. Outlawing this event would be a blow to The Foundation, since the proceeds account for a significant portion of their annual cash donations.

Mike Nolan has been active in the organization, planning, and execution of the event every year since the beginning. He tells of this particular insight into Fr. Fred's thinking:

> *In 1998, during a planning session for the Cigar Dinner, Father Fred asked me if I knew what the biggest benefit The Foundation received from the dinner was. I naively told him it was probably the funds we raised. He quickly corrected me, explaining that the dinner helped reach sections of the community that were previously untouchable—religious or not. He described the ways in which we brought connections to The Foundation that helped them achieve goals far more important than the financial benefits the dinner provided. He said The Foundation needed to become a part of the entire community if it was going to continue to help people. In that brief discussion, Father Fred explained to me the definition of networking better than any college professor I heard during any lecture. It became clear to me that his goal was not only to help those in need, but also to bring a sense of unity to the entire region.*

Mike goes on to tell of the involvement of the Hibernians. Each year, nearly every member of the local chapter works with this important fund raising event. It would not be possible without the significant and loyal input of every participant.

As with any other gathering of happy and contributing people, Fr. Fred thoroughly enjoyed the annual dinner. He was happiest when he was among friends. We don't know what was really on his mind those evenings. There may have been thoughts of his mother or the patients or his client visitors. In any case, as he compared the sweet smell of cigar smoke to the aroma of liturgical incense, he knew he wasn't the only one brightening the lives of others with a good cigar.

Let's Have a Garage Sale

Like a growing number of people in town, Nancy Larson heard about The Father Fred Foundation and began dropping things off at the Fourteenth Street location, then Griffin Street. She quickly realized two things: She was always put to work, and the place was a mess. It was jam-packed with a growing flow of donations.

By summertime of 1991, she was a regular volunteer at the young foundation, sorting clothes, furniture, and other donations. It was clear that it had outgrown the space they were in and needed to move to larger quarters. They were preparing to move to the new location on Cass and Griffin. "We need to have a garage sale," she told Fr. Fred. "Good," he said, which surprised her. "Why don't you do that?" She knew it would clear the place out and generate some money for Father to help the clients with gas money, utility bills, etc. It would also bring attention to the move to the new location on Griffin Street.

Nancy talked with her friend, Marie, and they rounded up a team to organize the first Father Fred Garage Sale. Up to that point, everything from Fr. Fred had come free to the clients, so there were some initial questions about selling donated items rather than giving them away. One example of this was when Nancy, in getting ready for the sale, set down her hammer and when she went to pick it up again, it and her other tools were gone!

Fr. Fred catches forty winks at a garage sale.

Prices were low, and the response was encouraging. Nancy saw a new revenue source coming from people who are just above the line of needing things for free and that cadre of regular garage sale prowlers who populate the streets and alleys on any given summer Saturday. They could find boots for a dollar, a sweater for seventy-five cents, a book for fifty cents, or an end table for three bucks. So, less than two years after the beginning of The Foundation, on

August 17, 1991, they cleaned house and raised $850. Fr. Fred was thrilled, and Nancy and her team knew they were on to something. They started planning the next one. Nancy tells:

> *The garage sale event was like a party, and Fr. Fred was happiest when he had money to give away and when he was around people. He liked to socialize with everyone and felt it was like missionary work, giving everyone a good representation of God. He loved the excitement of the garage sales, the cigar dinners, and the HOG rides, because he was around people—people who were helping others.*

Nancy also recalls how Father would pit each fundraiser against the others. He'd tell the organizers of the garage sale how much the HOG ride netted and challenged them to beat those guys. Then, with a chuckle, he'd tell HOG: "You aren't going to let those little old ladies running the garage sale beat you this year, are you?"

He would never ask anyone to do anything he would not do himself, and he was not afraid of hard work. "Late one Friday night before a garage sale," Nancy recalls, "I was working in the warehouse, getting ready for the sale the next day. I thought I was alone when through the darkness, I saw a man in blue jeans, walking toward me. 'Sorry, we're closed.' I told him. Then, I knew it was Fr. Fred when he said, 'Hello, Nancy, how can I help you?'"

Some folks called Fr. Fred the "Maverick Priest," because he often did what he knew was best, regardless of the "rules." One of the employees at the State Hospital who later volunteered at The Foundation tells this story about one of the early garage sales. A week or so prior to the sale, Fr. Fred realized there were No Parking signs all along the street where a huge crowd was expected on Saturday. An appeal to the City to rescind the parking ban for the day resulted in a simple response: "No." The administrator at the City went on to explain the request process and how it would take at least three weeks, get on the City Council agenda, approval, etc., etc., *blah, blah, blah.*

This didn't please Fr. Fred, so he called a friend of his, a sergeant on the city police force. "Okay, Father, here's what you do. On the night before the sale, cover all the signs with paper bags. Then, as soon as the sale is over, get rid of them. Park for free, as long as you need, but *please* don't tell anyone I told you to do it."

On Saturday, the street was jammed with parked cars. On Sunday, it was against the law to park there.

Over the years, the Father Fred Garage Sale has grown into a bi-annual event, spring and fall. While in the early years, Nancy and Marie paid for the newspaper ads and other costs out of their own pockets, it is now a regular part of The Foundation fundraising activities, with donated tents in the parking lot, concessions, entertainment, and a paid advertising plan. In the first ten years, by 2001, the garage sales had generated over $204,000. In 1999, they auctioned off a donated car and set a new record of over $20,000 in one day. That same year, in June, a public service announcement was made on the radio: "Due to space constraints, we cannot accept any more donations for the garage sale." By 2010, the average garage sale was netting around $30,000.

While the Garage Sale is a successful and important source of revenue for The Foundation, there is an on-going debate about setting the nicer things aside for sale. Does this deny the clients the dignity of having the nicer things that have been donated? This has never dampened the enthusiasm for the event, and Fr. Fred, at one point, asked Nancy if there could be four of these sales each year. While the debate continues and the balance of what to give away and what to sell is always in question, immediate client needs are not compromised, and those needs take precedence. There is no denying that the Garage Sales has become an important bi-annual event for The Foundation.

Frostbite Food Drive

In 1994, Matt Myers put together a publicity stunt to bring awareness to hunger in the region and also to the dwindling reserves in the Father Fred Pantry. He convinced a local disc jockey to camp out, in the middle of winter, in a semi trailer in the parking lot of a Traverse City strip mall. It was freezing cold. The idea was to fill the trailer with non-perishable food in order to re-stock the pantry. It worked, and Fr. Fred was thrilled. Since then, it has become an annual event. After freezing his way through the food drive, the disc jockey moved to Florida.

Sponsored by The Meijer Company and two Traverse City radio stations, WTCM and WCCW, the food is collected and stored in insulated heated trailers each fifty-three feet long. Each trailer holds twenty-four pallets of food. In 2010, the ten-day drive stuffed two and a half trailers.

Fr. Fred is amazed by the results of the 1999 Frostbite Food Drive.

The need continues to grow and so does the community response. A few years ago, the pantry needed an autumn food drive to stock the shelves, so one was established for October in conjunction with Spartan Stores and their annual "Spartan Sale." It was successful and in one three-day weekend, seventeen pallets of food were collected. In 2010, this effort evolved to the Virtual Food Drive, with participation from three local food chains: Oleson's, Tom's, and Glen's. The drive operated traditionally and added an online contribution ctomponent. By the end, twenty-nine pallets of food and over $50,000 in cash had been collected.

Some Well-Deserved Recognition

The work of The Foundation is what Fr. Fred lived for, after leaving the State Hospital. While he did things to bring attention to The Foundation and to "his people," he did not seek the spotlight for himself. There was no head table at any event he planned, and if there were, he would choose not to sit at it. Rather, he would find a place in the middle or back of the room, in with the crowd. In

Grand Marshall of the National Cherry Festival Heritage Parade.

1975, while he was still at All Faiths Chapel, WCCW radio station in Traverse City honored him with the "Good Guy Award." When interviewed, he told the reporter he thought that was "just dandy." If that were the only recognition he ever received for his work, it would be plenty for him. While he would be dismissive and a little embarrassed by a full listing of the recognition he received, these few seem appropriate.

Fr. Fred's official Distinguished Service Award portrait.

Traverse City Area Chamber of Commerce Distinguished Service Award

In late January of 1991, Fr. Fred was planning a vacation with a priest friend for a few days in the sun after the busy holiday season. He was characteristically gracious when a friend asked him to change his plans so he could be in town to give the invocation at the annual Chamber of

Commerce Dinner and the presentation of the prestigious Distinguished Service Award. He politely declined, explaining that his travel plans had already been made. After some considerable arm-twisting, he was convinced to change the plans. Little did he know it was part of an elaborate scheme to surprise *him* with the award.

The *Traverse City Record-Eagle* article tells of Helen Osterlin, the previous year's recipient, reading from prepared notes in the introduction to the surprise:

> *Father Frederick is a leader in serving the sick and needy. No one has touched more people, from our most destitute and desperate to our most professional and successful. He has given totally of himself to help all in need who have come to him for over 30 years. We have our own Mother Teresa right here in Traverse City," she said, quoting another nominator ... the courtly 65-year-old Catholic priest's face flushed red as Osterlin spoke and he slowly realized he was the person being named for the award.*

As she continued her remarks, Osterlin quoted from a few of the nearly fifty letters of nomination for the community's most prestigious award, that year:

> *One person observes that our recipient spends a good deal of time with folks who are hidden in the cracks, especially the sick, weak, hospitalized. And it is one-on-one. While there may be many in the Traverse Bay area who have done more spectacular things, this man has consistently dealt with matters most of us would rather put off to someone else. The stuff of our honoree is uncommon, and should occasionally find public celebration for us and for himself.*

> *Another person wrote, "I am absolutely amazed at his capacity for goodness, kindness and love. I have been in his office and seen for myself the unending stream of unfortunate humanity that passes through his doors. They are greeted with a big smile, a 'what can I do for you?' and then he does it. And all the time I have been there I have never heard him say no. If they couldn't come to him, he went to them."*

Another observes that "I have known him for over twenty years. He used to greet me in the parking lot of Munson Hospital with, 'How do you like this day I've arranged for you?' I've watched him on a number of occasions handle difficult and personal cases with great skill. No matter how tough or unpleasant, he always makes it look as though there is nothing to it."

Another person writes, "I am not trying to canonize him, the halo would continually slip off, and we are all more comfortable with another just human being. We have our own Mother Teresa right here in Traverse City. He always makes everyone feel that they are a worthwhile person and necessary part of our community. He helps everyone, regardless of faith, color, or situation."

The purpose of the Distinguished Service Award is to recognize the extraordinary endeavors of individuals who make the Traverse City region a better place. Rules governing the selection of nominees include character and ethical principles being prime factors in consideration. Other major considerations include contributions other than monetary to the cultural, economic, and social betterment of the region served by the Traverse City Area Chamber of Commerce. The first recipient was R. Floyd Clinch, in 1929.

In his acceptance remarks, Fr. Fred responded, "I have a job to do and no one else can take my place. My job is to help take care of the elderly, the sick, and the poor, and I'm happy to do it."

Thousand Points of Light

When President George H.W. Bush was campaigning for president in 1988, he referred to "Thousand Points of Light"—those average citizens who contribute to their community and country through volunteering. The National Association of Counties (NACo) initiated a program to bring a name and face to those citizens who have contributed to county programs. Representing Grand Traverse County, Michigan, Fr. Fred was honored at a "County Points of Light" ceremony at the annual NACo conference in Salt Lake City.

Fr. Fred's photo and a description of his service, along with more than 800 other honorees, are included in a book that was presented to President Bush and now placed in the Library of Congress and in the Bush Presidential Library.

Best of the Best

In a 1993 People's Choice Poll, conducted by the *Traverse City Record-Eagle*, Fr. Fred was named, along with Jerry Oleson and Bryan Crough, as the "Best Citizens." This was in a poll where responders also voted for the best cup of coffee, best fishing hole, best radio station, best outdoor sign, and best bowl of soup. As much as it was a tongue-in-cheek award, it showed that his work was on the minds of everyone in the community, as he was recognized for his work at All Faiths Chapel and his unmatched help to the needy.

Friend of AMI

In May of 1993, Fr. Fred was awarded a "Friend of AMI" award by the Alliance for the Mentally Ill of Michigan. He was one of eleven awarded that year at a banquet in Grand Rapids. The award recognized his pioneering work at the Traverse City State Hospital as well as his current work with the mentally ill at The Father Fred Foundation.

Sara Hardy Memorial Award

The Sara Hardy Memorial Award is named for the woman who gave birth to the Human Rights Commission in Traverse City. Through her work, she exemplified the ideals of the Commission: to promote amicable relations and mutual respect between and among the racial, cultural, religious, and other groups within the community. The award is given annually to the individual who best personifies these goals.

On Friday, December 9, 1994, the Traverse City Human Rights Commission celebrated its twenty-fifth anniversary in

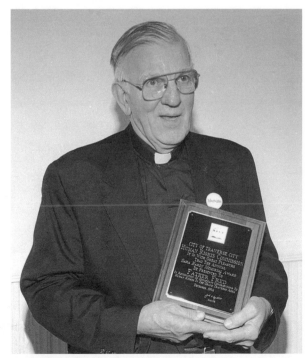

Fr. Fred accepts the Sara Hardy Humanitarian Award, December 1994.

a ceremony that also awarded the Sara Hardy Memorial Award to Fr. Fred for his work in helping the people of northern Michigan.

The letter of nomination, by a citizen who had worked with him at the Traverse City Regional Psychiatric Hospital, says:

> *Father Fred has lived in this community for over 25 years. He has consistently donated his personal and professional time to the less fortunate of our community. He has not taken on himself to judge others in need but has given of himself freely. Father Fred has been the champion of the mentally ill and used his many community contacts to assist them in the quality of their lives.*

From an article, in the next day's *Traverse City Record-Eagle*:

> *When Edwin Frederick was a little boy, he asked Santa Claus for a hammer, a saw, and some nails. The gifts arrived on Christmas Day. Frederick's father had visions of his son growing up to be a builder: Frederick and Sons. And it came to pass, but not precisely the way his father had envisioned.*
>
> *"We're all trying to build a community of love," said the Rev. Edwin Frederick on Friday evening as he received the Sara Hardy Humanitarian of the Year Award from the Traverse City Human Rights Commission. "Not with a saw, not a hammer, not any nails—but with three little words: listen, care, and share."*

Later, in that same article, he explains that The Foundation ministers to the physical needs of its clients, but does so in a way that meets their emotional and spiritual needs: "What he enjoys about the work is seeing someone who was isolated and lonely rejoin the community." He explained that it is a process he had gone through himself. When the Traverse City Regional Psychiatric Hospital closed, after thirty years of building and working there, he felt shattered, betrayed and unneeded. But that changed when some supporters helped him set up The Father Fred Foundation.

Do This in Memory of Me

It's going to be okay.

Father Fred

"Y ou're no Father Fred!" the longtime volunteer hissed, as she slammed the door behind her, coming out of Father Thome's office at The Father Fred Foundation.

This incident expressed the profound grief, frustration, and confusion of the volunteers when Fr. Fred died, and it signaled the years of difficult transition that were to follow. It also was symptomatic of the fact that The Foundation needed a solid, agreed upon organizational structure. After surviving and growing under the charismatic and nimble leadership of Fr. Fred, the successful and well-respected organization faced an unbelievable crisis. Without him, there was a precipitous and nearly fatal drop in donations to the ten-year-old Foundation. The organization came dangerously close to disintegration in the vacuum created by the absence of its benevolent and iconic founder. It was time to adapt to the new reality or go out of business.

Everyone had loved Fr. Fred. Volunteers were totally dedicated to him, clients were served in increasing numbers, and board members were there to support their good and generous friend. The problem was that when he died, many believed Fr. Fred *was* the organization, and that he had taken the whole thing with him. The volunteers ran the tasks of the operation, supporting his interviews and gifts, and the board had not evolved far from its role as the original steering committee. They were friends and met weekly as an unstructured breakfast group, not as a disciplined governing body. They always trusted Fr. Fred would do the right thing, since he made all the decisions.

Just two weeks after he died, Fr. Fred's brother Joe sent a letter to The Foundation board. In it, he wrote:

> *Finding somebody to replace my brother with his unique talents and abilities will be next to impossible, since no two people are alike. But I pray and have confidence that you will find someone who will have his or her own set of talents, abilities, and ideas to go forth and to build on what you have already established. I trust that the good Lord and my brother will be watching over you and guiding you and that they will in the long run be very satisfied.*

One of the original founding volunteers, Barb Lehnhard tells us: "When Fr. Fred died, we closed for a few days, but then we re-opened and kept on doing what he would have wanted us to do." She said it as though this unrealistic situation could have lasted forever. "There was little surprise when he died, because he had been so sick. He had not been coming in to the office regularly for a few months, and when he did come in, he was tired and would not stay the whole day. We were relieved for him that his suffering was over."

What followed was driven in an atmosphere of confusion and grief. Some of the people with longtime connections to the organization left, since their allegiance was to Fr. Fred on a personal basis, not to his mission or his organization. Many stayed and faced the new reality of not having their charismatic friend to guide them. It was this core of solid commitment and hard work that kept The Father Fred Foundation alive.

While Fr. Fred was not much for organizational dos and don'ts, he did a good job of inspiring the people around him, and the spiritual transactions he facilitated while he was alive continued to drive the volunteers. His spirit lives in the hearts of the volunteers and board members who stayed, and the fact that The Foundation has a spiritual component continues to set it apart from other human services organizations.

Since there was little established leadership or governance in the organization, there were differences on the decisions being made. There was second-guessing: "Father would not have done it that way." So, as the board began to adapt, they faced a really tough challenge: How do we bring order? Fr. Fred had not needed an executive director or administrator, because he called all the shots. He made all the decisions and seemed to run the whole thing out of his hip pocket.

Who's in charge? How do we move into the future? The board grappled with the difficult task of maintaining its momentum in the face of the loss of Fr. Fred. Challenges included maintaining the day-to-day work of the volunteers, service to the clients, and accounting for donor gifts, as the client needs continued to grow. Gradually and painfully, the board made progress toward becoming a truly responsible, non-profit governing body.

The Transition Team

The first step was to recruit a stable, recognizable persona to maintain a spiritual "presence" for The Foundation. They knew it would be impossible to replace the irreplaceable Fr. Fred. Several board members approached Fr. Edwin Thome, who was in the process of retirement from parish administration, after establishing Christ the King Catholic Church in nearby Acme. He had been just four years behind Fr. Fred at St. Joseph Seminary in Grand Rapids and served with him in the Diocese of Grand Rapids until they both transferred to the Diocese of Gaylord upon its formation in July 1971. Each had served the new diocese as Vicar for the Traverse City area. Fr. Fred and the chaplaincy at the State Hospital reported to Immaculate Conception when Fr. Thome was pastor. They even shared the same first name: Edwin. Most saw Fr. Thome's possible appointment as a good fit.

Blessed with organizational skills, Fr. Thome was known as a successful fund raiser, had served as superintendant and president of the local Catholic schools for twelve years, and played a major role in a successful $5.5 million capital campaign for the schools. He was the current Vicar General of the Diocese of Gaylord and had a good reputation, recognition, and acceptance by the community of Traverse City. After the coaxing and reflection, Fr. Thome accepted the position of Spiritual

Director in May 2000.

There was immediate relief that a new direction had been established. The community once again felt confident in their financial support of The Foundation. However, it was shortly after he arrived that the downturn in the economy was felt and local needs grew. This meant more space was needed. Fr. Thome petitioned to the board of directors to rearrange the limited office space to assure more privacy for the clients. Fr. Fred's original office was divided into four sections, and Fr. Thome made do with a much smaller, previously unused supply room. Eventually, the number of clients increased to the extent that Fr. Thome asked the board to appoint an administrator.

Mike Shockley was a teacher, working with expelled students and their community service obligations, and bringing them to work at The Father Fred Foundation. He was there when Fr. Thome came aboard and at the end of the school year, Mike joined The Foundation first as Volunteer Coordinator, then as Administrator.

Fr. Thome and Mike worked closely together. Mike was very personable and a hard worker. He was "all over The Foundation" and represented the organization well to the public. Together, they crafted new processes for the board and for the volunteers. A new order began to emerge, and it was not without the recognition that change is difficult for many people, especially for those who were protective of the independent, autonomous ways Fr. Fred had operated. The board supported the work of Fr. Thome and Mike as new processes were implemented, programs evolved, and budgets were established.

The Father Fred Foundation seemed to be growing day by day in a steady rhythm—more clients, more donations and, again, less and less room. When the adjacent building became vacant, Fr. Thome convinced the board to purchase it and sought out a donor for a favorable loan.

Mike attracted younger members to serve on the board. This was the beginning of a much-needed improvement in administration as these younger members brought new ideas and energy and called for strategic planning.

With new determination to meet the needs of the clients, Fr. Thome did what God seemed to have in mind for him when he was ordained, namely use his skills as a fund raiser. He and Mike brought in a firm to help with raising $2.5 million to pay off the loan for the second building and to buy another that became vacant. Soon, those who claimed, "Father Fred wouldn't approve" no longer spoke as loudly.

Moving Toward Greater Sustainability

The board, focused on good non-profit governance, made the commitment to confirm The Foundation's sustainability. They decided to ground the increasingly complex operation in practices that would assure a strong future to continue its mission.

Along with Mike, Norm Bamberg was another paid employee, charged with warehouse and volunteer oversight responsibilities. Norm also had a responsible hand in the beginnings of the capital campaign to raise funds to remodel the facilities on Hastings. Later, he was appointed Director of Operations, overseeing buildings and grounds and what has become the largest food pantry in northern Michigan. And, of course, there was Fr. Thome, as spiritual director and master fundraiser, who met daily with the clients, coming for financial help. In the background, LaVerne O'Neil provided client data entry and George Kuhn was "the computer guy." Able volunteers performed all other business and client services.

Mike Shockley served effectively and successfully in his position at The Foundation until the middle of 2006, when his father died and he had to leave and step into the family business. At that time, the board recruited and hired Martie Manty as Executive Director.

As one of the early Community Mental Health social workers, Martie speaks of plenty of opportunities, from the late 1970s, when she witnessed Fr. Fred's profound impact on State Hospital residents. As Executive Director, Martie's commitment has been to keep the "Listen, Care, and Share" focus primary in the daily workings at The Foundation, to maintain The Foundation's excellent reputation in the community. The human services community was appreciative of steps being taken to create a more responsive charity. In fact, staffing grants from United Way and Rotary Charities of Traverse City were funded and have allowed The Foundation to add to add a Director of Development who has successfully grown and diversified the revenue streams for The Foundation and a Volunteer Coordinator to fulfill the complex scheduling and management job for over 150 active volunteers. The final staff person added was Business Manager, who takes extreme care in managing the business of The Foundation as well as donation tracking and accounting.

As of this writing, the twelve-member board and the Executive Director have oversight over seven hard working regular committees and several *ad hoc* work groups—all focused on the sustainability of this unique organization.

Fr. Iakovos and Fr. Thome hang a portrait of Fr. Fred at the Hastings Street facility.

In July 2007, Father Iakovos Olechnowicz, a Greek Orthodox priest, arrived in Traverse City, moving his family from Binghampton, New York, with the charge of starting a Greek Orthodox mission in the community. As a way to integrate into the community, he volunteered in the food pantry at The Father Fred Foundation. He felt an immediate bond with Fr. Thome and the rest of the leadership at The Foundation.

By the following July, Fr. Thome had Fr. Iakovos appointed as his assistant. This split the spiritual work with the volunteers from fund development activities. It was also the beginning of an exit strategy for Fr. Thome since, in 2002, he had assumed the pastoral duties at the growing St. Joseph Parish on the Old Mission Peninsula. Fr. Iakovos also began having direct client contact, working with financial cases. His presence was successful with volunteers as well as clients. He challenged volunteers to grow and develop their thinking about serving the poor. He identified the paradigm that we as individuals need the poor to help us develop our own spirituality. This helps us to work out our own salvation (Fr. Iakovos says, "If the word salvation is too much for you, substitute character development"). Thus, we see the practice of virtue as volunteers.

In January 2009, Fr. Thome retired, once again, to devote full time to his pastoral duties at St. Joseph, and Fr. Iakovos assumed the title of Spiritual Director. By August 2010, work at his new parish, Archangel Gabriel Greek Orthodox Church in Traverse City, demanded more time than he could spend at The Foundation, so he thoughtfully and respectfully resigned his position. He left with an excellent reputation and the observation that, as The Foundation grows:

> *It is not about how we deliver services, it's about the heart—the delivery systems may be different, but the love is the same. As we grow, we need to fight to keep the small feel and remember that our work here is about our apostolate to the poor, regardless of religion.*

The search process for a new Foundation chaplain lasted four months and resulted in over 100 applicants from all over the country. Taking great care in this selection, the board of directors hired Pastor James Holwerda. He assumed his new full time position on Valentine's Day, 2011.

A View of the Current Foundation

Many are critical of the new environment. From the critics, we hear:

"Oh, Father Fred wouldn't go for all this fanciness and size. It was so nice when there were just volunteers and we all felt like family. He would have never gone for all the paid staff and computers. It's impersonal and not like the old days. My loyalty was to him, not the project. I had to leave when he died. It has become just another large social services agency."

These grief-driven statements are all variations on the theme: *I really miss Father Fred and the way it used to be.* It is as though they would only be happy if Fr. Fred, himself, walked through the door and asked, "How you doin'? What can I do for you?"

Other folks (some who have been there since the beginning) have a more positive reaction to the current direction. Sally Suprenant, says: "It is a big operation. I think Father Fred would be happy because we're serving more people, and that's what he was all about. We had discussions on the board every month. What about day care? Some of those things are now going on—good! Women need that so they can work. Change is always hard."

George Kuhn, the technical whiz who designed the first computer system for Fr. Fred, observes: "Among some of the older folks, there is a loyalty to Father Fred and the way it used to be. He'd love the way it is today, and he'd find a way to make it and keep it personal. He'd be happy with the number of people we serve."

Carl Madion, founding board member who is still serving on the board: "Every time I go into The Foundation I see what we are doing. We never thought it would be this big... I'm in awe every time I go in there... More growth? I hope not. We work on a strict budget because the need will continue to grow. Father Fred would be happy to see it today."

Arnie Ochs, longtime friend of The Foundation and board member: "If Father Fred were to walk into Hastings Street today, he'd be proud."

Fr. Fred may not have been interested in or capable of directing The Foundation to where it is today and would probably not have wanted to relinquish the level of control he enjoyed. However, it is difficult to believe that he would not be happy to see what is going on. Change is difficult for most people, yet wonderful results still speak for themselves.

The organization continues to evolve. It certainly evolved while Fr. Fred was running it, from a simple drop-in center to the current large and more complex facility on Hasting Street. Now, an active board and competent administration face the future with plans and means for sustainability. Would Fr. Fred have done it exactly this way? Probably not. Would he be happy serving so many vulnerable and needy families? You can count on it.

Fr. Fred would return to the basic question: "How will it help my people?" He would also want to examine the following issues that were important to him: Is the overhead low? Are we surviving on local donations, without the need for Federal and State funds? Are we treating people with dignity and respect? Do volunteers drive and deliver our services? Is there a spiritual component to what we are doing?

It is plausible that Fr. Fred knew it would be difficult for the organization to survive, yet he would have said, "It's going to be okay," knowing he had infused the community with a giving spirit and that the people left behind would find a way to make it all work.

Today, the community continues to hold a tremendous respect for Fr. Fred and The Father Fred Foundation because of who he was and what he started. It is not like other social services organizations, because its founder was a priest who gave his whole life to his work. It wasn't a job for him. It was his vocation. It is generally felt that a spiritual component will continue to be an essential part of the organization. Will a pastor or priest touch each visitor like Fr. Fred did? No. But a full time chaplain will have plenty of opportunity to influence and train volunteers and staff who will spend a good amount of time with clients as well as assure donors of The Foundation's stability. Today, The Father Fred Foundation is stronger than ever.

Fr. Fred would be happy to be serving so many.

St. Joseph the Worker

Spread love everywhere you go. Let no one ever come to you without leaving happier.

Mother Teresa

There is more than just a little bit if irony in the fact that Father Fred was named pastor at St. Joseph the Worker Parish in Mapleton, Michigan, on the Old Mission Peninsula. At sixty-five years old, he was named pastor for the first time. He was the grandson of hard working Polish immigrants, the son of a stonemason, a worker named Joseph. He was somehow destined for this assignment.

St. Joseph Parish is one of the oldest Catholic congregations in the Grand Traverse region. It was originally formed in 1841, in conjunction with the trading post and families at Old Mission, one of the oldest settlements in the area. Fr. Ignatius Mrak, an Austrian-born priest, served the Irish and French settlers and Ottawa and Chippewa Indians a few times each year in their homes and wigwams. Because of the scarcity of priests, he settled in Peshawbestown, across West Grand Traverse Bay, and travelled in a circuit

After Mass, the kids all wanted to hold Fr. Fred's hand for the recession.

Fr. Fred greets his parishioners at St. Joseph.

by canoe or Indian pony. His circuit extended along Lake Michigan, from Manistee, Michigan, to *L'Arbre Croche*, near Petoskey, Michigan, a distance of nearly 150 miles. Fr. Mrak left the area in 1869, when he succeeded Bishop Frederic Baraga in Marquette, Michigan.

In 1880, the first small, rustic wooden chapel (24'x30') was built on land donated by the Oliver Lardie family. The current church was dedicated July 14, 1908. The parish and church occupy a hilly, peninsula setting, surrounded by Grand Traverse Bay, fruit orchards, and vineyards. This area is widely recognized as one of the most beautiful areas in Michigan.

Fr. Fred's connection with this parish reaches back to his very early days in Traverse City, to 1961, shortly after his arrival at the State Hospital. It was then that the Ladies Guild of St. Joseph presented him with a new gold ciborium, the vessel used in Catholic liturgy to hold the consecrated hosts. The thank you note to the guild included:

> *We were all thrilled when Father Edwin J. Frederick, our beloved and zealous Chaplain, displayed the beautiful ciborium for use in our hospital chapel and told us at Mass that the ladies of St. Joseph's Guild, Mapleton, had donated this much needed and desired sacred altar vessel. Certainly,*

it is a grand church gift given to a grand priest of God, a true
personification of gratitude, if there ever was one.

A patient, representing all the Catholic patient-citizens in Fr. Fred's "little congregation" at the Traverse City State Hospital wrote the note and closed it with a promise to remember them in their humble prayers.

Recently installed Bishop Patrick Cooney appointed Fr. Fred pastor to help the oldest priest in the diocese, Fr. E. Francis Denay. On Sunday, March 24, 1990, the eighty-seven-year-old Fr. Denay administered the Oath of Fidelity to Fr. Edwin J. Frederick in front of a standing-room-only crowd at St. Joseph. Fr. Fred became pastor and Fr. Denay became an associate pastor. With an associate, Fr. Fred could continue his ministry at The Father Fred Foundation.

Fr. Fred was happy to have a parish of his own. He had not been totally happy with the arrangement at St. Francis of Assisi near downtown Traverse City. In a letter, dated May 22, 1990, he told a friend: "It's wonderful to 'own' a parish and to be my own boss. Those past seven months at St. Francis were something else."

It didn't take the new parish long to see the increase in attendance at Sunday Mass. Many of the Catholics who had found him at All Faiths Chapel followed him to St. Joseph, as well as several of the former patients.

One of the new parishioners commented:

> We switched parishes to St. Joe's when Father Fred was
> assigned there. This prompted our annoyed pastor, to call
> us up personally and lecture us that being a member of a
> parish and a Catholic was not a "cafeteria" style commitment.
> I'm sure that he probably had the same conversation with
> several parishioners who found Father Fred's ministry to be
> refreshingly simple and genuine.

The new attendees were well-received by the local parishioners and, during Fr. Fred's time there, the parish became a wonderful melting pot of older peninsula families and followers of Fr. Fred from his informal congregation at the State Hospital. The new pastor brought some of the traditions with him.

Dennis Carney, an All Faiths transplant recalls: "Father Fred continued his tradition of having outdoor masses at times, even after moving to St. Joe's. I remember more than once having Mass in the oddly beautiful and calming setting

Outside Mass was a favorite of Fr. Fred.

of the parish cemetery down the road from the church." Beginning in 1992, Fr. Fred had a Mass at the cemetery on the Fourth of July. The backdrop, behind the portable altar, was a large American flag that had been used in the final military services for his dad. A patriotic wreath was placed in front of the lector stand. On the wreath, people were able to write the names of loved ones who were at that time serving in the armed forces and deployed to the Persian Gulf. Fr. Fred always included prayers for military men and women.

Mary Lyon, longtime St. Joseph parishioner and parish historian, remembers two of Fr. Fred's characteristics. At the annual summer parish picnic at Bowers Harbor, Fr. Fred would circulate and talk with each person. He was often seen to sit down and eat next to someone who was alone. She also recalls that a special ceremony was held for couples celebrating their fiftieth wedding anniversary. Father furnished leis of red and white roses and put them around their necks: red for love and white for faith.

In the program for his retirement party, we read about his love for children of St. Joseph's:

> *Father Fred baptized more than 200 children while pastor*
> *at St. Joseph ... His love for children is very obvious. When the*

little ones bring up the "groceries." As he calls them, and put them in the basket near the altar, during the offertory, they learn giving and sharing at an early age... and it's always fun to watch them navigate the steps to put their food in the basket for the needy... after Mass, when he leaves the altar, the children run to him to grasp a finger or hold on to his vestments and walk out to the vestibule with him.

Fr. Fred initiated many needed improvements while pastor at St. Joseph: handicap and wheelchair access, dividers in Denay Hall to accommodate religious education class growth, an expanded parking lot, adding twenty-six acres adjacent to the cemetery, installation of a beautiful cedar ceiling in the church, and updating the electrical wiring and lights to meet current building standards. With the addition of the new ceiling, there are now four layers of ceiling above the congregants.

In November 1994, when he announced the plans for the new ceiling, many members of the Ladies Guild of St. Joseph were suddenly thrown into a real snit. He had not asked them if he could make such a change. So, they wrote a very strong letter of complaint to him in protest. He thanked them for their input and went ahead with the project. The feeling was not that it had to do with the cost, but rather a simple resistance to change. When the new cedar ceiling was completed a few months later, nearly everyone agreed that it was far superior to the old acoustic panels, now hidden.

During his time on the Old Mission Peninsula, Fr. Fred revived the annual spring tradition of the Blessing of the Blossoms, at Chateau Chantal. This prayer for a successful fruit crop was a tradition going back to 1923 and was of great significance to the cherry and apple farmers as well as the growing number of vintners on the peninsula.

Blessing of the Blossoms on the Old Mission Peninsula, May 1994

When some land adjacent to the St. Joseph Cemetery was for sale in a bankruptcy proceeding, Fr. Fred joined parishioners Whitney Lyon and Stu Hubbell to the courthouse to see if they could add an acre to the cemetery. The hearings went on all day before their parcel came up for sale. Whitney tells that during the entire day, Fr. Fred was anxious and could hardly contain himself, hearing the sad bankruptcy stories of the other people in court. He wanted to jump up and help them. Several times, Stu and Whitney had to tell him to sit down and talk him out of offering money to these poor people.

When their time came, the judge told the three of them he would not allow a single acre to be split out of the thirty-acre parcel, so they had to buy the whole thing. Today, after selling off four acres, that parcel is the planned site for a new St. Joseph Church.

Fr. Denay died on September 17, 1995, at age ninety-two. Two days later, Fr. Fred offered the Funeral Mass for his aged friend and mentor at St. Joseph Church.

Retirement from Parish Work

A few months later, on February 10, 1996, Fr. Fred announced to the parish that he would retire on August 1. In his announcement, he said:

> *Five years ago, I was permitted/appointed to assist Fr. Earl Denay at St. Joseph's and to learn from him. Now that Fr. Denay has died, I feel my mission has been completed. I did my job by serving the oldest saintly priest in the diocese, and by serving the parishioners.*

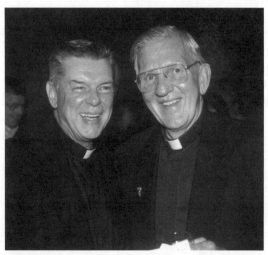

Bishop Cooney and Fr. Fred share a laugh at Fr. Fred's retirement party.

The parish planned a huge retirement party, and it was held on August 11 in the Governor's Hall at the Grand Traverse Resort. More than 570 attendees joined in the celebration dinner that was followed by tributes and gifts. Tributes included those from State Senator George McManus, State Representative Michelle McManus, and Traverse City Mayor Shelley Kester. Proclamations were read from Michigan Governor John Engler, and U.S. Congressman Bart Stupak.

St. Joseph Youth Group members tie Fr. Fred in a prayer web at his retirement party.

After dinner the Youth Group spun a "prayer web" around Fr. Fred. Standing in a circle, with Fr. Fred seated in the middle, about thirty children tossed a ball of twine over his head, exchanging prayers as they caught the ball. As more prayers were said, Fr. Fred became more and more entangled in the resulting web. Fr. Fred loved it. The Youth Group also presented him with a peace pole inscribed with "For Father Fred, in appreciation of your love and commitment to youth. God bless you." Later, the peace pole was installed and dedicated in front of The Foundation facilities on Hastings Street. The evening culminated with the surprise gift from the parish, the presentation to him of a new Oldsmobile.

In a farewell tribute, Fr. Patrick Barrett, his successor, wrote:

> *Whether with the hospital or with the foundation, Father*
> *Fred recognizes that service is of the very essence of religion.*
> *It can be said that service is religion and religion is service.*
> *Read again the parable of the Good Samaritan… I marvel*
> *at his ability in leading church services and dealing with the*
> *unexpected. He is imperturbable in his patience, devoted*
> *in his caring and able to make a person feel better just by*

*attending a "Father Fred" service. Father Fred, you are a man
of God. May you have many more years of beautiful service.*

His wonderful, productive time at St. Joseph's was over, and he could now concentrate on his work, full time at The Father Fred Foundation.

Here's One For You: Notre Dame Fan

Both Fr. Fred and his friend Jack Burns shared a passion for Notre Dame football. The Notre Dame–Boston College game was down to under a minute when Jack and Susan Burns pulled into the parking lot of St. Joseph's one autumn Saturday afternoon. The car radio reported that the score was close and Notre Dame had the ball with a chance to win the game. Five o'clock Mass was about to begin when Jack told Susan, "You just go on into church and get a seat. I'll be in as soon as the game is over. I can't leave this game now."

Fr. Fred met Susan at the church entrance and asked, "Where's Jack today?" She explained that he was still in the car, anxiously awaiting the outcome of a very close and dramatic game. A few minutes later, after Mass had begun, Jack joined Susan in a pew at the rear of the church.

Just before Holy Communion, when Catholics greet one another with a handshake as a sign of peace, it was Fr. Fred's custom to come off the altar and into the congregation, greet, and shake hands with the folks on the aisle in the first few rows. This day was different. Fr. Fred stepped down, off the altar, and began greeting and shaking hands with people on the aisle until he was way past his customary first few rows. Almost out the back of the church, he finally spotted his friend Jack. As he grabbed Jack's hand, he leaned in close, and in a very loud, audible stage whisper, asked, "Hey, Jack, who won the game?"

Here's One For You: Trip to Poland

Tim Carroll is a *bon vivant* and a raconteur of the first degree. He grew up on the Old Mission Peninsula and graduated from St. Francis High School in 1956. With a Master's degree in Anglo/Irish Literature from Notre Dame including a post-graduate year of study in Irish literature at Trinity College, Dublin, he knows how to tell a good story. After a stint in the Peace Corps; overseas duty at nine different postings around the world; and as Protocol Chief to the U.S. Attorney General for five years, he has a lot of stories to tell.

One of his postings, commencing in 1991, was at the U.S. Embassy in Warsaw, Poland, with the U.S. Peace Corps He was the country director of the agency with over 300 Peace Corps volunteers working throughout Poland. At that time, he didn't know Fr. Fred all that well, yet on a visit home, told him: "Father Fred, you're Polish. Why don't you come over to Poland while I'm assigned there?"

On October 3, 1993, Fr. Fred boarded a plane for Warsaw. In the diary he kept of the trip, we see an almost child-like awe of the wonders of an overseas flight and international travel.

During the ten days or so Fr. Fred spent in Poland, Tim saw to it that his staff drove and escorted him safely and comfortably around the country of his familial heritage. Tim made sure Fr. Fred did and saw what he should on a first-time whirlwind visit to Poland. While there was no particular effort to track down his roots, Fr. Fred must have had thoughts of his ancestry and the Polish traditions taught to him at his mother's knee, things his father told him, and what happened at the family's dinner table as a child. Tim explained, later, that if he had been looking for the town or region of his origin, he would have most likely been disappointed, since Polish vital records have been ignored, abused, or lost through generations of war and changing governments.

From Warsaw, he went as far north as Gdansk, on the Baltic Coast, and out to a resort area named Hel. (Later, Fr. Fred got a big kick out of telling folks back home that he'd been to Hel and back.) He also went as far south as Zakopane and was captivated by southern Poland. Along the way, he visited the holiest of all Polish shrines, the 800-year-old Shrine of Our Lady of Częstochowa. The Monastery of Jasna Góra in Częstochowa, Poland, is the third-largest Catholic pilgrimage site in the world. Home to the beloved miraculous icon of Our Lady of Częstochowa, the monastery is also the national shrine of Poland and the center of Polish Catholicism.

During the time in Poland, Tim got to know Fr. Fred. "He was a man completely without guile," Tim says. "He was not a worldly person. He had no agenda, other than what you saw, at face value." Tim's description of Fr. Fred's relative naïveté continues with observations that he did not present a particularly dazzling *persona* and there was no apology about it. People didn't understand how spiritual he was and he made no bones about simply being who he was—a compassionate priest. "I've found

Icon of Our Lady of Czestochowa, the "Black Madonna".

this to be true of many people I've met in my life who are 'other-worldly,'" says Tim, "and any motto he may have had would have been, 'Thy will be done.' It was that simple. He was an activist."

Accustomed to dealing with heads of state, high-level diplomats, and policy, Tim was almost apologetic in telling that he really didn't seem to have as much in common with Fr. Fred as he had thought he would. That all changed on the day Fr. Fred was to return to Traverse City. "Tim," he shyly professed, "the people of Traverse City have given me some money for my trip. You have been so gracious and accommodating and have looked after everything while I was here. I can't take this money home with me. You would be doing me a favor if you took this money and used it to help some of the poor people of Warsaw." With that, Fr. Fred took out a wad of twenty-dollar bills, amounting to around $500.

Tim was immediately uncomfortable on two levels. In his position and in his sense of propriety, it seemed unnatural to be taking money from a priest. As a life-long Catholic, he was more accustomed to having contributions flow in the other direction. Additionally, he'd never been one to simply hand out cash. Nonetheless, he took the money and saw Fr. Fred off to his flight home.

Tim said later that his real connection with Fr. Fred came when, over the next two weeks, he had a grand time watching the faces of the poor people he may have walked by previously, when he handed them a twenty. Beggars would begin to weep with his generosity. Street musicians and buskers would stop performing when they saw a U.S. twenty-dollar bill drop into the hat on the ground. In 1993, that amount was equivalent to a full week's pay for the average citizen in Warsaw.

Tim claims that the experience, for him, was a bit of an epiphany. It sensitized him more than ever to the poor people of Warsaw, who had previously been invisible to him. We wonder, after that, about Fr. Fred's motivation: Was he simply confident that the head of the U.S. Peace Corps in Poland would find a way to securely distribute the money he had at the end of his trip? Or, did he see that Tim might benefit from the experience? "That was the great mystery of Fr. Fred," Tim observes. "How complicated, yet very simple, was Jesus' admonition to love one another."

In either case, when the money was gone, Tim realized that he could now better understand the essential and irreducible goodness of this humble country priest who, after a memorable visit to his family's homeland, asked him to do a favor.

Here it is Sunday
Oct, 10 and getting ready
to attend St. Mary's church
at the Square. It's about
7:10 AM and Mass begins
at 8:00 AM. More on that
later. — I hope that it
does not rain today. We
want to see a Benedictine
Monastery and the church
underground made from
salt, — Like I said I
will tell you more later

9:25 Sunday — We returned
from Mass which took my
took 43 years ago. The priest did
not face the people. He distributed
communion to people who
knelt. Another priest hearing
confessions while Mass was in
session. They took up a collection
with a big basket. The
priest read all the readings
There was no homily. The
priest read a letter from
Cardinal Makarski. That
guy must be political
because he talked about

Excerpt from Fr. Fred's handwritten diary on his trip to Poland.

YOU ARE A PRIEST FOREVER

Jesus went around to all the towns and villages, teaching in their synagogues, proclaiming the gospel of the kingdom.

(Matthew 9:35)

T he title of this chapter is taken from the Catholic Rite of Ordination. Here, we explore Father Fred's priesthood, throughout his religious vocation, from the time of his ordination until his death. At the core of this story of his life, he was a priest. It defined him more than his Polish family heritage. As a priest, he flourished and excelled.

This chapter can only make sense after visiting the chronology of his pastoral life. We see his priesthood and witness his theology from multiple angles and perspectives: friends, fellow clergy, patients, and clients of The Father Fred Foundation. Perhaps the most compelling observations are those he makes about his own priesthood.

We are Jesus to Them

In the summer of 1970, a dozen or so deacons in the diocese were selected to participate in a unique Clinical Pastoral Training program at the Traverse

On Easter, 1995, Fr. Fred wears the vestments his sisters made for his ordination in 1950.

City Regional Psychiatric Hospital. Fr. Fred had designed and was supervising what proved to be an extraordinary program. As a Certified Mental Health Chaplain Supervisor, he brought an exceptional set of qualifications to the initiative.

The objective of the program was to help soon-to-be-ordained priests learn about mental illness and to be comfortable around the mentally ill. It also featured a component on how to minister to this often-invisible segment of our population. For ten weeks, participants lived on campus in employee housing. They spent mornings in a classroom setting and afternoons with patients in the hospital wards. Participants found the effects of the program to be valuable and lasting.

> **"Loneliness is the most terrible poverty."**
>
> *Mother Teresa*

Deacon Dennis Stillwell was assigned to Immaculate Conception Parish in Traverse City, working with his pastor, Fr. Edwin Thome. He was among the participants in the program. Now, as the pastor at St. Francis Xavier Parish in Petoskey, Michigan, Fr. Stillwell reflects on his experience:

> *All of us were inspired by how well Father Fred knew and loved the patients. He was Jesus to them. And he was Jesus to many of the hospital's employees. He gave his very heart. I learned about far more than mental illness. I learned the miracles that happen when a priest is Jesus to others. Setting yourself aside to totally serve others was something that Father Fred did so beautifully and heroically. I think of him and of what he has contributed to my priesthood to this very day... Father Fred has been my hero in priesthood for thirty-nine years. God rest his beautiful soul.*

Father Francis Murphy, now pastor at St. Ann's Parish in Cadillac, Michigan, was the assistant pastor at Immaculate Conception that same summer and remembers the program, as well:

> *What I saw in Father Fred was a very welcoming and calm man, who was gifted with troubled folks. He had a real gift of compassion and patience and that was especially evident among the mentally ill. It was also evident among the participants in our program...*
>
> *Years later, I watched as his compassion and patience moved in a slightly different direction, as he moved to The Father Fred Foundation. I watched and admired his work with people who society had swept aside—his ministry to those who fell through the cracks... He was rock solid.*

Currently, Fr. Stillwell oversees what began as a tiny food pantry in the rectory basement and is now a major food pantry and outreach center for the city of Petoskey, Michigan. Folks throughout the city support the pantry, and it helps anyone who comes in need. As Fr. Stillwell explains, "It was done as a result of having been inspired by The Father Fred Foundation in Traverse City. Just as he taught us in the summer of 1970, 'We are Jesus to them.'"

Administration of the Sacraments

Administering the sacraments of the Catholic faith is a significant, and perhaps the most important, part of priesthood. For most of his life as a priest, Fr. Fred did not have the responsibilities of a parish to administer. Consequently, a focus on the administration of the sacraments was a greater percentage of his activities as a priest.

Sister Ann Goggin knew Fr. Fred since he arrived in Muskegon in 1953 and kept an active correspondence with him throughout the remainder of his life. Because of her advanced degrees in theology, he found her to be an articulate and informed correspondent and an effective sounding board for matters concerning Catholic theology. She says:

> *He had an unerring instinct for the core of religion and for the core of the Gospel.*

> *He told me once: "Often I find more Christianity in the State Mental Hospital than I do in the parish. They will often give each other their last cigarette and that's all they have."*

> *He knew to treat all people as human beings; he didn't stand on a lot of ceremony, even though he was a priest, from head to toe. He was able to get to the center of what religion is supposed to be and he never strayed from that. That's why he was adamant at the hospital that people had to be treated with respect and dignity—basic things like getting them a comb.*

Fr. Fred focused on bringing the comfort of God, faith, and the sacraments to people in need. He had, perhaps, a little wider and gentler definition of how to do this, compared to other priests. Sadly, however, this may have been mistaken by a few for a lax or even disrespectful treatment of the sacraments. This definitely was not the case.

As Sister Ann observed:

> *As an experienced and mature priest who was well*
> *acquainted with human suffering and the frailty of human*
> *experience, Father Fred was known to welcome people back to*
> *the sacraments who were found to be in intractable situations.*
> *He did this quietly and judiciously, without fanfare, using the*
> *right of priests to make decisions using "internal forum" after*
> *he became well acquainted with a particular pastoral need.*
> *He had great respect for the sacraments and never trivialized*
> *right reception of the sacraments, but he also was pledged to*
> *ameliorate human suffering and faith that had been tested.*

The few stories that follow are presented as diverse selections to characterize Fr. Fred. They are not intended to portray the total commitment Fr. Fred made to each sacrament, yet they illustrate his unique understanding and adaptability of the human condition.

Eucharistic Administration

The Eucharist, or Holy Communion, is the center of the Catholic Mass. It is the liturgical transformation of bread and wine into the body and blood of Christ. During his priesthood, Fr. Fred must have offered thousands of masses. That means administration of the Eucharistic Communion hundreds of thousands of times. He especially loved First Communion events.

Church teaching is fairly specific about the committed requirements needed for the reception of Holy Communion, because of the Catholic belief that Christ is truly present in its reception. Many people talk about how Fr. Fred did not judge anyone who presented for the reception of Communion. He would give them Communion, even if they were not Catholic. "Who am I to judge?" he would ask. "If someone comes to me to receive Christ, how can I deny them?" He was never known to invite communicants inappropriately. "After all, they're not asking to commit adultery—they just want to receive Christ."

When artist Paul Welch, who is not a Catholic, was working with Fr. Fred on the design and construction of the windows at All Faiths Chapel, he made some observations on the topic of Catholicism and Fr. Fred's administration of the sacraments. He would observe patients as they worshipped, and he saw

Fr. Fred celebrates a wedding Mass.

how Fr. Fred responded to them and served them:

> *Catholics are different from other denominations. I believe Catholics have a deeper feeling that suffering is an essential part of life. As a general rule, they accept suffering and loss differently. Consequently, their concept of a Eucharistic Sacrifice brings the reality of suffering closer to the heart of their belief. So, then you see Father Fred and his attitude of acceptance of everyone, giving Communion to a mental patient, putting Christ in the suffering patient's mouth—just imagine that. It is a very powerful image.*

> *I think Father Fred's spiritual work inside and out of the hospital environment made him more effective in working with everyone, both patients and "regular" people. This duality was a significant source of his empathy.*

Sara Dennis attended Mass at All Faiths Chapel on the campus of the State Hospital with her parents. When she was about to make her First Communion, she had many questions about the mystery of it all. Fr. Fred answered her questions and would let her taste the unconsecrated hosts, after Mass. On her big day, a beautiful summer Sunday, Mass was held outside All Faiths Chapel at one of the "Mass in the Grass" events. Patients wanted to get in front of her for Communion, and in a rare denial to the patients, Fr. Fred told them, "No, this is Sara's big day.

You'll have to wait." As an adult, she now says she grew up with a greater tolerance for disadvantaged people because of Fr. Fred, what he did for them, and how he treated them: "We saw his compassion firsthand as children."

One last Eucharist story comes from Sister Ann Goggin, and involves an elderly couple who came to see Fr. Fred when he asked them about their regular attendance at Mass, but noticed they did not receive Communion. They explained that even though they were in a stable forty-year marriage, each of them had been married previously. There was no way for an annulment, at that point, since they could not have located the other partners by then. So, when they told him why they didn't go to Communion, they had tears in their eyes. Fr. Fred told them they would receive that very day. The details of this were something they kept quiet, under the concept of internal forum. They received Communion for the first time in over forty years, and they were so thrilled; it was as if they were on fire with the Holy Spirit.

Weddings

Grant and Paulette Parsons were married at All Faiths Chapel in October 1975 on a Friday night. "It was the neutral ground we needed," Grant explains, "because I wasn't Catholic and Paulette was. It was a good compromise. The only issue was that we wanted to keep the patients out of the Chapel during the wedding, and Father Fred would not hear of it." Fr. Fred explained that it was the patients' facility, and they could come and go as they pleased. And they did. The other thing Grant tells is that he and Fr. Fred had a gentlemen's agreement to keep everything short because of the football game that night. Knowing this, Fr. Fred extended the ceremony considerably with stories of Grant's family, building All Faiths Chapel, etc.

They weren't the only ones who wanted the Chapel to themselves during their wedding. There are several stories about how nervous brides didn't want "those people" wandering through their celebration. Fr. Fred always sided with the patients, although he had to draw the line in one wedding when a patient wanted to kiss the bride.

The story of Vince and Paula Prusick's wedding in 1977 is similarly unconventional. In order to marry Vince, Paula took classes to convert to Catholicism. After finding their meeting with another priest uncomfortable, they approached Fr. Fred. Paula took her classes at the Chapel, and Fr. Fred did her conversion. Still, however, to make the ceremony ecumenically comfortable for both families, they were able to plan their wedding at the Presbyterian Church in Traverse City, and both Fr. Fred and Reverend Homer Nye were on the altar for the Catholic celebration in a Protestant church. Everyone was happy.

Bill Maxbauer served as an altar boy with Fr. Fred at All Faiths Chapel. He says: "I'll always remember the joke that Father Fred told in his sermon at weddings. It's about a boy who wrote a story about the early life of Benjamin Franklin, but hadn't learned to punctuate yet. The story read like this: 'Benjamin Franklin grew up a poor boy in Pennsylvania until one day he got married and discovered electricity.' That story always got a good laugh!" Bill tells that his relationship with Fr. Fred was formative in his life and made Catholicism come alive for him.

Joe and Barb Novak had been married for several years, had two teenagers, and got divorced. They still loved each other, however, and that was the basis for their discussions with Fr. Fred about reconciliation. For nearly eighteen months, Fr. Fred met with them and helped them re-define their relationship. He helped them work out the issues that had earlier divided them and re-married them in All Faiths Chapel in a very private, quiet ceremony with only one friend and Joe's parents present. Joe and Barb recently celebrated the twenty-fifth anniversary of their second marriage. "Something was coming from God, through him," Joe says. "His relationship with each person was unique and a meaningful conduit of spirituality—different from the kind of relationship we have with friends. He was a great listener."

Last Rites

Before it was called the Anointing of the Sick, or the Sacrament of Healing, it was called Last Rites. Before that, it had the ominous name of Extreme Unction, due to the use of holy oil in the sacrament. Now, it is emphasized as a healing sacrament. Previously, it has only been administered in cases of imminent death. Who could find comfort in these extreme situations? More than that, who could find humor? Fr. Fred could.

This story about a fellow employee at the State Hospital is illustrative. He was called to the hospital to visit with *Art*, who was not a Catholic, and with whom he had had a friendly, long-standing, on-going discussion about religion. There was never any animosity, but Art was always trying to pin him down with esoteric and puzzling theological questions. Shortly before he died, Art asked for Fr. Fred to come and administer Art's first and last Catholic sacrament. Just before he administered the Last Rites, Fr. Fred said, "Okay, Art, now I've got you right where I want you." The smile on Art's face told the whole story. "Yes, Father," he said, "you've got me—right where I need to be. Thanks for being such a good friend."

Another employee in a similar situation called for Fr. Fred. This fellow had always tried to get Fr. Fred with a joke and never could. When Father arrived at his hospital bedside, Fr. Fred offered him Communion. "No thanks, Father, I don't eat between meals," and with a wink, received the Holy Eucharist as they prepared for administration of the Last Rites.

When Peg Bruen was just twenty-five, Fr. Fred made house calls to be with her dad who had been diagnosed with lung cancer. She tells this touching story:

> *Toward the end of my father's illness Father Fred came to the hospital to visit him and I happened to be there at one of those visits. Father Fred bent down and whispered in my father's ear and said, "Remember, Leon, your middle name is Joseph and he was a carpenter. You are going to heaven ahead of your family to build a house for them. It is okay to go now to build a place for them to live someday with you, and I know it will be beautiful." What more can I say about that sentimental conversation except that at the age of twenty-five, I decided that death is not to be feared.*

Baptism

Fr. Fred was good at meeting the basic needs in people's lives, so it is no wonder the sacrament of baptism was so important to him. It is the egalitarian universal gateway to Christianity. It is the basic need, the first sacrament. There are hundreds of baptism stories connected to his legacy, which cannot all be told here.

His first baptism after ordination was in July 1950, when he baptized infant Suzanne Kaczmarek in Saginaw. She is the daughter of his first cousin, Marge. Photos of the day show a proud family gathered around the two new stars in the family, the newly ordained young priest and the newest baby in the family.

In 1990, Barb and Jack Lehnhard were Episcopalian and met Fr. Fred when they went to the funeral of a friend's mother. Jack liked him right away. Later, when Jack was diagnosed with cancer, he called his friend Jim Lizenby and asked him if he thought Fr. Fred would come visit him in the hospital. Before he knew it, there was Fr. Fred.

A friendship between them strengthened rapidly as Jack's body weakened with equal rapidity. His new friend, Fr. Fred, came to the house and visited him with increasing frequency, often as late as ten at night, after a long work day. Jack found himself drawn close and comfortably to Fr. Fred as he realized his time might be running out. "With all he has going and all his responsibilities, how does he have time to come visit me?" Jack wondered.

In November, on a Saturday visit, Jack asked his visitor what it would take to convert to Catholicism. "Well, that's not hard, Jack," Fr. Fred answered. "When are you thinking of doing that?" When Jack explained that he'd be happy to do it anytime, Fr. Fred asked, "How about this afternoon at two o'clock?" Surprised, by the response, Jack agreed and had just four hours to prepare for the event. *Why the four hours?* Jack may have thought as Barb helped him get cleaned up and dressed.

A few hours later, Barb and Jack arrived at St. Joseph Church to see the parking lot filled with cars, and they walked into church to see many of Jack's friends gathered to celebrate with him. Fr. Fred had left their home and called many of Jack's friends and asked them to join him that afternoon. The event was emotional, since everyone who watched Jack get baptized, receive Communion, and get confirmed knew he was very ill. When they were leaving the church, Fr. Fred told him, "Jack, you are as white as snow—the best since you were a pup." Jack told Barb that he had never felt better in his entire life.

Three weeks later, Fr. Fred celebrated Mass for Jack's funeral. The fact that many of the same people joined him that day, were the same who were with Jack three weeks earlier, did not get overlooked. They had just celebrated Jack's life, twice.

By February, Barb had become a regular at St. Joseph Church, but was not taking Communion. So, one Sunday after Mass, she told Fr. Fred: "I'd like to be baptized, receive Communion, and be confirmed."

"When are you thinking of doing that, Barb?" Fr. Fred asked her, in exactly the same way he had responded to Jack. A few minutes later, after the congregation had left, the two of them walked through the empty church into the sacristy and took care of business. No classes. No questions. No problem. While other priests may not see this as particularly good pastoral policy, it was typical Fr. Fred.

The son of one of The Father Fred Foundation volunteers and his fiancé were pregnant before they got married. The volunteer talked to Fr. Fred about baptizing the baby. Of course, he would do it. He told the young father a lot of priests would not do it. For Fr. Fred, that was a manmade rule, not the way Jesus would do it. After the baptism, the family invited him to join them for Mexican food at a local restaurant. The celebration of life and Christianity goes on—casually, naturally.

Often, the same story would play out in the wards of the local hospital. New parents approached him to baptize their newborn. The parents were often of mixed religions or unmarried. No problem. He'd get some water out of the faucet and baptize the child. There you go.

Eileen Heck tells of being raised Catholic, yet, in the early 1980s, she had no church affiliation. Her husband had been raised Lutheran. She knew she wanted her last two children baptized and was conflicted as to where or how. Fr. Fred was happy to accommodate the situation with his characteristic wisdom. A Catholic priest baptized their children at All Faiths Chapel in the Protestant chapel. All the families were happy.

The primary purpose of All Faiths Chapel was to serve the patients and staff of the State Hospital, so when there was a wedding or baptism for the visitors, the patients could not be excluded. When Vince and Paula Prusick's daughter, Ashley, was baptized there, some of the patients were present. As was his custom, Fr. Fred would hand the newly baptized infant off to the parishioners. When the child was about to be handed to one of the patients who appeared quite unsteady, both parents were quite nervous about it. Fr. Fred simply nodded to them and they were at ease, trusting his judgment. He knew the patients and would not let harm come to the baby. By not excluding them from the ritual, he brought some dignity and normalcy to the patients.

Adam was born with Down syndrome and life-threatening holes in his heart. Because chromosomal analysis was not in use yet, doctors didn't tell his parents much about it. It wasn't until twenty-four hours after Adam was born that doctors broke the sad news: "We don't know if he will survive." The parents immediately called Fr. Fred, who had married them a few years earlier, to please come to the hospital. "I'll be right over," he reassured them.

When he got there and heard about Adam's condition, Fr. Fred told them, "We'd better get him a baptism." With that, he took a Styrofoam cup into the bathroom, got some water, came out, and baptized the newborn. Immediately after, he administered the Last Rites to the vulnerable infant. When he finished, he headed for the door. "Where are you going?" asked the father. "I'm going back to work, now. The doctors can do a better job than I can with his body, and his soul is in God's hands." It was all over, just ninety minutes after they got the original distressing news.

Adam survived surgeries and treatment at University of Michigan Hospital, and graduated high school on time with a 3.6 GPA in an adjusted curriculum. He was a member of the National Honor Society and has grown into being a big-hearted, friendly, and lovely young man, known and loved by many. His parents now talk about what a joy it has been to raise him.

Lorraine Laird has a similar story of when her daughter was born, gravely ill and unknown whether she would survive. When Fr. Fred arrived at the Neo-Natal Intensive Care Unit (NICU), he told them he was mowing his lawn when he got the call, and that he always prayed to Mary when he was mowing his lawn. He said he prayed for their daughter then because he figured Mary was Jesus' mother, so she knew the joys and sorrow of motherhood. Happily, after a couple of weeks in NICU, the baby was released from the hospital with a clean bill of health—the family's "miracle baby."

Jean was a nurse at Munson Hospital in the NICU and tells of the time Fr. Fred announced to her he had to baptize a child in her unit. "You have to gown up and scrub before you can go in there, Father," she told him. "However, you can use this water. I've already boiled the hell out of it." And she handed him a cup. She then goes on to say that nobody enjoyed telling that story more than Fr. Fred.

Bill Kildee told another classic Fr. Fred story that involved a group baptism at All Faiths Chapel. There were several babies being baptized in one ceremony. All their names were on slips of paper that Fr. Fred held while he baptized each one. Realizing that some of the children had been baptized by the wrong name, someone brought it to his attention. "Oh, don't worry about it," he replied, "God will keep track of all that and sort it out eventually."

Baptism Letters

When you mention Fr. Fred and baptism in the same breath, the person you are talking with is likely to respond with, "Do you know about the letters?" One of the most endearing things Fr. Fred did was write a letter to the newly baptized on the day of their baptism—not a note, not a card, but a letter often three or four pages long.

The sealed letter arrived in the mail usually, along with the official baptismal certificate, with instructions to hold it and give it to the child on his/her thirteenth birthday. Everyone who tells of these letters tells of the impact it had on the thirteen-year-old's life. Each letter had a listing of the family members who attended the baptism, along with the readings, weather, national and local news, sports news, hymns played at the Mass, and often a movie suggestion or a reference to current pop culture.

Each letter held a piece of advice for the teen. There was no preaching, just a straightforward conversation at the young person's level, telling how to incorporate goodness and love into his or her life. He always closed by blessing that person and his or her family and wishing them well.

He also never missed the opportunity to thank the person who typed the letter for him. In the early days, it was LaVerne O'Neil. Later, there were others. Ina Falkowski, an intermittent patient at the hospital, would often work in his office and typed a few of the letters. She knows, in some small way, her efforts live in a few of these letters that carried Fr. Fred's message to these children and their families.[9]

Breaking News: Father Fred Invents the Eighth Sacrament

One of the aspects of Fr. Fred's personality that made him an effective priest, along with a near-photographic memory for names and faces, was his ability to listen. He found it to be the most important form of communication. He honed this skill while at the State Hospital, working with the patients. While he was there, he studied psychology, psychiatry, and social work under several of the staff and perfected his listening. He felt it was important for everyone. Throughout this book, and attached to nearly every Fr. Fred story ever told, is the impression that he was a good listener.

So, we can assume that if he were to invent an eighth sacrament for the Church, it would be *Listening*.

Observations on His Priesthood

One aspect nearly everyone who attended his masses talks about is his homilies. They say he didn't talk about himself. He always talked about how to get to God.

---

9 As this book goes to press, the last few of the unopened letters are still in the hands of parents, since his last baptism was nearly thirteen years ago. While we were able to identify his first baptism and a few in between, we have not been able to accurately determine the name of the last person he baptized.

His homilies were typically short and to the point. They had a beginning, a middle, and an end, with a punch line and a message to remember. At the end, he would usually announce: "Okay, here's a little something to take home with you." With that, he'd tie it all together with a memorable, short, often amusing message. Even though he usually included a funny story to get and maintain the attention of the listener, he was genuinely devout. He had a innate feel for the true meaning of the Gospel. Some say that's why he was such a fan of Pope John XXIII. He didn't put on airs, either.

Sister Katherine Murphy knew Fr. Fred, but didn't get much of a chance to work with him:

> *If he weren't a priest, he would have been a good social worker. He was a good listener and he was inspirational. I'm sure he got tired, but he never lost that beautiful smile. He was not aloof, like some priests can be. He was down-to-earth and human. Father Fred was simply Father Fred. He didn't fit in a pattern. He was very accommodating and always available to help anyone who asked.*

Reverend Dr. Gary D. Hogue, now retired Sr. Pastor at First Congregational Church in Traverse City, was brand new in town the first time he met Fr. Fred, in 1984. It was when the legendary Traverse City High School football coach, Jim Ooley told him about a local tradition that took place at the church he had just been assigned to. Even though the team was from the local public high school, before each home football game they would gather at First Congregational for a prayer and a meal. Local ministers and priests took turns leading the prayer. Coach Ooley told Gary the first leader he would meet is Fr. Fred, that week's prayer leader.

Gary remembers his first impression: "That great smile." He was surprised at the ease with which Fr. Fred spoke to these guys, at their level. He spoke of character and compassion, shook hands with each player ,and joined the meal in the fellowship hall. He found him to be engaging, personable, and friendly as he quietly addressed the concepts of faith and football.

> *Later, I realized he was a local legend, not just with the Catholics. He attracted the people in town, many in my own congregation.*

He was a public religious figure and a community leader who spoke to the heart of the community about taking care of the least of those among us... He was ecumenical at a time before it was as fashionable. He was impressive from the first moment I met him and he was in foreign territory.

Father Francis J. Murphy knew Fr. Fred's ministry at the State Hospital as sort of a third parish in town. Parish priests were always moving in and out of town, but he was a constant. His ministry developed for the people who came to him and to Mass at All Faiths Chapel. He didn't seek parishioners. They found him. He remembers:

If he got twenty requests for help a day, he would do as well on the twenty-first.

He was fair and responsible in his giving, but don't abuse it. He'd give you the shirt off his back, but he would also put an end to a scam.

He was just rock solid. There was no pretense, no soapbox. His ministry was to those who fell through the cracks. This was true, even at the State Hospital, in those situations where the normal routine didn't meet the needs of the patients. He'd go to bat for them.

Father Jim Gardiner began serving Mass for Fr. Fred at Immaculate Conception Parish in Traverse City, as a boy. Later, Fr. Fred was the Vicar when Jim was assigned to the Native American parish at Gill's Pier. As he did with many of the people he knew, he referred to Fr. Jim with a nickname. Fr. Gardiner recalls with a chuckle: "When I was working with the Native Americans, he called me 'Little Eagle.'"

He was a man of peace and joy and was everybody's best friend. His own spiritual qualities were something he recognized, and he used them to help people. When you were with Father Fred, he made you feel as though he had all the

time in the world, and that you were the most important
person in the world.

Father Fred enjoyed hearty laughter and saw the silver
lining in everything and he would hang on to it—not
unrealistically, and he truly celebrated people's goodness.

Since he wasn't tied down by parish work he was a bit
of a maverick. He respected all religions and was everyone's
pastor, no matter what denomination they were... Last time
I saw him, he was quite sick, but told me, "God always takes
care of everything."

Father Ron Gronowski was pastor at St. Francis Parish when the State Hospital closed. He offers the following observations on Fr. Fred's priesthood:

Father Fred was the Godfather of all the parishes, having
been assigned to this area longer than any other pastor and
also because of the prestige and love held for him in the
hearts and minds of both Catholic and non Catholics alike ...

At times Father and I disagreed on liturgical issues. Being
young, I followed the book, the rituals as written. On the other
hand, Father Fred improvised a lot and always put the people
before the rules and regulations. In the end, I believe he did
the more pastoral thing. Everyone in the community knew,
that if for whatever reason they could not be married or have
their child baptized or receive first Eucharist in their own
parish, Father Fred would find a way to make it happen at
the Chapel. The church, he felt, was a big tent, large enough
for everyone.

If we could hear his voice from Heaven he would say, "Hey,
none of this is about me, it's about the people. It is their light,
which must shine, not mine. But if using my name helps to

*feed the hungry, clothe the naked, and shelter the homeless
then let it shine, shine, shine."*

Grant Parsons, a Traverse City attorney, remembers Fr. Fred as a warm, gregarious, authentic personality, who worked outside the local culture. "He was a real guy who wore his religion and his collar comfortably and openly and was probably the only person who could have made All Faiths Chapel happen. He worked in a closed and orderly community, yet was unafraid to cross the line, representing the 'outcasts' of society. That also marked his congregation at All Faiths Chapel."

In His Own Words

Both humor and ecumenism added spice and flavor to Fr. Fred's priesthood. He loved telling the story about a catechism class he was teaching when one little first-grader told him, "Father, when you're dead, I want to be just like you." His pastoral and life philosophy are one in the same, which he explains well in a 1994 piece from the *Grand Traverse Business Journal*:

> *There is a little story, a powerful story, in the spiritual writings of the Islamic religion where a holy man was bowed in prayer and he had all these thoughts of the difficulties in the world: poverty, war, crime, and everything else. And in his prayer and meditation, he would say, "Why, Lord, why do you allow all of this? Why don't you do something?" And according to the writings, God responded: "I did do something. I made you." So I know I've got some things to do, whether they be feeding the hungry, taking care of addicts, or getting someplace for the homeless to stay.*

> *I never ask what religion people are. Even if they are atheist, it doesn't make any difference. They get hungry, and they've got pain and sorrow, just like you and I do. I treat everybody with dignity, or at least I try to get people to find a dignified way of living.*

Here's One For You: Does It Really Matter?

This story comes from the Spring 1991 Foundation Newsletter. It is one written by Fr. Fred.

Never have I asked "religious preference" from requesters, but it happened twice in one day that people said, "I'm not Catholic" or "I used to be Catholic." That is not of immediacy when hunger and deprivation of fuel gas/oil is the issue. But I have to tell you how one of these answered came about. A distraught female phones that her fuel gas tank was empty. She and the kids were cold. Other agencies were drained and she did not know what to do. To bring the reader up to date, I have contributors who emphasize their conviction, "Don't let anyone be without heat." In a matter-of-fact listening mood and trying to find out with which fuel company this lady was affiliated, I questioned, "Who does your service?" "Oh, I used to be Catholic, now I go to the Baptist Church." After a smile to myself, I said, "I mean who services your fuel tank?"

Happy New Year!

Alan Buell, a longtime volunteer at The Father Fred Foundation, tells the story of *Ginny*, a woman he and his wife, Sharon, met when they were on a couples' retreat a few years ago. During the course of the retreat, Fr. Fred's name found its way into the conversation. Alan and Sharon could see Ginny's face flush with the reference to Fr. Fred, and her eyes began to fill with tears.

Ginny had known Fr. Fred from her days as a patient at the State Hospital. Several years after her release, she was living in Petoskey, Michigan, about an hour's drive north of Traverse City. It was late afternoon on New Year's Eve. She was depressed and sad over the recent death of her husband and in need of some consolation, so she called Fr. Fred. After a few minutes on the phone, he could tell she was suffering.

Even though he had made other plans, he drove from Traverse City to Petoskey through some hard, northern Michigan, snowy, winter weather to meet with Ginny.

They spent the evening talking and praying, until after midnight when the New Year arrived. It must have been a long drive home for him that night.

Then, years later, Ginny meets Alan and Sharon and her memory of that comforting and meaningful experience is as crisp and fresh as if it had been yesterday.

Go Now, to Love and Serve the Lord

For I am already being poured out like a libation, and the time of my departure is at hand. I have competed well; I have finished the race; I have kept the faith.

(2 Timothy 4:6)

Even though, in some ways, Father Fred was a noticeably public figure in the community, there was a very private side to him. In many ways, he was still just Bud, and it was essential to him to maintain his privacy. With his friends, he also expressed a warm, personal side that the public did not see. After all, he was a man in the community with responsibilities like any other. He voted and got his hair cut. He traveled and wrote letters. He laughed and had disappointments. He bowled with friends and rooted for the Detroit Lions and Notre Dame football teams. He went to the doctor, the bank, and the hardware store, like any wage-earning homeowner. He hunted, fished, and did home repairs. In these ways, he was a regular guy. He was a man's man. He was Bud.

Having fun while traveling with friends in California.

As we close the story of this incredible man's life, in a chapter whose title is taken from the closing words of the Catholic Mass, we briefly glimpse into a bit of his private life, an area not addressed earlier.

His House on the River

For the first few years he was in Traverse City, Fr. Fred lived in the Carmelite Monastery on Tenth Street. Then he bought a home on the Boardman River, a few miles south of town. It was his retreat, his peaceful spot. It was his *sanctum sanctorum.* Although his out-of-town family visited him there, he kept it very private and few of his local colleagues visited or even knew where it was. He very intentionally kept it to himself. He received his personal mail at a Post Office box in Traverse City, and when asked where he lived, he'd reply with a vague reference to "out south of town" or, "I live out near Mayfield."

The home was a 1950s-era brick ranch house with a breezeway attached to a two-car garage. It had been a modest fishing cabin when he bought it, and he and his father, the stonemason, remodeled it. During the remodeling, there was a period of about two weeks that he slept in the new part, even though there was no roof over it yet. He owned a nice stretch of frontage on the Boardman, in one of the finest trout fishing areas of this nationally known river. The river is about thirty

This piece hung in Fr. Fred's home on the Boardman. It shows all his grandparents. On the left are Paul and Myrtle Frydryszek and their son Frank. On the right are Ursula and Joseph Szczepanski. The inscription reads, "Far or near to mem'ry dear."

feet wide and only a few feet deep as it passes by the home, which is positioned close to the riverbank. There is a very well-done stone embankment and cement steps going down to the river in front of the home. These are the result of a couple work bees with his brother, Joe, and his nephews who hauled the stones from Grand Rapids in a truck.

The sounds of the river were a constant part of his reverie there. A creek separates the property into two parts, and in the mid-1990s, Matt Myers and his two sons built a bridge across the creek to the marshy, spiritually private area away from the house. The bridge still crosses the little tributary. Neighbors, who always respected his privacy, report he could be seen sitting on a bench in the part away from the house in meditation and prayer. He enjoyed the wildlife and fed the wild turkeys and deer. He referred to them as his "cattle."

Bud's nephew, John tells of the time he was working side by side with his uncle and learned this bit of woodsy wisdom:

> *... there were deer in the morning in the front yard of his home, and Uncle Bud told me, "If you don't make eye contact with them, you can walk right next to them and they won't move." I still try that trick today.*

One friend tells when, on a visit, saw Fr. Fred's artificial Christmas tree up in July. "What's this all about?" the friend asked. "Oh, I'm the only one here, so why take it down, since I'm going to just have to put it back up again next Christmas. Besides, it makes me happy to have it up. I love Christmas."

Another poignant home story is about a patient at the State Hospital. Patients loved him so much they didn't want to be separated from him, even when he went home at night. "Hey, Father Fred, can I come home with you sometime?" Or, "Where do you live, Father? We'd like to come visit." As kind as he was, he wasn't going to have any part of that.

One night, after a long and tiring day on campus at the Hospital, he got in his car and went home. As he pulled in the driveway, *Chet* popped his head up from the back seat. "Hey, guess what, Father, I came home with you." Startled, Fr. Fred came back with, "C'mon, Chet, you know you can't do this. They need you over there at the hospital. They're counting on you." "Please, Father," he begged. "I don't want to go back there." Fr. Fred turned the car around, and returned the crying, begging patient back into town and back to his ward. The man meant no harm to his good priest friend. He simply couldn't bear being separated from him, even for the night.

When they arrived back at the ward, Fr. Fred, tired as he was, patiently helped the man get into his pajamas and gently tucked him into bed. Then, just before he left the ward to drive back home, he told him: "You go to sleep, good friend. I'll be down in my office, waiting for you. Everything's going to be okay."

Everyday Life

In 1989, Dolly Cataldo got a call from her friend Nancy, a volunteer at The Foundation, "Can you do me a favor? Father Fred's haircut is just awful. I don't know where he gets it cut, but could you do something with it?" Thus began a long friendship with Dolly, who has run a beauty salon in Traverse City for the past thirty-five years. Fr. Fred baptized her children. She cut his hair. She would have him bait and set the mouse traps in the salon for her. Just before setting down the peanut butter trap, he'd bless the trap and the mouse about to be caught. "Gotta give 'em the mouse Last Rites," he'd joke. Once, a kid in the salon with fashionable holey jeans met with his humor when Fr. Fred asked, "You mean you paid for those? You need to come over to The Foundation and we can get you a pair without holes."

Dolly's favorite is the one about the "Swearing Jar." Each spring, during Lent, Fr. Fred would put out a little jar in the salon and tell everybody that every time they swore or spread some gossip, they had to put a quarter in the jar for "his

people." When he would leave, he'd tell them "Okay, girls, don't be too good, or we won't make any money."

The mechanics in the garage where he had his car repairs done still tell how he would come in and announce to them: "God's chariot needs fixing."

For several years, Fr. Fred would take a three-week trip to Arizona to relax and recharge his batteries. He spent time in the desert, staying in modest surroundings, praying and relaxing. He told friends that

Fr. Fred, relaxing in Arizona.

after a week or so, he'd be ready to come home, but stayed, knowing the break was essential for him. Barb Lehnhard describes that he would leave The Foundation each year physically exhausted and return home refreshed after he walked in the desert, meditated in peace, and "touched base with God." Often, he'd bring simple yet precious souvenirs back for some of his friends, who still keep them.

Home Health Care

In the early summer of 1997, Fr. Fred had just turned seventy-two and was suffering the painful effects of osteoarthritis in both knees. He was scheduled for simultaneous bilateral total knee replacements. His friend and orthopedic surgeon, Dr. Vince Prusick was going to be doing the surgery. He explained the surgery to Fr. Fred and went on to tell him about the debilitating and painful recuperation. "You're going to need total care for several weeks," Vince explained. "Bathing, toilet, grooming, dressing, physical therapy—the whole thing." Vince laid out the options for him. He could either go into a facility, like a nursing home; he could get some live-in help; or he could go live with his brother's family in Eaton Rapids.

"What other options do I have?" he asked Vince. "Let me think it over."

Hearing about the situation, Vince's wife, Paula, who had by then, been working at The Father Fred Foundation and serving on the board for several years, spoke up. "He's coming to live with us," she declared. "He'll live with us while he recovers." So, after the surgery, Fr. Fred moved into a room at the Prusick's home, already set up to accommodate the patient.

"It gave me a fresh and unique perspective, as a surgeon," says Vince, when recollecting this memory. "Living with the recuperating patient gave me a whole new understanding. It was a difficult recovery because it was bilateral, made more difficult by his age." Fr. Fred had a goal that gave him a special incentive and determination to recover. He wanted to go to Paris, with the St. Joseph Parish Youth Group, in July to see the Pope at World Youth Day.

Fr. Fred became an intimate part of their family as he worked through his recovery. The Prusick kids—Ashley, Vince, and Parker—witnessed a new kind of love and made a new friend. The family dog, Mike, became his personal assistant. Fr. Fred was moved to the huge, cushy leather recliner in the family room during the day and Mike would fetch things for him. This friendship was going well, until one day, when Fr. Fred's lunch, prepared by Paula, was just out of reach from the

Bud relaxes with Prusick's dog, Mike, in their home.

recliner and Mike decided to gobble it up. Fr. Fred couldn't move fast enough to stop it, and after that, he and Mike came to a new understanding.

As he recovered, Fr. Fred accepted the generous gift of love from this family. They have precious family memories of him in their home. There are even some memories of him saying Mass at their kitchen table on Sunday mornings, in his pajamas.

Vince recalls that saying prayers with Fr. Fred never got monotonous or routine. He always changed the rhythm and pace of the prayer to make sure we thought of it as fresh.

Fr. Fred met his goal and traveled to Paris with the youth group, along with friends Barb Lehnhard, Matt Myers, and Ken Neyer. He walked with the aid of a cane or two, and in Paris, Ken made arrangements for a wheelchair, but he made it. "He did it,"

Fr. Fred brings his ministry home, as he celebrates Mass at Prusicks' breakfast table.

remembers Vince, "through will and by having a goal. I've never seen anything like it."

Trip to Paris

Before he left St. Joseph Parish, he had promised the Youth Group that he'd go to Paris with them for the World Youth Day celebration, August 21-24, 1997. He must have been eager, also to see the Polish Pope, born Karol Józef Wojtyła. Barely recovered from his surgery, he boarded the first plane with the group and embarked on a series of flights that would take them to Paris. As the group waited in the passenger boarding lounge area in Houston, Barb Lehnhard heard her name called by the gate agent. Thinking there was a problem, she met the woman behind the counter who asked her to surrender her tickets. Quite concerned, as the woman was tearing her tickets and Fr. Fred's to pieces, Barb asked about the problem. "Oh, there's no problem. I just saw that you were travelling with that elderly priest who is having trouble walking, so I upgraded your seats to Paris to first class." After the same thing happened on the way home a week later, Barb says, "I think I'll make it a point to travel with an aging priest from now on."

It was 100 degrees on Sunday, August 24, when they joined nearly a million others as Pope John Paul II celebrated Mass. Fr. Fred enjoyed being with the kids and at one point, inside a basilica, he told the group to go ahead on the short tour. He'd wait for them, because his knees made walking uncomfortable. When the group returned, a few minutes later, there was Fr. Fred, on the altar celebrating Mass with a group of about fifteen other priests. He just loved group celebrations. Throughout the trip, the entire group wore French *berets*.

For Everything, There is a Season

After the trip, his life began to slow down even more than it had when he retired from St. Joseph Parish in 1996. Stories of the last few weddings he did include him sitting in the front pew of the church to preserve his waning strength, with the bride and groom facing him and the congregation as they exchanged vows. Baptisms were more and more of a chore. After he left St. Joseph's, he said Mass in the conference room, upstairs at The Father Fred Foundation. He had young volunteers, children of friends, help him in his garden for the last few summers. He was tired, his knees hurt, and his health began to fail.

In early 1998, Bud was diagnosed with a low-grade prostate cancer. "We'll keep an eye on the PSA," his doctor told him, with confidence that it was a slow-moving process that he would outlive. By early 1999, however, the PSA levels escalated and the cancer became more aggressive. Treatments ensued and this lion of Traverse City began to weaken. His spirit and humor didn't, however. Dolly tells of a visit to her shop after one of his radiation treatments. "Well, your color looks good, Father. Your cheeks are nice and rosy." He shot back with: "Oh, that's not where they're treating me, dear."

The Last Time I Saw Father Fred

Gil, a self-described tough old buzzard, was a naive Buckley farm boy who grew up Methodist and got a job at the State Hospital in 1959. He was totally unprepared for what he experienced over the next thirteen years that he worked there. He was a nurse and, later, a nursing supervisor. He relied on Fr. Fred for some guidance, and they developed a very close friendship.

The friendship was close enough that, even though he was not a Catholic, he one day asked Fr. Fred if he would preach at his funeral. "What's wrong?" Fr. Fred asked him, in his characteristic caring manner, as he held his friend's arm. "Oh, nothing," Gil replied. "I just hope that you outlive me, so you can do me that favor." Fr. Fred assured his friend by saying, "If I can, I will; but I hope you live to be a hundred."

Fr. Fred didn't outlive his friend. In fact, in a coincidental circumstance, years later, they were both being treated for the same cancer at the same time. They would often meet each other after their post-surgical radiation treatments at the cancer clinic.

The last time Gil saw his friend, Fr. Fred, was after one such appointment. They shook hands in the parking lot, and Fr. Fred asked how he was doing. After a brief update response, Fr. Fred told him, "I'll say a prayer for you."

"And I'll do the same for you, Father," was Gil's reply.

Fr. Fred paused and said to him, "That's really good, Gil. We need to do that for one another." Years later, Gil wipes a tear from his eye, and emotionally adds that Fr. Fred's prayers must have been more powerful than his, because he has outlived his friend for these many years. "No," another clergyman told him, "we all have a direct connection with God. We simply have to use it."

"That," Gil reassures us, "is the true Christian message of Fr. Fred."

In between stays in the hospital, Bud moved in with a friend who lived in

Traverse City to be close to doctors, treatments, and the hospital. With respect for his privacy, only a few close friends and some family came to visit. Each tells of their last contact with him. One story stands out.

Sally Suprenant went up to the hospital to see him, and his face brightened when he saw her. He told her he was disappointed he would not get to go to Arizona this year. A week or so before he died, Bud called her and asked if she would come and take care of his feet, since she had worked in the office of a foot doctor. She took her equipment to the friend's home, washed and rubbed his feet and trimmed his toenails for him as he sat on the sofa and thoughtfully asked about her grandson. With understandable emotion, and knowing his time was short, she tells of quietly crying at his feet, with an inescapable reference to the parable of Jesus washing the feet of the apostles. "We loved him," she says. "We all loved him. We loved the man he was—everything about him."

Other stories from the small group of friends have a common thread to them. He was only afraid of two things, he told one visitor: motorcycles and dying. He explained the fear of dying was not because of what was on the other side for him, but what was on the other side for "his people." To the end, he worried about what would happen to The Foundation and to the families it was serving after he died.

Each of his visitors tell how they felt a special grace that came with comforting the man who had brought comfort and well-being to them and so many others in his life. Consoling him seemed lovingly and peacefully appropriate for them. Most of these friends have names we have already seen in this book. Stories of their last words or touch or how they bathed or soothed him are highly and individually personal and will only be shared elsewhere.

Father Jim Gardiner was pastor at St. Francis of Assisi, just a short walk from where Fr. Fred was resting. Daily, he stopped by for a pastoral visit during this end period in the life of a man for whom he served Mass so many years ago. He brought the Eucharist to him, and administered the Sacrament of Last Rites to him in a prayer of Final Commendation and Farewell. Even in his exhaustion, Fr. Fred never strayed from his gracious and cheerful demeanor and continued to call his friend "Little Eagle," a nickname he had given him because of Jim's work with the Indians. Fr. Gardiner recalls that Fr. Fred was characteristically concerned for Jim's welfare during the busy holiday season and was upbeat, showing no signs of morbidity—even until the end.

On the morning of January 4, 2000, there was a small, intimate group gathered at his bedside when he died: his brother and sister-in-law, Joe and Colette, and two others. Bud was in and out of consciousness, and the last thing he told Joe is that the Blessed Virgin was standing at the foot of his bed, inviting him to let go and come with Her. With that, he peacefully smiled, closed his eyes, let go, and stepped into Eternity.

Saying Goodbye

Later that day, Mike Shirley was on his way to the monthly meeting of the Ancient Order of Hibernians and decided to stop by the house and check on his friend who had been the chaplain of the local chapter of AOH for many years. When he learned that Fr. Fred had died, he removed the green sash he was wearing and wept, as he draped it over the foot of Fr. Fred's bed. When Mike entered the meeting without his green sash and announced the news to this group that met regularly to celebrate Irish life and culture, he faced the first thirty-five men in Traverse City to cry and mourn the sad news of the passing of their chaplain and friend. The group was happy to learn that the Frederick family accepted their offer to bury the green AOH sash with their inspirational colleague.

Bishop Patrick Cooney immediately sent a letter to all the parishes in the Diocese of Gaylord, commenting on the sadness of Fr. Fred's passing. He wrote, too, "… there is also a sense of joy and happiness. Fr. Fred not only heard but visibly put into practice the Great Commandment. He knew that everyone was his brother or sister and treated them accordingly. No better statement can be said about anyone."

Fr. Fred's Funeral Mass, on January 7, 2000, was at St. Francis Church in Traverse City, with Bishop Cooney as celebrant. There were over a thousand attendees. Fr. Fred's friend, Dr. Vince Prusick, was asked to read the first liturgical passage from scripture, selected from the Book of Isaiah. "It was as hard a thing as I ever had to do," says Vince. "I was physically locked up for a moment, not able to move. Then a peace came over me and I was able to read the piece."

Bishop Cooney read the Gospel selection, from the Gospel according to Matthew. The most poignant and relevant verses seemed to be verses 35-36 from chapter 25:

> *For I was hungry and you gave me food, I was thirsty and*
> *you gave me drink, a stranger and you welcomed me, naked*
> *and you clothed me, ill and you cared for me, in prison and*
> *you visited me.*

There could not have been a better Gospel selection for the celebration of the life of Traverse City's Mother Teresa.

The next day, in a story in the *Traverse City Record-Eagle*, we read:

> *In the pews sat people of many denominations and social positions. Some wore the newest styles, the most elite of brand names. Others donned boots worn ragged from years of use ... All of them sat together, celebrating the life of this simple man with gleaming blue eyes and a quick smile who loved sports, his plow truck and every person he met whether they came bearing gifts or asking for handouts.*

The *Traverse City Record-Eagle* also quoted Dan Dingeman from his comments as spokesman for The Father Fred Foundation:

> *He bridged the haves and the have-nots. He didn't just enrich the lives of the needy, he also enriched the lives of people who have greater blessings, greater resources, and he showed them the light of how they can help those less fortunate ... I would think he is perhaps one of the greatest community servants northern Michigan has ever seen.*

Arnie Ochs, Foundation board member and longtime friend, spoke at the funeral, commenting on what made Fr. Fred such an inspirational leader. He remembered his friend's short, simple, effective sermons and the summer outside masses that reflected his patriotism, as if the picture were out of a Norman Rockwell painting. He recalled visits to The Foundation office:

> *... it didn't matter if you were bringing in a substantial donation or asking for help with your utility bill, he saw Jesus Christ in you—and everyone was treated with the same respect and dignity.*

> *Father Fred often talked of his great love for Mother Teresa and her work and her constant message of loving Jesus and how that message sustained her in her work of helping the poor and destitute on the streets of Calcutta. I feel sure Mother*

> *Teresa was a role model for his work ... My memory of Father*
> *Fred is one of his deep and compassionate love of his fellow*
> *human beings—that love made possible accomplishments*
> *that seemed impossible.*

Two weeks later, Bud's brother, Joe sent a letter to the board of The Foundation, and in it he, commented on some of the things he heard at the funeral:

> *As I listened to the many comments that were made, I*
> *couldn't help but think of Mother Teresa when she said that*
> *she was "merely a pencil in the hand of the Lord." So, too, (it*
> *was) with my brother. He wasn't trying to be the important*
> *one even though his picture often appeared in the newspaper*
> *and on TV, rather he tried to help people realize that God*
> *alone was the "giver" and that He alone had the answers.*

On Tuesday, February 15, 2000, Michigan Congressman Bart Stupak made the following entry in the Congressional Record in Washington, D.C.:

> Mr. Speaker, I and many, many residents of northern Michigan continue to mourn the passing of the Rev. Edwin Frederick, our beloved Father Fred, who affected so many lives by the simple act of tending and caring for those in need.
>
> It may be misleading, Mr. Speaker, to describe Father Fred's work as simple. The simple act of sharing is to offer a hungry man half one's loaf of bread. The simple act of caring is to put one's own coat over the shoulders of a child shivering with a cold.
>
> Father Fred went much further than that. The foundation he created has provided food, clothing, and other basic necessities to literally thousands of families. The Father Fred Foundation now distributes more than a million dollars in aid each year to individuals and families in the Traverse City area. It is, at its heart, the story of the loaves and the fishes, a miracle being worked by our Savior through this simple man of the cloth who was willing to ride on the

206 • *The Heart of a Priest*

back of Harley Davidson motorcycles and oversee garage sales to build this sustaining fund.

I was fortunate, Mr. Speaker, to have been one of Father Fred's instruments in his performance of good works. I looked forward each year to assisting him in serving Thanksgiving dinner to those in need. In this most basic of act of charity, helping to provide sustenance to another human, I learned that most basic of Christian lessons, learning to love a stranger.

My heart was heavy this year at Thanksgiving, because as I left, I knew I would never again see Father Fred alive. His smile was as wide as ever, but the cancer that was killing him had left this once powerful man very frail. Father Fred died in January at the age of 74.

We in Congress have an opportunity to meet many stately, strong, wise, and wonderful people. But in those quiet moments when I can reflect on the individuals who have really had an impact on my view of the world and my feelings for my fellow man, it is Father Fred who marches at the forefront of that long procession of men and women whose lives at one time or another intersected with mine.

He will continue to live among us in the foundation he created, and in the special place in our hearts and memories he created.

Fr. Fred is buried in St. Joseph Cemetery on the Old Mission Peninsula. It is a little country cemetery, belonging to the little country church where his incandescent love shone for six years in his only assignment as pastor. The simple inscription on his black granite headstone, under the broken heart Foundation logo reads:

Listening – Caring – Sharing

Father Fred

1925 -2000

Reverend Edwin Frederick

Three years after his death, a new entrance to the cemetery was built and dedicated in his honor.

Amen

When Fr. Fred died, the headline on the *Traverse City Record-Eagle* read, "The Faithful Father Fred: TC's 'Mother Teresa' leaves lasting legacy." This comparison was not something Fr. Fred, himself, had not thought of, as he used her life and work as a model in his life and work. In his November 22, 1994, written report to the board of directors, he wrote: "I ask you to pray for me to reflect Jesus to all. I have a long way trying to catch up with Mother Teresa, but I won't give up."

For many of the people who were helped by his lifelong, daily acts of compassion, he did catch up with Mother Teresa. For those who made contributions, and for volunteers, the feeling is the same. For all of us who knew him or knew of him, whose lives are continually inspired by Fr. Fred, who with the heart of a priest, taught us all how to listen, care, share, and give people the dignity they have a right to.

Bless you

Fr. Fred

Christ has no body now on earth but yours,

No hands but yours, no feet but yours,

Yours are the eyes through which is to look out

Christ's compassion to the world;

Yours are the feet with which he is to go about doing good;

Yours are the hands with which he is to bless men now.

St. Teresa of Avila, 1515-1582
Carmelite Nun, Doctor of the Church

ACKNOWLEDGEMENTS

If the only prayer you say in your whole life is "Thank you," that would suffice.
Meister Eckhart, Thirteenth-Century Dominican Mystic

When I was growing up, there were always two questions someone in my family would ask in special situations. One came after a series of questions that seemed to be pestering one of them: "What? Are you writing a book?" The other one that comes to mind was often asked when I had forgotten to do something, such as write a thank you note or a letter home: "What? You got a broken arm and can't write?" So, I open this acknowledgement with answers to my parents. Yes, I did write a book and no, I don't have a broken arm. So, my first thanks goes to my parents, Fran and Larry LaPorte who, in their own way, taught me to give. I wish you were both still here to see this work. In your name, it is my gift to the Traverse City community and a tribute to you.

Thanks to the hundreds of people who shared their Father Fred stories with me. Without you, there would be no story. I hope I did it well for you.

To Jerry Carlson, who reassured me that I had the support of the community, then proved it. Thanks to Dave Abeel, who originally asked me to write the book and helped me hatch the idea. And to Sue Bauer and Martie Manty and their volunteers: Anna Coles, the bright, young face of the future, thank you for your tireless research and transcription; and Judy Nisbett, for your organizational skills in scanning and organizing the hundreds of images considered for this project.

Gratitude goes, in huge proportion, to the Traverse City community and the wonderful people who saw me through the process: Doug Stanton for telling me to "Just write the book, Paul. It is an important story." Thanks to Peg Siciliano and the staff at the History Center of Traverse City and the Traverse City Area Chamber of Commerce. When I needed the Frederick family door opened, Bernie Moritz opened it so Tom McCarthy and I could walk through it. Tom BeVier: as I whined my way through this process, your support, friendship, and professionalism taught me more than you may ever know. Speaking of professionals, I owe so much to Doug Bishop who expertly navigated this project through the legal domain. To you, Doug, I dedicate the copyright page of this book.

Thanks to Tom Dilley for your invaluable help in making the Grand Rapids connection and facilitating the advancement of research on that end; and to Fr. Dennis Morrow, the archivist and historian for the Diocese of Grand Rapids; and to Orchard Lake St. Mary's, Cecile Wendt-Jensen, and the MiPolonia Project. Thanks to the staffs at the parishes of St. Josephat in Saginaw, Sacred Heart in Grand Rapids, St. Michael's in Muskegon, and to Mary and Whitney Lyon at St. Joseph Parish in Mapleton. Thanks to the Traverse City Record-Eagle: Mike Casuscelli, Bill Thomas, and Loraine Anderson; and the people at Village Press: Scott Lizenby, Steve Smith, Jill Swan, and Mike McCatty for your help and guidance. You've made this project shine with your excellence. Thanks, too, to those production folks who did so much without my asking: John Robert Williams, "photo phenom" and friend—being with you is more fun than therapy—and to Rich Brauer and Bob Tomlinson at Brauer Productions, along with Travis Miller, the bright, young filmmaker. Colleen Zanotti, you are amazing. Smiling, you came running into this project in the eleventh hour and became our wonderful cover girl. Your design for the jacket presents this book stunningly and beautifully to the reader.

Thanks to the Frederick family, starting with Suzanne Rehmann and Marge Kaczmarek. You were my first sources of family information and photos. To Colette Frederick and your beautiful family. You were gracious in allowing me into your family during a difficult time. I wish I'd gotten to meet Joe.

There are four people who have helped me immeasurably and who defy categorization. First is Mike Nolan. Thanks, Mike, just for being Mike Nolan, one of the gifted thinkers in Traverse City—a true gentleman and a wonderful, gracious friend. Second is Sister Ann Goggin. Your insight, wisdom, candor, and theology were like beacons for me, guiding this project through the process. Next is Tom McCarthy, the genealogy genius who took to this project like a dog on a bone and found and organized far more genealogical information than we could ever jam between the covers of this book. Tom, you are more than a genealogist—you have become a good friend. Finally, thanks to my friend and mentor, my spiritual director, Fr. Ed Thome. Without your unique and caring guidance and friendship, this would have been an even more difficult project.

My family deserves all the gratitude I can express. Thanks for standing by me through this project. Dave and Kate—you and your families are the light of my life. Carol, you have graciously hosted Fr. Fred in our home for the past two years. Thanks once again for your love and support in the face of another one of my great ideas. I love you.

Paul LaPorte
June 2011

Appendix A: Bibliography and Sources

BeVier, Thomas, "When There's No Place Else." *Detroit News*, 2 February 1992.

Bodus, Tom, "Too Much Unfinished Business." *Grand Traverse Business Journal*, 1994: 9.

Carr, Tom, "Crowd Turns to Prayer to Save Chapel." *Traverse City Record-Eagle*, 25 September 1989: 1A.

Coates, Rick, "Cigar Politics: Despite Smoking Ban, 15th Annual Cigar Dinner is a Go." *Northern Express Weekly*, 10 May 2010: 16.

Conners, Diane, "Hospital Chapel Pushing to Keep Facility Open." *Traverse City Record-Eagle*, 3 July 1989: 3A.

Decker, William A., M.D., *Northern Michigan Asylum: A History of the Traverse City State Hospital*. Traverse City, Michigan: Arbutus Press, 2010.

Delserone, Alicia, "HOG WILD," *Traverse City Record-Eagle*, 23 July 1993: 1D.

DeVal, Robert P., "Fr. Denay and Fr. Fredrick(sic): A Team." *The Catholic Weekly*, 13 April 1990.

Echlin, Bill, "Chamber Honors 'One of a Kind' – Father Fred." *Traverse City Record-Eagle*, 26 January 1991: 1A.

Frederick, Edwin J., "I Had More Fun than the Kids – The Party was Great..." *The Catholic Weekly*, 5 January 1979: 1.

Frederick, Edwin J., *Ah, Nostalgia!* A collection of unpublished stories about his time at the Traverse City State Hospital. 59 pp (incomplete).

Frederick, Edwin J. A collection of unpublished stories about his time at the Father Fred Foundation. 7 pp.

Frederick, Joseph. Letter to Board Members of the Father Fred Foundation. 14 January 2000.

Hall, Lori A., "Chapel's Last Mass Full of Emotion." *Traverse City Record-Eagle*, 21 August 1989: 1A.

Hall, Lori A., "Best of the Best: Readers Rate Their Favorite People, Places and Things." *Traverse   City Record-Eagle*, 23 May 1993: 1F.

Lyon, Mary, *St. Joseph Parish, 1900-1995*. A scrapbook history of St. Joseph Parish, Mapleton, on the Old Mission Peninsula.

Lyon, Mary, *St. Joseph's Catholic Church History: 1850-1996*. An unpublished history of St. Joseph Parish, Mapleton.

McGee, John W., *The Catholic Church in the Grand River Valley 1833-1950*. Lansing, Michigan: Franklin Dekleine Company, 1950.

Miller, Chris, *Images of America: Traverse City State Hospital*. Chicago: Arcadia Publishing, 2001.

Mother Marie Therese, OCD. Letter from the Sisters at Jefferson City. Carmel, Jefferson City Missouri, 17 June 2010.

Mother Mary of Jesus, OCD. Letter from Carmelite Monastery. Traverse City, Michigan, 6 July 2010.

Neiman, Joseph C., "A Chaplain Has Skills to Help Make Persons Whole: Future Role Pondered at Psychiatric Hospital." *The Catholic Weekly*, 10 March 1978: 3G.

Noga, Cari, "Faithful Father Fred: TC's 'Mother Teresa' Leaves a Lasting Legacy." *Traverse City Record-Eagle*, 5 January 2000: 1A.

Norton, Mike, "The Thunder was On Them." *Traverse City Record-Eagle*, 31 July 2000.

Raymer, Marjory, "Father Fred to Ride Again in Harley Fund-raiser." *Traverse City Record Eagle*, 16 July 1999: 1C.

Raymer, Marjory, "'He was Important to Us and He was Loved by Us': Father Fred's Funeral Mass at St. Francis Catholic Church Draws More Than 1000 People," *Traverse City Record-Eagle*, 8 January 2000: 1A.

Reisig, Greg, "Hope For the Needy." *The Gazette, Fen's Rim Publications*, 5 March 1993: 4.

Russell, Olave Walker, "H.O.G. Wild about Father Fred." *Preview Community Weekly*, 16 June 1996: 1.

Skendzel, Eduard A. , *The Sacred Heart Story, A History of Sacred Heart Parish in Grand Rapids, Michigan, on the Occasion of its Diamond Jubilee 1904–1979.* Grand Rapids, Michigan: Foremost Press, Inc., 1981.

Steele, Earle E., as told to Kristen Hains in *Beauty is Therapy: Memories of the Traverse City State Hospital*. Traverse City, Michigan: Denali and Co., 2001.

Van hulle, Lindsay, "Annual Thanksgiving Meal Canceled." *Traverse City Record-Eagle*, 19 November 2009: 1A.

Wertz, Rick, "Fr. Fred Honored for His Efforts: Priest Presented with Sara Hardy Humanitarian of the Year Award." *Traverse City Record-Eagle*, 10 December 1994: 1A.

No Author. "St. Therese of Lisieux." (2008). *Catholic Online*. www.catholic.org/saints/saint.php?saint_id=105.

No Author. "History of the Discalced Carmelite Nuns." (2003). http://www.ocd.pcn.net/hista.htm.

No Author. *Golden Blessings 1960-2010: Carmel of The Sacred Heart and Saint Joseph.* Jefferson City, Missouri, 2010.

No Author. Letter from the Sisters at St. Agatha Carmel. St. Agatha, Ontario, Canada, 16 June 2010.

No Author. "City Smokes Up: Nineteen Million Cigars Are Made Here Annually." *Grand Rapids Press*, 16 August 1910.

No Author. "Info Poland." (2010).University at Buffalo, State University of New York. http://info-poland.buffalo.edu.

No Author, "Treating the Mentally Ill: Dreams and Realities in Transition." *Traverse City Record-Eagle*, 11 August 1981.

No Author. www.cenaclesisters.org.

No Author, "New Carillon Installed at St. Michaels," *Muskegon Chronicle*, undated.

No Author, "Faithful Toast Father Fred." *Grand Traverse Herald*, 14 August 1996: 3A.

No Author, "'Father Fred' to Leave Pulpit." *Traverse City Record-Eagle*, 10 February 1996.

No Author. www.kirkbridebuildings.com.

Who's Who in Religion, 2nd Ed. Chicago, Illinois: Marquis Who's Who, Inc., 1977.

The New American Bible. Catholic Bible Press, 1987.

Appendix B: Photo Credits

Chapter	Page number	Credit
Dedication		History Center Traverse City
1	3	Courtesy of the Kaczmarek family
1	5	Courtesy of the Kaczmarek family
1	6	From the collected memorabilia of Sister Agnes of God, Carmelite Monastery, Jefferson City, Missouri
1	9	Courtesy of the Frederick family
1	10	Courtesy of the Kaczmarek family
1	11	Courtesy of the Kaczmarek family
1	13	Courtesy of the Frederick family
1	15	Courtesy of the Frederick family
1	16	From the collected memorabilia of Sister Agnes of God, Carmelite Monastery, Jefferson City, Missouri
1	17	Courtesy of the Kaczmarek family
1	18	Courtesy of the Frederick family
1	21	Courtesy of the Frederick family.
1	22	Courtesy of the Frederick family.
1	23	Courtesy of Jim Frederick
1	27	Courtesy of the Frederick family
1	27	Courtesy of Suzanne Rehmann
1	27	Courtesy of the Carmelite Monastery in St. Agatha, Ontario
2	29	Courtesy of the Kaczmarek family
2	29	Courtesy of the Frederick family
2	31	Courtesy of the Frederick family
2	31	Courtesy of the Kaczmarek family
2	32	Courtesy Hector Sifuentes
2	33	Courtesy of the Kaczmarek family
2	34	Courtesy of the Frederick family.
2	34	Courtesy Ann Goggin and Marilyn Mapes
2	35	Courtesy Ann Goggin and Marilyn Mapes
2	41	History Center Traverse City
2	42	Courtesy Ann Goggin and Marilyn Mapes
3	45	Courtesy of Gordon Cornwell and the Cornwell family
3	47	Courtesy Hector Sifuentes
3	51	From the collected memorabilia of Sister Agnes of God, Carmelite Monastery, Jefferson City, Missouri
3	56	Traverse City Record-Eagle
2	69	Courtesy History Center Traverse City

2	74	Courtesy of Susan Im
2	75	Courtesy of Susan Im
3	95	Courtesy of the Frederick family
3	107	History Center Traverse City
3	108	History Center Traverse City
3	109	History Center Traverse City
3	109	History Center Traverse City
3	116	Courtesy of Matt Myers
4	129	With permission from Bob Ashmun
4	131	Courtesy of Matt Myers
4	131	HIstory Center Traverse City
4	132	Courtesy of Matt Myers
4	133	History Center Traverse City
4	136	History Center Traverse City
4	137	Courtesy of Mike Nolan
4	140	History Center Traverse City
4	143	History Center Traverse City
4	144	History Center Traverse City
4	144	Curtis R. Frook
4	147	Traverse City Record-Eagle
5	151	History Center Traverse City
5	156	History Center Traverse City
6	161	History Center Traverse City
6	162	From the collected memorabilia of Sister Agnes of God, Carmelite Monastery, Jefferson City, Missouri
6	164	Mary and Whitney Lyon
6	165	Traverse City Record-Eagle
6	166	History Center Traverse City
6	167	Mary and Whitney Lyon
6	171	Courtesy of Jerry and Linda Carlson
7	173	Courtesy of Matt Myers
7	174	History Center Traverse City
7	178	Courtesy Hector Sifuentes
7	191	Courtesy of the Lyon family
8	193	Courtesy of the Im family
8	194	Courtesy of Suzanne Rehmann
8	195	Courtesy of Colette Frederick
8	197	History Center Traverse City
8	199	Courtesy Vince and Paula Prusick
8	199	Courtesy Vince and Paula Prusick
8	207	History Center Traverse City

Appendix C: About the Authors

Paul LaPorte retired in 2004, after nearly forty years in the computer software business. In 1990, he opened his own company, Mission Communications, to write for and with technology-based companies around the world. He earned an undergraduate degree in English from the University of Michigan. He took nearly two years off from his watercolor painting avocation to write *The Heart of a Priest*. Paul and his wife, Carol, previously published Life in the North Lane, a popular guide to living and working in northern Michigan. They live in and travel from Traverse City, Michigan. They have two grown children and six grandchildren.

Fr. Edwin Thome, at 82, was described by the *Traverse City Record-Eagle* as "Forever Priest." He knew Fr. Fred from his early seminary days in Grand Rapids, Michigan. They share more than a common given name of Edwin. Each of them stepped out of the stereotypical understanding of a priest to assist the disadvantaged. Fr. Thome has reached out to the deaf and the migrant population while serving as a parish priest. He has served as pastor, vicar, superintendant of the Grand Traverse Area Catholic Schools for twelve years, and as Vicar General for the Diocese of Gaylord for four years under Bishop Patrick Cooney. When Fr. Fred died, he was the perfect fit to step into The Father Fred Foundation as Spiritual Director and sit behind the desk of his senior priest-mentor and friend. He currently serves as pastor at St. Joseph Parish on the Old Mission Peninsula in Traverse City, where Fr. Fred also once served.

For more information on the genealogy of the Frederick, Frydryszek, and Szczepanski families, contact:

The History Center of Traverse City
322 Sixth Street
Traverse City, MI 49684
phone: (231) 995-0313
email: *gthc@gtheritagecenter.net*